THE FIRES

THE FIRES

How a Computer Formula Burned Down

New York City—and Determined

the Future of American Cities

JOE FLOOD

RIVERHEAD BOOKS

a member of Penguin Group (USA) Inc.

New York

2010

RIVERHEAD BOOKS

Published by the Penguin Group

Penguin Group (USA) Inc., 375 Hudson Street, New York, New York 10014, USA • Penguin Group (Canada), 90 Eglinton Avenue East, Suite 700, Toronto, Ontario M4P 2Y3, Canada (a division of Pearson Penguin Canada Inc.) • Penguin Books Ltd, 80 Strand, London WC2R 0RL, England • Penguin Ireland, 25 St Stephen's Green, Dublin 2, Ireland (a division of Penguin Books Ltd) • Penguin Group (Australia), 250 Camberwell Road, Camberwell, Victoria 3124, Australia • (a division of Pearson Australia Group Pty Ltd) • Penguin Books India Pvt Ltd, 11 Community Centre, Panchsheel Park, New Delhi–110 017, India Penguin Group (NZ), 67 Apollo Drive, Rosedale, North Shore 0632, New Zealand (a division of Pearson New Zealand Ltd) • Penguin Books (South Africa) (Pty) Ltd, 24 Sturdee Avenue, Rosebank, Johannesburg 2196, South Africa

Penguin Books Ltd, Registered Offices: 80 Strand, London WC2R 0RL, England

Library of Congress Cataloging-in-Publication Data

Flood, Joe, date.
The fires : how a computer formula burned down New York City—and determined the future of American cities / Joe Flood.
p.   cm.
Includes bibliographical references and index.
ISBN 978-1-59448-898-6
1. New York (N.Y.). Fire Dept.—Appropriations and expenditures—History—20th century.   2. Fire investigation—New York (State)—New York—History—20th century.   3. City planning—New York (State)—New York—Statistical methods—History—20th century.   4. New York (N.Y.)—Politics and government—20th century.   5. Drugstores—Fires and fire prevention—New York (State)—New York—History—20th century.   I. Title.
TH9505.N509F58   2010   2010001987
363.3709747'1—dc22

Printed in the United States of America
1   3   5   7   9   10   8   6   4   2

BOOK DESIGN BY MEIGHAN CAVANAUGH

FRONTISPIECE PHOTOGRAPH COURTESY HARVEY EISNER

While the author has made every effort to provide accurate telephone numbers and Internet addresses at the time of publication, neither the publisher nor the author assumes any responsibility for errors, or for changes that occur after publication. Further, the publisher does not have any control over and does not assume any responsibility for author or third-party websites or their content.

We must be aware of the dangers which lie in our most generous wishes. Some paradox of our nature leads us, when once we have made our fellow men the objects of our enlightened interest, to go on to make them the objects of our pity, then of our wisdom, ultimately of our coercion.

—LIONEL TRILLING

I'm eighty years old, and after thirty-two years in the fire department, I can say there isn't anything as exciting as responding to a fire. Nothing. Nothing I have experienced or read about as exciting as getting on that truck with lights blazing, sirens going, then turning the corner and seeing the red demon coming out of that building. It's a strange group of men, and I was proud to be one of them. If sociologists and psychologists would have studied us, they would have been shocked at what they found. . . . No one runs into a building that everyone else is running out of without one or two screws loose, constantly facing death and danger like that, but it's what we did. They call it the War Years, but I also call it the Glory Days.

—RETIRED FDNY CAPTAIN VINCENT JULIUS

CONTENTS

A NOTE ON SOURCING AND PHRASING

All dialogue in this book is from the memory of the participants, and has been checked with multiple sources wherever possible. To distinguish between the sources, quotations taken directly from interviews conducted by the author are referred to in the present tense (. . . says) and those taken from books, articles, or archives are quoted in the past tense (. . . said). Because the events described take place before women joined the FDNY, fire*fighters* are generally referred to as fire*men*.

The Waldbaum's collapse, Sheepshead Bay, Brooklyn.
(Photo courtesy FDNY Photo Unit)

ONE

The War Years

We cannot understand firemen; they have risen to some place among the inexplicable beauties of life.

—Murray Kempton, *New York Post*, August 3, 1978

Just after eight-thirty in the morning on August 2, 1978, a small fire broke out on the mezzanine level of a busy Waldbaum's supermarket in the Sheepshead Bay neighborhood of southern Brooklyn. "I saw flames coming from a large wooden beam right next to the men's room wall," said plumber Arthur Stanley, who was part of a construction crew adding an extension to the mezzanine. "I told somebody to tell the store manager and then I hooked up this garden hose I keep in my tool kit, and tried to put it out." Store managers delayed calling the fire department and evacuating customers from the market, but when the flames spread to a storage room they relented, and employees had to convince reluctant customers to leave their carts and exit the store. At 8:39, the call came in to the fire department, and within three minutes the first fire engine was on the scene. The units at the scene quickly radioed for backup, and after an eight-minute delay, dispatchers complied, calling a "second alarm" just after nine o'clock, and a third and a fourth alarm soon after that.

Across the street from the fire, Louise O'Connor stood with her three children—five-year-old Billy Jr. and his little sisters, Lisa Ann and Jean Marie. A few minutes earlier, Louise had arrived at Brooklyn

Ladder Company 156 to pick up her husband, Billy O'Connor, after the nine a.m. shift change, but saw that the house's garage was open and empty. One of her husband's friends from the house saw her waiting outside and told her Billy was out at a fire. It was contained, he'd said, nothing to worry about, and gave her directions. When she reached the supermarket, the blaze was far from out. Waves of heat radiated from the building, and thick clots of dusky smoke oozed into the sky. A dozen or so engines and ladder trucks idled in the parking lot, and the arm of a big tower ladder was telescoped out over the roof of the building. Standing across the street from the fire, Louise was distracting the kids to keep them calm—pointing out things to look at, explaining what was going on—when she spotted a familiar frame striding out the front door of the Waldbaum's.

"We're standing in front of the building, and I'm watching and I'm watching," says Louise, "and now we see Billy come out of the building, and the kids are calling him but he doesn't hear. Then he went up the ladder and onto the roof and I guess he must have heard the kids or maybe he just—I don't know, he turned around and they were yelling and waving and he waved and he stepped on the roof."

Just as Billy walked out of sight, a sudden flash shone through the windows of the market and the roof hemorrhaged thick streams of jet-black smoke. A security guard standing next to Louise told her it was nothing the firemen couldn't handle, but she had a bad feeling. A fresh wave of heat rippled from the building and Louise—muttering "God, Christ the fire," to herself over and over—took the kids across the street to a pay phone to call Billy's father, a captain in a nearby Brooklyn firehouse.

STANDING ON THE ROOF OR FLOOR ABOVE A BLAZE IS THE most dangerous place a fireman can position himself. Before the terrorist attacks of September 11, 2001, the deadliest day in the history of the Fire Department of New York came when the first floor of a brownstone apartment building collapsed into a burning basement below, killing twelve firemen. Most of the deadliest blazes for American firefighters—twenty-one killed in a Chicago stockyard in 1910; fourteen in a Philadelphia factory that same year; thirteen killed in a Massachusetts theater in 1941—were all collapses. But getting above the fire is precisely what the "truckies" of a ladder company like Billy O'Connor's do for a living. Engine companies put water on a fire. Along with rescues, a ladder crew's job is to vent the heat and smoke from the blaze. Without venting, fire crews run the risk of a backdraft, when an oxygen-starved fire gets a sudden burst of air—say from another fireman, axing his way through the door—and the fire explodes outward. More often, the heat and smoke from a blaze radiate back into the room to cause a rollover, when carbon monoxide and unburned hydrocarbons smolder in dancing blue flames that roll along the ceiling like northern lights in the winter sky. In the engine of a car, the exploding gasoline isn't hot enough to burn off these gases, so a catalytic converter is used to change their chemical structure to burn at lower temperatures. In a rollover, there is no chemical catalyst, just heat blasting the molecules apart. Without venting, a rollover can quickly turn into flashover, when everything in the room is heated to the point of ignition and suddenly bursts into flames.

The easiest way to vent a fire is to break out windows and doors, but the most effective method is to tear holes in the roof or ceiling above the blaze. Truckies have a few tricks for spotting and preventing collapses. Once they're actually above a fire, they look for sudden puffs of smoke coming up through the vents, and check the roof they're standing on for increased warmth or softness. But the most important work happens before ladder crews even set foot on a roof, when they scout the fire from below. Some of their methods are by-the-book: checking the severity of the fire, cutting small holes in the ceiling and walls to see how far it has spread, studying the building's construction for weaknesses. Others are harder to quantify, the almost subconscious process of stacking up the countless, tiny details gleaned from the blaze at hand—the smell, shifts in air currents and pressure—and comparing them with the accumulated wisdom of a career spent fighting fires. It all happens so quickly that most firefighters describe it as little more than a gut feeling, but, like hitting a curveball or making a no-look pass, it's a matter of skill and experience, not divine inspiration.

Before Billy climbed onto the roof and waved to Louise and the kids, he and Ladder 156 had been inside the market scouting the blaze, probably cutting holes in the ceiling and walls for signs of fire extension, checking how far the heat and smoke had "banked down" from the ceiling to gauge how long and how hot it had been burning. Radioing back to headquarters, chiefs inside the market said the fire was nothing out of the ordinary, but they didn't know that an inferno was blazing above them, hidden in an illegally constructed section of the attic. The first hint came when a ladder crew on top of the building cut a hole in the center of the roof, to find not flames but another roof. Unbeknownst to firemen, the Waldbaum's was built with what's known as a "truss roof," which has a tendency to sag in the middle and collect heavy rainwater. To fix the problem, the contractors added a thin, sloped "rain roof" on top of the original roof to divert water to gutters on the side of the building. But management never told the buildings department or the fire department about the rain roof.

In New York in the late 1970s, keeping City Hall in the dark about building renovations was standard operating procedure. The city had gone all but bankrupt in 1975, and the cash-strapped buildings department and fire department didn't have the time or manpower to perform many inspections or enforce codes. With no one to stop or fine them, building owners routinely cut corners to save money. In the case of Waldbaum's, the fire department had never even done a serious inspection of the building—chiefs on the scene knew nothing about the truss roof, the rain roof, or the out-of-code attic that hid the main fire from both the firemen inside the store and those on the roof above.

After cutting through the rain roof, truckies had to use long hooks to punch smaller holes in the original roof below. Initially the openings didn't show much fire, but just after Billy and Ladder 156 reached the roof, someone cut a hole above the hidden inferno in the attic. With the sudden rush of oxygen, smoke and flames shot into the air and caused the burst of sparks that sent Louise to the pay phone to call Billy's father. With the previously hidden flames now vented, Billy and the crew on the roof faced two facts that had initially escaped them: that the roof they stood on was actually above the original roof, and that there was a very serious fire burning below a section of that lower roof. There was a third fact they were still unaware of, though: the truss-style construction of the original roof. One of the big advantages of a truss roof is that the trusses (usually steel or wooden beams) work together to evenly distribute the weight above them to the side walls of the building, removing the need for load-bearing columns below. For decades, column-style construction had been the FDNY's primary collapse problem—an uneven distribution of weight or fire damage would cripple one or two columns and down they'd come. Collapses were particularly common with the cast-iron architecture of many factories and warehouses south of Houston Street in Manhattan. By the late 1970s, the cast-iron district was being rechristened as SoHo (for "South of Houston [Street]") and TriBeCa (for "Triangle Below Canal [Street]") by the area's budding artist population and the enterprising real estate developers who followed them, but in the fire department, the neighborhood was still known as Hell's Hundred Acres. Trusses cut the risk of collapse by distributing excess weight from one truss to the entire roof. But if that distributed weight is too much for the trusses to bear, they can all crumble in an instant (which happened with the collapse of the World Trade Center towers).

LOUISE O'CONNOR HUNG UP A PAY PHONE DOWN THE BLOCK from the Waldbaum's supermarket as the heat of the fire and the August sun bore down on her and her three small children. Billy's father had told her not to worry about the fire, but said he'd come down to the scene if it would make her feel better. It did, and she tried to calm herself as she led little Billy, Lisa Ann, and Jean Marie back down the street to watch the blaze.

"We're standing there and it's starting to get real, real hot where we were standing," she says. "So I'm getting scared now for the kids, because they're starting to get scared because it's so hot. So I say, 'Let's go across the street,' where there was a butcher shop. But before I could walk away, before I knew it . . ."

The building gave out a loud crack, and a ball of flame leaped into the air. Firemen on the ground looked for cover, and shouts rose from the growing crowd of onlookers. Above the burning market, half of the roof had given way, and a dozen of the twenty or so men standing on it had fallen through.

"All of a sudden there was a terrible burst of flame," said Leonard Stone, who lived across the street from the market. "They all went down just like they were infants. It was a shame to see those fellows blown into the air, and then they just fell into the fire."

From his shoe store across the street, Walter Fullenwider watched the scene descend into chaos. "It happened fast," he said. "It looked like hell to me. The flames were shooting very high, and the smoke was so thick in the street that you could hardly see. I heard a loud noise when the roof caved in and I saw five or six firemen running on the ledge. They looked like they were going to jump, and other firemen and people in the street started shouting, 'Don't jump, don't jump.' None of them jumped, and they got them down."

The firemen who made it down from the roof and the fifty or so already on the ground quickly formed up along the supermarket wall and attacked it with a steel battering ram, punching a hole in the bricks just large enough to squeeze through. Once inside, they used power saws and axes to cut through fallen steel beams and flaming truss supports to clear a path to the victims.

"When the roof collapsed, four or five guys fell straight through to the floor," said fireman Tom Murphy, who was inside the market when the roof came down around his company. "The other six guys got trapped in the crawl space. They didn't go all the way through to the floor and they got tangled up on the wire supports for the floor space. Down on the floor, the one guy's face is all on fire. He's on fire here and here," Murphy said, grabbing at his arms and shoulders. "Fire all over him. You couldn't see the fire burning him, you could just see the fire all over him, you know? We got him out and all he said to us was 'There's others in there in the third aisle. The third aisle of the supermarket.' That's all he said. He's got flames all over him and he tells us about others."

As firemen pulled survivors from the building, Billy's uncle Phil Ruvolo and his fire company pulled up to the scene. "We responded," said Ruvolo, "and when I got there I went to guys I knew and said, 'Where's Angel?' that's the name we called Bill. A guy said to me, 'He was on the roof when it went.' I said, 'What part?' The guy said, 'Center.' I went in. I couldn't find anything."

Outside the market, Louise, tired of being stonewalled and told to "get back to the fucking firehouse!" by every panic-stricken, confused fireman she saw, ran over to Ruvolo. "Uncle Phil," she told him, "I'm looking for him." Not sure what to say, Ruvolo headed back to the market to search.

"I went back in and couldn't find anything," he said. "I came out and the father was standing there and he saw my eyes and he knew. I told him, 'There's no hope.'"

BY THE TIME FIREFIGHTER'S UNION PRESIDENT DICK VIZZINI reached the scene, the survivors of the collapse had all been rescued. In the parking lot, a fire department chaplain was preparing to go inside the still-burning building to perform extreme unction, the last rites, on the six who hadn't made it out.

The scene was crawling with reporters, department brass, politicians. Commissioner Augustus Beekman was in operational control of the fire and rescue efforts. Chief of Department Francis Cruthers was supposed to be on vacation, but he'd heard the mayday calls over his scanner and rushed over from his Brooklyn home. Even the new mayor, Ed Koch, was there, offering his condolences to firemen and family members who had rushed to the scene. Like the mayor, Vizzini had started the day at City Hall, preparing for contract talks with Koch's labor negotiators. Seven months earlier, Koch had blown into City Hall like a breath of fresh air. After three years of near-bankruptcy and almost daily embarrassments (the Son of Sam murders, sanitation strikes that left the streets filled with trash, exploding rates of crime and drugs), Gotham was desperate to regain some of its swagger, and Koch, a brash, bald, wise-cracking Army vet, seemed like the man for the job.

Koch promised to be a tough negotiator, but the pressure of the city's fiscal crisis was finally starting to ease, and things were looking up for the union for the first time in years, as the city was just starting to come out of a fire-plagued decade that firemen had taken to calling "the War Years." Hundreds of thousands of people in the Bronx, central Brooklyn, and Manhattan's Lower East Side and Harlem neighborhoods were burned from their homes, as once bustling neighborhoods were turned to little more than ash and rubble. Civilian deaths doubled to more than three hundred per year, and that was only for people who died shortly after the fire, the department all too happy to not count those who hung on in the hospital for a few days. Firemen were dying at an unprecedented rate, too, about ten a year on duty and plenty more at home from heart attacks, strokes, and cancer caused by too many bellies full of toxic smoke.

Firemen were used to the dangers. Some of the most coveted station assignments, like Vizzini's old company, Engine 41 in the South Bronx, were actually in the most fire-ravaged sections of the city. What was killing morale—and, as far as Vizzini was concerned, killing firemen and civilians—were budget cuts. Every municipal department had taken its lumps in 1975, when the city was more than $12 billion in debt and on the verge of bankruptcy. But the fire department had started making cuts years before that, closing dozens of busy fire companies in the same poor, black, and Puerto Rican neighborhoods that were burning to the ground. Vizzini and the union sued to stop the cuts, saying they were dangerous and racially motivated, but judges threw the cases out at the first opportunity.

It all seemed so backward to the union boss, almost like City Hall wanted the neighborhoods to burn. Plenty of firemen thought as much—that it was a conspiracy to chase the blacks and Puerto Ricans from the city, some kind of convoluted real estate grab or gerrymandering scheme. The conspiracy stuff was a bit far-fetched—the bureaucracy was far too disorganized and inept to carry out a plot that complex. But still, you had to wonder. The urban planner Robert Moses, now retired to his Long Island beach house, but still an influential writer for *The New York Times* and a bevy of magazines, wanted to blacktop the whole South Bronx—with the buildings burned down and the land abandoned, most of the heavy lifting was already done. City planning commission studies from the late 1960s had recommended the same thing, taking advantage of the burnout to acquire abandoned lots on the cheap and redevelop them. Roger Starr, the head of the city's housing department in the mid-1970s, had actually proposed a policy of "planned shrinkage," closing hospitals and fire, police, and subway stations in places like the South Bronx and pushing out whoever was left living there. A few years later, a friend of Vizzini's from the union recounted an interesting conversation he had with a high-ranking mayoral aide about the fires and how the city hadn't done anything to stop them, had, in fact, encouraged the destruction with all the cuts. "Well, you can always look on the bright side," the aide had said. "The city got rid of a million and a half undesirables."

"And he was right," says Vizzini's union colleague. "All those people burned out of the Bronx and Brooklyn and Harlem, they moved. Back to Puerto Rico, to Paterson [New Jersey], Newark, Jersey City. It was like they had a clean slate to rebuild on."

The conspiracy theorists were bolstered by the puzzling fact that the cuts cost far more money than they saved. The city itself lost countless millions in real estate taxes from the fires and had to shell out millions more to put fire victims up in welfare hotels or move them into public housing projects, to say nothing of the businesses and jobs lost to the flames. The cuts barely even saved money for the department, which had to foot the bill for all the extra injuries, disability, and widows' pensions, and compensate for the lack of manpower with time-and-a-half overtime pay. To help rein in that overtime, the department had devised a series of policies, some official, others too controversial to put into writing but nonetheless enforced down the chain of command. The number of men on an engine was cut from six and sometimes seven to as few as three or four. Firemen were denied sick leave. Dispatchers sent fewer and fewer fire companies to blazes. Previously, if a unit was out fighting a fire during a shift change, they stayed until it was out and collected overtime. Suddenly, dispatches from headquarters started mysteriously coming in moments after a shift change.

Vizzini thought about those overtime cuts as he watched Koch talk to fire department brass and address the gaggle of reporters and photographers. Twenty-two men had responded to the initial fire alarm instead of the thirty who would have been there if it weren't for the manpower cuts. Despite getting a call for backup from firemen at the scene at 8:54, headquarters hadn't issued a second alarm until 9:02, just minutes after the shift change, eliminating the need to pay overtime. And Vizzini thought there was something fishy about the whole affair—supermarkets didn't just collapse like that. Along with the rain roof it was a pretty safe bet there was plenty more about the building that the cut-to-the-bone buildings department and fire inspectors didn't know about.

It wasn't the first time Vizzini blamed budget cuts for deaths. A little girl had died in Harlem recently after overtime cuts delayed the response by ten minutes. The department took so long to respond to another fatal Harlem fire that residents jeered the mayor and fire commissioner when they arrived on the scene. Some people in Queens had died when unserviced fire alarms malfunctioned. There'd been dozens, maybe hundreds, more deaths in the past few years where if a nearby fire company hadn't been closed, if a fire hydrant had worked, if the men hadn't been exhausted and dehydrated and sick with carbon monoxide poisoning from fighting fires all day, things would have turned out differently. But Vizzini had never made charges on this scale before. Six firemen, not civilians, were dead—Charles Bouton, James Cutillo, Harold Hastings, James McManus, George Rice, and the youngest, Billy O'Connor. Each had a wife and family, eighteen kids among them. "We charge that the city stalled on the second alarm for needed manpower in order to avoid paying overtime," Vizzini later told reporters. "Death was the grim paymaster."

ON THE MORNING OF OCTOBER 5, 1977—TEN MONTHS BE-fore the Waldbaum's collapse—a cream-colored limousine followed by a phalanx of dark sedans and a trio of helicopters made an unexpected appearance in the South Bronx. Early risers did double takes as the cavalcade rolled past the Art Deco apartment houses of the Grand Concourse, a few realizing with a start that the limousine at the center of the commotion was ferrying President James E. Carter. "We want jobs!" a few people shouted after the convoy. "Give us money!"

Turning east onto the dilapidated commercial drag of East Tremont Avenue, Carter was treated to his first glimpse of the ruins of the once mighty Bronx, resplendent in the warm autumn sun. He passed row upon row of burned-out buildings, the brick façades scorched black, windows hastily boarded up with cinder blocks, plywood, and—where scavengers hadn't gotten to it yet—tin flashing. On Third Avenue, stray dogs nosed through bags of garbage in weedy, rubble-strewn lots. On Claremont Parkway, junkies nodded out in vacant buildings as the motorcade rolled wordlessly by on its circuitous route, eventually coming to a stop on Charlotte Street, a short, hooked road in the middle of an uninhabited stretch of land just southeast of Crotona Park.

The neighborhood hadn't always been so empty. Until recently, Charlotte Street had occupied a somewhat enviable rung on the ladder of New York City neighborhoods, a stepping stone for working-class immigrant families looking to escape the tenement slums of Manhattan. (In America's first full-length talkie, *The Jazz Singer*, Al Jolson promised to move his family from their cramped Lower East Side apartment if he can make it as a vaudevillian: "Mama dahlin'," he says, "if I'm a success in this show, we're going to move up to the Bronx!") The neighborhood around Charlotte Street was home to fine apartment buildings and townhouses, good public transportation, a bustling open-air market on nearby Jennings Street, the swimming pool and ball fields of Crotona Park, and most important, two fine public schools, P.S. 61 and Herman Ridder Junior High. By the 1950s and 1960s, Yiddish and lox mixed with Spanish and *bacalao* in the Jennings Street markets, as Puerto Rican families began to replace Eastern European Jewish families (just as they had replaced Italian and Irish families before them), but still the area thrived. "There had been so much life," Louis Lugo later said of the neighborhood he moved to in the 1960s, "so many people and so many stores. Everything was busy, busy, busy." In the late 1960s, the city made plans to build new elementary and junior high schools to accommodate the growing population, one Board of Education surveyor noting in March of 1970 that, despite a few burned-out buildings and two vacant lots, "this entire area has high-density housing that is in fair condition."

Seven years after that Board of Education report was written, Jimmy Carter stepped from his limousine into a world almost impossibly removed from that once bustling, optimistic neighborhood. Most of the handsome five- and six-story apartment buildings were completely gone. What buildings were still standing had been gutted by flames, home only to rodents, packs of roving dogs, and the occasional junkie or squatter. Everywhere Carter looked, there were piles of rubble and whatever charred artifacts of mid-twentieth-century American domesticity had been deemed unworthy of hauling to the scrap yard: smashed-up televisions, wheel-less roller skates, cracked bathtubs. Neighborhood kids did an admirable job making use of the flotsam, turning mattresses into trampolines and landing pads, scavenging electrical parts for homemade sound systems. "You know that nice park in the South Bronx?" a character in Grace Paley's short story "Somewhere Else" asks. "We have some film if you ever want to see—the block is burning down on one side of the street, and the kids are trying to build something on the other."

Just a week after Carter's visit to Charlotte Street, the Yankees hosted the Los Angeles Dodgers in the second game of the World Series. An hour before the first pitch, an abandoned Bronx schoolhouse just a few blocks past the right-field bleachers of Yankee Stadium caught fire. With dispatchers initially able to send only one engine to fight the blaze, and an icy October wind whipping the flames, and some nearby companies too busy fighting other fires to respond to the second alarm, 60 million viewers were treated to their first glimpse of a roaring Bronx cookout. "That's the very area," said broadcaster Howard Cosell, "where President Carter trod just a few days ago."

Until the World Series, most Americans—most New Yorkers, even—were largely unaware of the condition of New York's poorest neighborhoods. People knew there were frightening slums in Harlem, the Bronx, and parts of Brooklyn. They even knew about fire to some extent, thanks to the smash success of fireman Dennis Smith's 1972 book *Report from Engine Co. 82* and, just a couple of months before Carter's visit and the World Series, an overnight blackout in New York that touched off an orgy of looting and arson in the city's slums. But nothing prepared the casual baseball fan for the sight of a massive fire left to burn amid the kind of ruins you usually had to hack through a Yucatán jungle to see.

After the blackout riots, Carter's visit, and Cosell's weary lament, the image of the South Bronx was forever fixed in the American popular imagination, "a spectacular set of ruins, a mythical wasteland, an infectious disease," in the words of one historian. "Even the gangs who once claimed this turf—the vicious Turbans and the feared Reapers—were now gone, as if they had been blown to dust by the forces of history."

In 1970, Bronx County census tract 2, in a neighborhood called Soundview, held 836 residential and commercial buildings. By 1980, there were nine left. Statistically, it wasn't even the most devastated area in the borough—that was tract 173, home to the schoolhouse left to burn during the World Series. Seven different census tracts in the borough lost more than 97 percent of their buildings to fire and abandonment; 44 tracts (out of 289 in the borough) lost more than 50 percent.

Among those left to live in what buildings remained, conditions were oppressive. "Everybody was gone from Charlotte Street but us," remembered one resident. "We ran the boiler on old tires and got something like heat. After three winters like that, finally it was just too cold and we decided to move. We made a thousand dollars stripping all the pipes from the building and selling everything we could from it." Youth unemployment rates hit 80 percent. A thousand teenagers camped like would-be concertgoers outside the South Bronx Neighborhood Youth Corps Center one night in the hopes of landing one of fifty summer jobs being offered the next morning. Life expectancies fell. Rates of low birth weight, infant mortality, and malnutrition reached Third World levels. To one local doctor quoted in *The New York Times*, the borough was a "Necropolis—a city of death." To the *Times* editorial page, seeing the Bronx was "as crucial to an understanding of American urban life as Auschwitz is crucial to an understanding of Nazism."

After Carter and the World Series, camera crews, visiting dignitaries, Ronald Reagan, even Mother Teresa, came to marvel at the dissolution. Around the world, the Bronx was anathema, "a condition of poverty and social collapse, more than a geographical place," wrote architectural historian Robert Jensen. In Catania, Sicily, a run-down slum near the docks became known as the "Bronx." In French slang, the phrase to describe not just disorder but utter dysfunction, irreparable fuckedupedness, became *"C'est le Bronx,"* literally, "It's the Bronx." The Métro shut down at rush hour? The pipes froze and flooded your apartment? *C'est la vie*, and *c'est le Bronx*.

In New York City itself, though, thinking about the Bronx was the last thing anyone wanted to do. A few years later, along the Cross Bronx Expressway—a 225-foot-wide, seven-mile-long trench carved through the heart of the borough in the 1950s to provide a direct link between the suburbs of Long Island and New Jersey—the city tried to create a Potemkin village, a gilded ghetto. "I remember driving on the Cross Bronx with my dad when I was a kid," says borough native Anthony Loscalzo, "and him telling me to look up at the buildings along the road, tell him what I saw. 'I dunno Dad, windows?' I told him. 'No,' he said, '*look* at them.' I looked and I saw it, all the boarded-up windows, they'd put posters or wallpaper over them, so it looked like there were plants and blinds in the windows, like people lived there." The postering campaign cost the city the same amount as keeping three or four closed fire stations open for a year.

The Cross Bronx Expressway, wrote Marshall Berman, was a particularly excruciating commute for those "who remember the Bronx as it used to be . . . until this road cut itself through their heart and made the Bronx, above all, a place to get out of. For children of the Bronx like myself, this road bears a load of special irony: as we race through our childhood world, rushing to get out, relieved to see the end in sight, we are not merely spectators but active participants in the process of destruction that tears our hearts. We fight back the tears, and step on the gas."

And it wasn't just the Bronx. While their collapse wasn't quite as spectacular or nearly as famous, the same thing was happening in Harlem and the Lower East Side of Manhattan, and Brooklyn's Bushwick, Brownsville, Bedford-Stuyvesant, and East New York neighborhoods. Throughout the 1970s, the city hemorrhaged jobs by the hundreds of thousands, prompting nearly a million people to leave for the suburbs, and more than a million to stay put and go on welfare. Heroin flooded the streets; muggings, burglaries, and armed robbery were rampant; the murder rate nearly quadrupled. A new breed of rat, a foot and a half long and immune to conventional poison, took over subway tunnels. There was even pestilence, as diseases believed to be all but conquered by modern medicine, like measles and tuberculosis, staged a spectacular comeback in the city's slums.

Underpinning New York's woes was its mounting fiscal crisis. Twelve billion dollars in debt and unable to secure loans to pay its workers, the city was put into de facto bankruptcy, its purse strings held by "Big MAC," the Municipal Assistance Corporation, a state authority run by investment bankers and unelected political power brokers. In the midst of the crisis, a spokesman for MAC laid out their basic contention as to what drove New York to the poorhouse. "It's the fucking blacks and Puerto Ricans," he told journalist Robert Fitch. "They use too many city services and they don't pay any taxes. New York's in trouble because it's got too many fucking blacks and Puerto Ricans." While few officials employed such colorful phrasing (terms like "jobs-skills mismatch" were generally preferred), their basic argument was the same. Liberalism, in the form of social welfare programs and lenient jail sentences for the unruly poor, and lavish contracts for civil service unions, was driving the city into bankruptcy and turning the ghettoes into lawless, welfare-dependent dens of iniquity.

The timing of this explanation couldn't have been better, New York City fast becoming the example par excellence of the excesses of New Deal and Great Society liberalism. "In the 1960s," Ronald Reagan became fond of saying, "we fought a war on poverty, and poverty won." That war on poverty, and its controversial "community action" programs, were born in New York City. Along with Sargent Shriver and his brother-in-law, New York Senator Robert Kennedy, the American politician most closely associated with inner-city poverty programs and "liberal white guilt" was New York's mayor, John Lindsay, the man who made the 1968 Kerner Commission Report on inner-city riots famous with its conclusion that the United States was "moving toward two societies, one black, one white—separate and unequal." The neoconservative movement, usually associated with activist foreign policy, actually cut its teeth criticizing such activist domestic policy. "A neoconservative," journalist Irving Kristol famously quipped, "is a liberal who has been mugged by reality." With the movement's intellectual forefathers—Kristol, *Commentary* editor Norman Podhoretz, sociologist Nathan Glazer, and political ally Daniel Patrick Moynihan—all longtime New Yorkers, it doesn't take much to guess which city they were mugged in.

It was a perfect storm of political, economic, and social misfortune for Gotham, its worst stretch since the Revolutionary War, when half the city burned to the ground and Redcoats occupied the rubble. From 1970 to 1980, roughly 600,000 people's homes were lost to fire and abandonment. The city's economic output fell by 20 percent; average income dropped by 35 percent. Even Johnny Carson left for greener pastures, moving his *Tonight Show* to Los Angeles—but keeping his New York jokes ("Some Martians landed in Central Park today . . . and were mugged."). And just as in the 1770s, fire was the central actor in the tribulations of the 1970s. In a single decade, fires killed thousands, injured tens of thousands, and destroyed the homes of hundreds of thousands. It chased white New Yorkers to the suburbs, destroyed neighborhood economies, and emptied out the tenements of the South Bronx neighborhood of Mott Haven, where that new, poison-resistant strain of rat first bred. Fire rates, epidemiologists have found, were a determining factor in the spread of previously contained diseases, rising infant mortality, and falling life spans. And while those blights stayed largely in the ghetto itself, within a few years a new epidemic, HIV-AIDS, fostered among the intravenous drug users and prostitutes of those same burned-out neighborhoods, spread to the population at large.

The pat explanation for the scope of the fires is arson-for-profit. Howard Cosell blamed arson for the fire that raged outside Yankee Stadium during the World Series. Fire marshals and police investigators uncovered enormous landlord arson rings that set fire to thousands of buildings and collected tens of millions of dollars in insurance. Arson graft went right up the political and economic food chain, from kids who were paid twenty dollars to spread the gas and light the match to landlords, real estate title companies, insurance agents, federal urban renewal bureaucrats, even high-ranking politicians. "The one place you couldn't talk was City Hall," says a veteran fire marshal. "If word got out about your case there, it was all over." And it wasn't just landlords; tenants got in on the act as well. Firemen routinely pulled up to burning buildings to find families waiting outside, surrounded by luggage and neatly stacked furniture, after setting the fire themselves to take advantage of welfare programs that handed out thousands of dollars to fire victims and put them at the front of years-long waiting lists for public housing.

From a media and political standpoint, the arson story comes with the added bonus of appealing to both liberal and conservative moralizing. For liberals, the argument was that greedy landlords, corrupt businesses, and lax government agencies destroyed neighborhoods for profit. For conservatives, that well-intentioned welfare and public housing benefits created perverse incentives for ghetto arson. This helped the arson explanation worm its way into nearly every account of the city in the 1970s. In-depth academic histories, popular books, magazine and newspaper articles, even novels, movies, and television shows set during the period, make at least a passing reference to the "arson epidemic," or "plague of intentionally set fires," that burned down the city's ghettoes. But for all its ubiquity, the arson story is ultimately fiction.

Certainly by the *late* 1970s, arson was taking its toll on the city and fire department, particularly in devastated communities like the South Bronx, East New York, and Bushwick. But arson was never the major cause of fire damage in New York. During the 1950s, city fire marshals attributed less than 1 percent of fires to arson. Until 1975, that ratio never rose above 1.1 percent. At its peak in the late 1970s, arson made up less than 7 percent of fires. What's more, arson occurred primarily in already burned-out, abandoned buildings—after all, it made more sense to torch a building without rent-paying tenants than one that had at least some revenue coming in.

"You know, in some ways the job became easier after 1975 or so, because even though there were all those fires, they were mostly in abandoned buildings," says retired Fire Commissioner Thomas Von Essen, who worked out of Ladder Co. 42 in the South Bronx during the War Years. "Before then, you actually had people living in all of them. God, it was awful."

Arsonists were little more than vultures, picking over the bones of dead and dying communities. What killed those neighborhoods was an earlier wave of conventional fires, which spread over the poorer quarters of the city like a contagion. The first stage of accidental fires was not only more damaging but more easily preventable—whether by stepping up fire prevention or simply maintaining levels of service in fire-ravaged neighborhoods. Instead, thirty-four of the busiest engine and ladder companies in the city were closed.

Liberalism was, in fact, at the heart of both the fire cuts and the city's fiscal crisis. But it wasn't the tax-and-spend liberalism of activist civil service unions and no-questions-asked welfare, it was the paternalistic liberalism of can-do interventionism, the notion that cities, countries, and economies should be controlled from the top down by educated elites and number-crunching technocrats who could use the scientific method to bring greater order and stability to society.

There was ample reason for the belief. From the 1930s to the 1950s, America's central planners, engineers, and efficiency experts fought the Depression, built the most powerful army the world had ever known, split the atom, reached outer space, and dominated the world economy, all of it on the strength of new inventions and corporate efficiency. To American eyes, the world seemed an increasingly rational, predictable, and prosperous place. During the two decades following World War II, the average American's income doubled. In the longest continuous economic expansion in the country's history, the Gross National Product grew from $503.7 billion to $807.6 billion in just seven years. Even the compilation of such encouraging economic data was something of a modern marvel. Before World War II, gauging the American economy was a murky enterprise at best. Take unemployment figures for the Great Depression, which approached 25 percent at its peak, according to most estimates: those figures are just that, *estimates*—unemployment was officially tallied only once a decade by the Census Bureau. By the 1960s, the vast array of economic data suddenly available made even complex fields like economics seem fairly predictable. The Council of Economic Advisers' forecast for the 1964 GNP was off by .06 percent. Their unemployment forecast was spot-on.

Blinded by their recent success, American politicians and planners believed they could reshape American cities and society along similarly rational, organized lines, and no group was more optimistic than the leaders of New York City. At the vanguard of this movement was the FDNY and the man who dominated every aspect of firefighting in New York City during the War Years, John T. O'Hagan, one of only two men to simultaneously hold the titles of chief of department and fire commissioner in the FDNY's nearly 150-year history. (In the FDNY, the chief of department is responsible for day-to-day operations, while the commissioner handles the politics.) Chief for fourteen years and commissioner for four, O'Hagan initiated and fostered the development of some of the most important advances in firefighting technology since the invention of coal-powered steam engines and fire hydrants—arguably, the man most responsible for the 75 percent decrease in American fire fatalities over the last four decades. For his fellow firefighters, O'Hagan helped usher in the first practical air-masks, telescoping tower ladders that could extend out and over burning buildings, a super-pumper engine so powerful it could knock down a brick wall with water, handy-talkie and walkie-talkie radios, early versions of the "jaws of life" steel-cutting saw, shatter-resistant eye shields, and the use of a special polymer that, when added to the water in a fire engine, reduced the friction enough to pump nearly twice as many gallons per minute. For the public at large, O'Hagan pushed the first home smoke detectors, fire-resistant building materials and furnishings, self-extinguishing cigarettes, and sprinkler systems. A self-taught engineer and architect, O'Hagan literally wrote the book on how to fight fires in modern high-rise buildings, and created the building codes that help prevent and contain them, since copied around the country and the world.

The greatest setback of his career came when he failed to force the powerful designers and builders of the World Trade Center to follow those codes. His warnings proved eerily prophetic when a car bomb exploded in the North Tower in February of 1993. Just as O'Hagan had predicted, without an adequate sprinkler system, fires burned out of control and the building's poorly designed ventilation system spread poisonous smoke throughout its 110 floors. He had larger concerns than the sprinklers and vents though, railing against the Twin Towers' truss-style construction, inadequate fire-proofing, and susceptibility to collapse. "You go into those pieces of shit," he used to tell his men, "you watch your back."

"In 2001, I was at home, watching as those buildings fell," says retired FDNY chief Vincent Dunn, an expert on building collapses. "For that kind of collapse, I'm supposed to be *the* guy who understands how that happens—insurance companies and architects, they pay me big bucks to give talks about this kind of stuff. But watching it, I had no idea how. It just didn't make any sense—a pancake collapse? So I grabbed my copy of O'Hagan's book and I saw why it happened. The trusses, the fire insulation, having all the weight on the exterior frame—O'Hagan saw all of that."

John O'Hagan also ran the FDNY during the worst fire epidemic in modern urban history, and oversaw the systematic withdrawal of fire protection from the areas that burned. During O'Hagan's reign, the national fire fatality rate fell by nearly 40 percent, thanks in large part to the technological innovations he helped bring about. In the city that he was charged with protecting, fire fatality rates more than doubled thanks in large part to the managerial innovations he enacted, namely a series of statistically determined budget cuts and fire company closings. The first round of cuts, billed as actually improving fire service by creating a smaller, more flexible and responsive department, significantly reduced fire protection in the neighborhoods that needed it the most. But the dangerous results were buried in piles of fire department statistics far from the view of the public, and as the city went into economic freefall, the cuts only deepened. Not only were dozens of the busiest engine and ladder companies in the city closed, but units that provided extra lengths of hose, air tanks, and logistical support at fire scenes were slashed, fifty companies in all. Fire inspections were cut by 70 percent, and the fire marshal program was gutted.* Without new fire engines and ladder trucks, the fire department garage in Queens became known as "Red Square" after the sea of crimson-hued apparatus sitting idle in its sprawling parking lot, and ancient rigs with outmoded safety features and rickety wooden ladders were pressed into service. Every time one South Bronx fire engine went up a sloped section of Freeman Street, the men would jump off and sprint ahead in full gear and heavy rubber boots, laughing and waiting at the top of the hill while the engine struggled up behind them like a whip-weary pack mule not long for this world.

"I'd say a quarter to a third of the hydrants didn't work," says Jerry DiRazzo, who fought fires in the Bushwick section of Brooklyn. "Everything cost money, and without it we lost manpower, we lost equipment. . . . You can see the way an area changes when they don't repair a neighborhood. Every day I drove over the border from Queens to Brooklyn to go to work, and it was like this imaginary line was crossed. Almost like suddenly the sun wasn't shining, like it was darker somehow. I drove extremely careful, looking out for kids running wild in the street;

---

*Cuts in the number of fire marshals even set the stage for one of the darkest moments in the city's history. "I remember there was a stretch," says retired Bronx firefighter Tom Henderson, "where someone was setting trash fires, usually happening under the awnings of buildings, in the early morning out on City Island [in the Bronx]. So one morning we're on our way to one of these fires and I see this yellow car that I'd seen at another fire just like it, so I tell the chauffeur [the driver of the rig], who radios the other company to handle the fire, and he turns around and goes after the guy. His car was faster than us and he got away, but we got the license plate."

"A yellow sedan," says retired fire marshal Mike DiMarco, "license plate 561XLB, belonging to one David Berkowitz. He lived off Pelham Parkway, and we had him under surveillance for months, watching his car late at night when we didn't have any fires to run off to, but we never caught him in the act. Then he moved off to Brooklyn, and at that time there wasn't any coordination between the fire marshals from the different boroughs, we just didn't have the time to talk and compare notes, and he slipped through the cracks."

The next time DiMarco heard the name David Berkowitz was the summer of 1977, when he was arrested for the Son of Sam shootings, after police tracked down a yellow Ford Galaxy, license plate 561XLB, that was ticketed for parking too close to a fire hydrant just a few blocks from the eighth Son of Sam shooting. "And you know, the funny thing is," says DiMarco, "I'd been talking to a reporter I knew just a few weeks before, and he asked me, just to make conversation, what kind of a guy the cops should be looking for, and I told him a pyromaniac. A lot of serial killers, that's how they start—the same kind of a thrill, I guess."

I always made sure the window was up. And it was like no one cared. We'd go to a car fire where the car is fully involved, and you'd come back a month later and that same car would be in the exact same spot where it burned. In many cases, it was flipped over and it would lay there in the sidewalk for weeks. People would ask me, 'How can you deal with this, seeing that every day?' And I'd tell them, 'I have a front row seat to the greatest show on earth.' This was history being made, a city collapsing."

As chief and commissioner, O'Hagan was the man most responsible for what happened in the department, but he was also a cog in the larger political and intellectual machinery behind the cuts. The technical justification for the closings came from the New York City–RAND Institute, a joint endeavor of the mayor's office and the Santa Monica–based military think tank, home to dozens of Nobel laureates, the strategists behind America's nuclear defense policy, and the designers of the first modern computer and the hydrogen and neutron bombs. RAND's hallmark was a process known as "systems analysis," which tried to replace fallible human judgment with cool rationality by looking at an organization, turning all of its components into hard numbers that could be plugged into models and equations, and determining the optimal way of running that system.

Convinced that their statistical training trumped the hands-on experience of veteran fire officers, RAND analysts spent years building computer models they thought could accurately predict fire patterns and efficiently restructure the department based on those patterns. The models were deeply flawed—closing busy ghetto fire companies and opening new units in sleepy suburban-style neighborhoods—but they benefited from the sheen of omniscience coming from the whirring supercomputers and whiz-kid Ph.D.'s behind them.

But governance is more than just a matter of bureaucrats and big ideas: for those big ideas to be enacted, there must be politicians with a vested interest in them—in this case, liberal Republican mayor John Lindsay. A product of New York's progressive reform and good-government movement, Lindsay's dream was to do away with the city's cynical, corrupt governance, run from the bottom up by Tammany Hall ward bosses and horse-trading politicians, and replace it with an honest, efficient system, the dual "gospel of morality . . . [and] gospel of efficiency," as New York's greatest reform politician, Teddy Roosevelt, once put it. Lindsay shared the RAND Corporation's belief that the biases of human judgment and corruptions of power politics could be replaced with hard numbers, rationality, and scientific management. Like John Kennedy and his "best and brightest" cabinet, Lindsay, O'Hagan, and RAND believed they were ushering in a new era in government, when programs would be administered from the top down by nonpartisan technocrats and a mandarin class of meritocratic elites culled from the nation's finest colleges and business schools, not local clubhouse hacks and ill-educated civil service bureaucrats.

And so, for all the paradoxes inherent in closing busy fire stations while the neighborhoods around them burned, the greatest irony would be the who and the how and the why of those closings: John Lindsay, an ardent supporter of civil rights and a key figure in the passage of the Civil Rights Act, overseeing policies that burned down New York's black and Puerto Rican ghettoes; John O'Hagan, the most influential and forward-looking fire chief in the country, gutting his own department; and the RAND Corporation, an organization devoted to logic and rationality, recommending the most illogical of policies. A city burned by brilliance, idealism, and the best of intentions.

Mayor John Lindsay with New York's bravest.

(Photo courtesy FDNY Photo Unit)

TWO

The Fireman and the Reformer

Thus the city presents in microcosm all the contrasts of our modern life, its worst and its best aspects. Here are the broad avenues, and here the narrow lanes; here the beautiful parks where landscape gardening has done its best, and here the fetid streets whose festering filth pollutes the atmosphere. Here are the noblest men and women . . . and here the most hopeless specimens of degraded humanity, in whom, so far as human sight can see, the last spark of divinity has been quenched forever. What shall we do with our great cities? What will our great cities do with us?

—The Reverend Lyman Abbot, Plymouth Church, Brooklyn

John O'Hagan was raised above a liquor store near the southwest corner of Brooklyn in a neighborhood called Bay Ridge. Named for a narrow glacial spine that runs south along what is now Ridge Boulevard, Bay Ridge straddles the upper and lower bays of New York Harbor. Connecting the two bays and separating Brooklyn—the southwestern terminus of Long Island—from Staten Island, is the Hudson Narrows, a calm shipping channel formed six thousand years ago, when the glacial melt–swelled Hudson River burst through a thin strip of low-lying land to reach the sea. In 1524, Giovanni da Verrazzano entered the Narrows and became the first European to set eyes on the New York that F. Scott Fitzgerald would later call "a fresh, green breast of the New World." But Verrazzano did not venture farther into the harbor, instead dropping anchor in the Narrows and holding a brief meeting with a group of befuddled Lenape Indians, who rowed canoes carved from tulip trees out to his hulking ship, before he set sail for New England. It was another eighty-five years before Henry Hudson entered the Upper Harbor and sailed the river that bears his name, and seventeen more years before a permanent settlement of Dutch fur traders sprang up on the southern tip of Manhattan, the island purchased from the Lenape by Peter Minuit, according to legend, for $24 worth of trinkets.

Michael and Mary O'Hagan welcomed John, their only child, into the world on April 7, 1925. The family moved from apartment to apartment over the next few years, but always within Bay Ridge. Unlike most future firefighters, there were no smoke-eaters in O'Hagan's family, nor was he one of the neighborhood's "fire laddies" who hung around outside firehouses and chased after engines on their way to blazes. Still, firefighting families were common in Bay Ridge, and the job—particularly during the Depression, which struck the O'Hagans and the neighborhood hard—was an attainable ticket to the middle class, a respectable profession with decent pay and good benefits, staffed by men with familiar-sounding Irish last names. "The nuns," New York fireman Dennis Smith once wrote, "never spoke to us about becoming doctors, or lawyers, only about becoming President of the United States, or a fireman, or a cop. Any of us could become President, it was our birthright, for we were all second-generation Irish or Italian, but we could become firemen or cops only if we applied ourselves, and managed in one way or another to get through high school."

With his family settled in the apartment above the liquor store, young John O'Hagan was sent to Catholic school in St. Ephrem's parish, a mile away. He did well in class, drawn to numbers, facts, and figures. Not well educated himself, and struggling to provide for his family, John's father, Michael, fixated on his son's schooling and work ethic. When John's favorite boxer, Joe Louis, came to Madison Square Garden, his father promised the boy tickets if he scored well on an upcoming test. When John came up two-tenths of a point short, his father sold the tickets and wouldn't let him listen to the fight on the radio. For decades, John recounted the story to his children, assistants, and firefighters in his command, anyone from whom he expected hard work and accountability, the tale simultaneously serving as a lesson and an apology for his hard-driving tendencies. "He was a real taskmaster," one assistant remembers, "but he never wanted more from you than he expected of himself. He could be tough but it was the way he was brought up. I hate to say it, but cold Irish."

The basis of religious education in American Catholic schools like St. Ephrem's at the time was the Baltimore Catechism, a synopsis of Catholic doctrine and philosophy relayed by way of hundreds of plainly asked and concisely answered questions, from Bible trivia (Q: What is forbidden by the Ninth Commandment? A: The Ninth Commandment forbids unchaste thoughts, desires of another's wife or husband, and all other unlawful impure thoughts and desires) to great existential conundrums (Q: What is man? A: Man is a creature composed of body and soul, and made to the image and likeness of God).

The questions and answers were memorized and recited in class at the peril of your knuckles, giving students a thorough, if rigid and unreflective, understanding of Catholicism. But the real advantage of memorizing the Catechism had more to do with test-taking and writing than with theology. Beyond the very literal lessons in Catholic dogma, there was the implicit lesson that persistent study and memorization yielded tangible results: better grades, fewer wrathful ruler-strikes from the nuns, afternoons and weekends not wasted in JUG (Justice Under God, the Catholic school equivalent of detention). It's no accident that the dramatic rise in the economic fortunes of American Catholics and Jews (who grew up memorizing lengthy passages from the Talmud) in the middle of the twentieth century coincided with the sudden rise in importance of standardized testing in college admissions, civil service hiring, and placement in the military—without even realizing it, they'd been studying all along.

The second advantage of the Catechism was that it contained, conveniently organized by topic and theme, hundreds of complicated questions about society, morality, and religion, all answered in succinct, lucid prose that even a child could understand (or at least memorize). It didn't inspire abstract poetry, but as a model for how to organize subjects and synthesize complex ideas into clear writing, it was hard to beat. A knack for math and science made O'Hagan a natural test-taker, but the writing skills he developed helped translate that analytic aptitude into his greatest intellectual strength, the ability to turn abstract quantifications into useful concepts, to give numbers the power of narrative.

After St. Ephrem's, O'Hagan was accepted into the prestigious Brooklyn Technical High School, and found himself on the verge of things no one in his family had ever achieved—college, a professional career, middle-class comfort, perhaps even affluence. Like most able-bodied men of his generation, O'Hagan had to put those plans on hold for World War II, when he was sent to the Pacific with the Army's 11th Airborne Division. The "Angels" of the 11th were thrown into a series of brutal, sometimes hand-to-hand, battles in the Philippines. After a successful airborne raid by the 11th on a Japanese prison camp, Japanese forces went out into the countryside to punish the local Filipinos for not helping repel the Americans. They tied whole families to the stilts that held their wooden homes high above the swampy ground and set the buildings on fire, O'Hagan and the 11th returning a few days later to find more than fifteen hundred crushed and charred bodies.

WHILE O'HAGAN WAS PARACHUTING BEHIND ENEMY LINES in the Philippines, his future boss, John Vliet Lindsay, was just offshore, escorting U.S. aircraft carriers and launching artillery strikes as a gunnery officer aboard a Navy destroyer. Tall, elegant, and educated amid the patrician finery of St. Paul's School and Yale (where John rowed crew and joined the prestigious secret society Scroll and Key; his twin brother, David, was Phi Beta Kappa and joined Skull and Bones), Lindsay fit the bill of the well-to-do WASP from Manhattan's Upper East Side.

When war broke out, Lindsay stepped up his coursework and finished his honors thesis in time to graduate a year early in 1943, shipping off soon afterward aboard the USS *Swanson*. After three years of combat in Italy and the Pacific, and five battle stars, Lieutenant Lindsay left the service in 1946, ski-bumming across the American West and coasting through an unhappy stint as a bank clerk in Manhattan. After the war, Lindsay rarely spoke of his combat experiences, but his time in the service helped stoke an already well-developed sense of moral purpose. "The war played a part in my entering politics," he later wrote, "there is no doubt that three years of active service in the navy contributed to my decision. Postwar frustrations—the restless strivings to find direction and moorings—led me toward government service."

After returning to Yale for law school, Lindsay and his new bride, Mary Anne Harrison—a schoolmate of Jacqueline Kennedy (née Bouvier) and a relative of presidents Benjamin Harrison and William Henry Harrison—moved to Stuyvesant Town, a massive, whites-only, middle-class housing project built for returning GIs at the northern edge of Manhattan's Lower East Side. After a few years at a white-shoe law firm, Lindsay joined the Justice Department, where he worked on civil liberties cases and the 1957 Civil Rights Act, two of the defining issues of his early political career. In 1958, he decided to run for Congress in Manhattan's "Silk Stocking" Seventeenth District, which covered the Upper East Side, Midtown, and bohemian Greenwich Village. A virtual unknown in politics, the thirty-five-year-old gained quick attention for his tireless campaigning and fiery street-corner stump speeches on bringing integrity and progressive ideals back to Washington. Winning the long-shot campaign convincingly, he was hailed by *The New York Times* as "one of the bright hopes of the Republican Party."

Just like his decisions to graduate early and volunteer for World War II, and to take on controversial civil rights and civil liberties cases for the Justice Department in the days of Jim Crow and McCarthy Red Scares, Lindsay's urge to enter politics was rooted in not just a patrician sense of noblesse oblige but a true moral obligation, what his friend August Heckscher called "a dominant, rather cheerless compulsion—to act according to what he thought was right." Friends and colleagues invariably describe Lindsay as a moralist, a man with a

"Puritanical" sense of right and wrong. In fact, he wrote his Yale thesis on radical Puritan reformer Oliver Cromwell, who overthrew the English monarchy in the mid–seventeenth century and was the de facto dictator of the Commonwealth of England for ten years. Cromwell was a fervent moralist and government reformer, and his rise to power included beheading Charles I, banning Catholicism, imposing harsh morality codes on his subjects—dancing, dice, the theater, and Christmas were all banned—and massacring Irish peasants. (Winston Churchill called his impact on Anglo-Irish relations "the curse of Cromwell.") Yet to Lindsay, Cromwell's zealotry was a sign of admirable integrity, and the young student wrote reverently of Cromwell's moral vision: "completely individualistic, guided by a sense of the immanence of God which made his will, once resolved, an inflexible cutting instrument which was to clean through tradition and opposition with irresistible force."

  With the unquestioning confidence of a man who believes in his own honor, Lindsay embarked on quixotic quests to disband the House Committee on Un-American Activities, impose stringent ethics rules on Congress, and block popular bills that infringed on civil liberties. He angered Republican Party elders by shepherding Lyndon Johnson's Civil Rights Act of 1964 through the House and supporting the president's liberal social agenda. When the right wing of the party nominated Arizona senator Barry Goldwater for president over liberal New York governor Nelson Rockefeller later that year, Lindsay took his name off the Goldwater ticket in New York and ran for reelection as an "independent Republican." With a campaign slogan of "The District's Pride—The Nation's Hope," he won in a landslide.

  Lindsay's outspokenness earned him a reputation as a truth-telling maverick with the press corps. When Goldwater was trounced by Lyndon Johnson, the then liberal *New York Post* celebrated the defeat of the "lunatic fringe" and hailed Lindsay as the "GOP's Big Winner." Along with his reputation for integrity, the congressman's patrician good looks and energetic liberalism had the papers calling him the Republican JFK. With right-wing Republicanism pronounced dead by the chattering classes after the Johnson landslide—Lindsay's own description of the Grand Old Party as "a pile of rubble" was quoted widely—his brand of socially liberal, economically conservative politics was seen as the future of the Republican Party, and Lindsay himself was considered a serious contender for the party's 1968 or 1972 presidential nomination.

LIKE JOHN LINDSAY AND MANY OTHER MEN FROM THEIR generation, John O'Hagan had trouble readjusting to civilian life. A top student in high school, O'Hagan was admitted to Rensselaer Polytechnic Institute in upstate New York on the GI bill, but dropped out after a semester. His father had died during the war, and O'Hagan returned home to live with his mother and grandmother. For months he seemed lost, his former focus gone, mind adrift. Then, in 1946, an uncle on the police department told John's mother, Mary, that the firemen's exam was going to be offered, a long hiring-freeze imposed during the war finally lifted. Perhaps Mary O'Hagan saw in the fire department's military-style training and esprit de corps a lifestyle her son had missed since leaving the Army. But most likely, she simply saw a decent job that would get him out of the house.

"You've got to think about this in terms of where he was from," says O'Hagan's oldest daughter, Catherine. "No one in the family history had graduated from high school. This was a Brooklyn Irish family that struggled for generations, and every time they got a foot up on the economic ladder, there would be a sudden death or some other tragedy and they would be back down again. So John"—she refers to her father always as John—"goes to war, survives it, and comes home to a widowed mom, just her and his grandmother at home. There's no male influence, so when the maternal forces gather and say, 'You went to college and it didn't work out, your uncle says you need to take the fire test,' he went and took it. And he found something there, whether it was the structure or the environment, or that he saw he could study and really move up, and it worked for him. He was a very analytical guy and he saw room for progression."

Having scored well on the test, O'Hagan was accepted into the department's training academy on April Fools' Day in 1947, and was soon a probationary fireman, or "probey," in a Coney Island fire company. The firehouse has a reputation for not exactly being a font of learned conversation, more construction site than Algonquin Round Table. But the occasional working-class "dese" and "dem" accents, profanity-centric diction, and constant riffing and insults tend to obscure a rapid-fire repartee, jabs and jousts that toughen the uninitiated and bring a hard edge to a romantic's profession. "Guys on the department used to get intimidated by politicians, lawyers, all these educated types," says Captain Tom Henderson, who worked as a union lobbyist in New York City, Albany, and Washington, D.C. "And I always told them the same thing: if most of those guys came into the firehouse and had coffee with you guys in the morning, while everyone's breaking balls and making jokes, they wouldn't last five minutes; they weren't smart enough to handle the give-and-take."*

Just like Lindsay, O'Hagan thrived as a public servant, and drew inspiration from his time in the military. Though he rarely spoke of the war, his rare moments of candor were telling. When he discussed combat, it was only obliquely: days of tense boredom waiting for the next drop became descriptions of the heat and humidity of the South Pacific, how

---

*With a probey in the house, all the wit and wisdom are trained on him. The harassment, chores, and occasional sleep deprivation—probeys have to cover the "twelve-by" (midnight to three a.m.) and "three-by" (three to six a.m.) night-watch shifts while vets catch a few winks—serve roughly the same function as military hazing. The probey's sense of self (self-reliance, self-preservation, self-absorption) that was fostered in the civilian world must be broken down, and a new identity, one subservient to the fire company and the job, built up. For all the legitimate reasons behind the hazing, though, the life of a probey can bear a marked resemblance to that of a new fraternity pledge. "I remember one night," says retired fireman Richard Schofield, "the probey was holding down the house watch, and the aide to the battalion chief, an old-timer, goes [upstairs] into the borough command office and gets an assistant chief's uniform. He puts it on, goes out the side door of the firehouse, and comes back in at the house watch. The probey jumps up and salutes and stands there as the 'chief' looks at the book and asks questions—lots of harrumphing and such—and tells the kid to carry on and walks out. This johnnie comes into the kitchen all flustered and excited that an assistant chief came in. The old guys tell him it's no big deal, the borough command is in the same building and it's just an excuse for a chief to say that he made a firehouse visit. 'But,' says this probey, 'he didn't have any pants on. . . .'"

he had to shave his thick beard twice a day, and developed an irritating skin condition on his back that stayed with him the rest of his life—plot replaced by detail. Lindsay tended to discuss the overarching ideals and public goals he adopted during his military career. O'Hagan's wartime references focused on the tactics and detailed minutia by which such goals are achieved. He turned stories about fierce battles with Japanese units holed up in mountainous caves into dry discussions on the importance of strategy and theories on leadership. When he spoke of midnight drops onto Japanese-held islands, he didn't talk about falling through the sky into a blackness pierced only by the flash of cannon fire and glowing tracer rounds of ammunition tearing through the air. He discussed ways of measuring the success of those missions. Drop numbers. Success ratios. Kill rates so high he was promoted to platoon sergeant in a matter of weeks because he was the most senior man still alive.

With his analytic mind, test-taking prowess, and combat leadership skills, John O'Hagan was a perfect fit for the FDNY. In his day, a probey became a first-grade fireman after one year and was eligible for promotion to lieutenant after two more (today it takes four). In most municipal departments, promotion tests were only used for middle management, the upper-echelon jobs appointed by department brass and their political patrons. But the FDNY was the purest meritocracy in the city, with every rank, even chief of department, determined by test scores, not political appointment.

It hadn't always been that way. In their first incarnation as volunteer clubs, New York City fire companies were the social and political center of a neighborhood, second only to Democratic Party clubhouses. (At the time, Manhattan's Democratic Club was coming to be known as "Tammany Hall" after the eighteenth-century social club it had grown out of, itself named after a Lenape Indian chief.) When the city's Democrat-controlled Board of Aldermen fired a popular fire chief in 1836, half the department resigned and joined forces with the Whigs to form the city's first anti-Tammany "Fusion" party, trouncing Tammany men in elections for City Register and the state's General Assembly.

After the embarrassing defeats, Tammany was convinced that firemen were better allies than enemies by a brawny young volunteer fireman and former gang leader named William Marcy Tweed. Six feet tall and well over two hundred pounds, Tweed cut a dashing figure, a red-suspendered, bellowing Brobdingnagian always at the center of the fights that routinely broke out between rival fire companies racing each other to fires for bragging rights (and the first crack at any goods that could be pilfered from the burning buildings). In 1849, Tweed and his cohorts formed their own firehouse, Americus Engine Co. 6 (named after Americus, aka Amerigo Vespucci), which Tweed turned into his own personal Tammany-allied political club. Tweed eventually became the "Grand Sachem" of Tammany and—thanks to political cartoonist Thomas Nast—the bearded, corpulent face of Gilded Age corruption.*

In 1865, the volunteer force was turned into a professional department run by the state, but in 1870, Tweed turned it into the city-run Fire Department of New York, which he and Tammany could use to dispense favors to politically connected firemen and steer contracts for new engines and equipment in the proper direction. Tweed's control was short-lived though: he was arrested in 1871 by a fireman-turned-city-sheriff, after a *New York Times* exposé detailing Tweed's corruption. After a series of arrests, convictions, and escapes, fifty-five-year-old Tweed eventually died in the Ludlow Street Jail in Lower Manhattan in 1878. In 1883, progressive reformers set up the nation's first Civil Service Commission to cut down on Tweed-style patronage jobs in the bureaucracy, and in 1894 required a series of tests for civil service jobs. The FDNY was now officially open to any man who fell within

---

*For years Tweed had used Engine Co. 6's mascot, a fierce Bengal tiger painted on the back of the engine, as his unofficial symbol. Nast turned it into the original fat cat, the Tammany Tiger, supposedly prompting Bill the Boss to complain that someone needed to "stop the damned pictures. I don't care so much what the papers say about me. My constituents can't read, but, damn it, they can see pictures!" Despite the connotations of corruption, Tammany made the tiger its official symbol after Tweed's death, a practice repeated by the national Democratic and Republican parties, which turned Nast's mocking donkey and elephant depictions into their mascots.

the height and weight requirements and could pass the physical and written test.

The FDNY's test-taking path to promotion suited O'Hagan perfectly, and he set up a study group of young firemen as soon as he was on the job. An early, if brief, member was a hulking six-foot-three veteran, helicopter pilot, military reservist, and engineering whiz named Elmer "Bud" Chapman. Eventually the head of the department's Bureau of Planning and Operations Research, Chapman did pioneering studies on the physics of smoke- and fire-spread in high-rise buildings, became an editor of *Fire Engineering* magazine—a post usually reserved for Ph.D. chemists and engineering professors—and conducted the first study to definitively prove that the accelerants used in cigarettes, which keep them lit even after they fall from the fingers of soporific smokers, were the single largest cause of preventable fire death in New York. "Physically and intellectually the most intimidating guy on the department," says Chief Vincent Dunn. "This was a guy who in the 1980s was writing about how fiber optics were going to be used for communications in office buildings—just way ahead of his time." Says Chapman of O'Hagan and his group: "I tried to study with John and those guys. I just couldn't keep up with them."

O'Hagan and his fellow upstart World War II vets rose with almost unprecedented speed through the department, becoming the foremost experts in New York, and in many cases the world, on an array of topics—electrical fires, building collapses, subway fires, blazes in modern, supposedly fireproof, steel-and-glass high-rises. To professionalize the department's training, they turned their knowledge into standard operating procedures for handling different kinds of fires, and passed that information on to younger firemen.

"They used to run training classes for probeys and firemen," says Captain Cesar "Sandy" Sansevero, who was O'Hagan's personal assistant for four years. "And each would present on whatever topic they were an expert on. One did ducts, another did grease traps or ventilation. It all sounds like small stuff—guys would think, 'You're an expert on ducts, or grease traps?' But hey, if you've got a grease trap on the fourth floor of a high-rise and the duct runs up twenty more floors and it catches, you *better* have an expert on grease traps and ducts."

O'Hagan and his cohorts challenged the conventional wisdom on how to structure the department, train firemen, and fight fires. It won them the respect of the fire department's younger generation, tired of risking their lives with antiquated equipment and outmoded tactics, but irked the older, tradition-bound chiefs and officers. "These guys were real old-timers," retired chief Edward Jonat, who joined the department with O'Hagan in the years after World War II, says of the older generation O'Hagan looked to supplant. "When we came in, all the chiefs spoke with brogues. Until they started Social Security, those guys never left, they worked into their eighties. The old department was staid, the motto was, 'We did it this way, we're always gonna do it this way.'"

There was an aura forming around the entire group (some firemen called them the "Whiz Kids," after the team of Air Force statistical control officers who went on to revolutionize the Ford Motor Company after World War II), but the light gleamed brightest off the brass of John O'Hagan. Once he was on the department, the studying he had drifted through during his brief stint in college became almost an obsession. At the firehouse between calls or during his days off at home, he could usually be found squirreled away somewhere with a book in his hand, studying structural defects in new skyscraper designs, pressure differentials in the city's water mains, or the latest trends in business management and organizational theory. O'Hagan so thoroughly outclassed the competition on every exam he took that rumors began swirling that he had an inside connection at the Civil Service Commission, someone sneaking him previews of the test. But the rumors were baseless, akin to what Satchel Paige once said of accusations that he scuffed and spit on the baseball to make his pitches dance and dive: "I never threw an illegal pitch. The trouble is, once in a while I toss one that ain't never been seen by this generation."

O'Hagan was promoted to fire captain in 1957 and moved from a

Brooklyn firehouse to Manhattan, where he took over the elite Rescue Company 1, responsible for handling collapses, multiple-alarm fires, smoky basement blazes, and any other unconventional fires in the borough. The glory jobs in the FDNY at the time tended to be in "ghetto" firehouses located in poor neighborhoods where most of the attention-grabbing blazes and daring rescues occurred. But working for the first time amid the skyscrapers of Midtown and Lower Manhattan, O'Hagan found a cause to match his ambition.

IN THE 1940S, ARCHITECTS DEVISED A NEW STYLE OF SKY-scraper. Instead of distributing weight throughout the building with widely spaced, load-bearing columns, trusses would shift the burden to a central core of elevator and air shafts made of reinforced concrete. The buildings would be lighter and cheaper to build, able to take on bold new architectural styles and, without load-bearing columns, could offer large swaths of unobstructed floor space. The only problem was that the new buildings violated every major fire code in the world's largest skyscraper market. After a wave of disastrous fires in the late nineteenth century, New York started requiring that high-rises be built with heavy masonry tiles to protect load-bearing beams, standpipes on each floor for firefighters to hook their hoses to, fireproof walls at regular intervals to compartmentalize fires, and reinforced air and elevator shafts to stop fires from spreading between floors.

As O'Hagan would later write, "builders, developers, and designers began to charge that we in fire protection were guilty of overkill. That we were adding unnecessarily to the cost of construction. Inflation was a problem, construction worker's contracts were costly. There was a need to create more jobs and a desire to renew some of the older sections of our cities." And in New York City, the real estate industry rules like oil in Texas and cars in Detroit; the regulations were quickly rolled back to allow for a new generation of ultra-light steel-and-glass high-rises.

A self-taught expert on engineering and architecture, O'Hagan quickly spotted dangerous flaws in the new buildings: inadequately fire-insulated steel beams that could flex and bend in the heat of a serious blaze; thick, climate-control windows that radiated heat back inside and made venting almost impossible; elevator and air shafts that could spread smoke and fire throughout a building. But O'Hagan also knew that as meritocratic as the FDNY was, it still relied on City Hall for funding, a city hall that in turn relied on the real estate industry for its tax base and, more important, the campaign contributions that kept the mayor, borough presidents, and city councilors in office. O'Hagan had already raised the ire of some chiefs in headquarters for his ambition and challenges to the department's status quo. They couldn't stop O'Hagan from acing promotion tests, but step on the wrong toes at headquarters or in the real estate industry, and he'd end up the highest-ranking paper-pusher in an administrative back office somewhere, or the chief in charge of fighting Staten Island brush fires. So O'Hagan was cautious in his dealings with the real estate industry, speaking to them not in the blunt terminology of a fire chief looking to save lives but that of a businessman looking to limit liabilities. The young chief made friends with progressive real estate developers who were open to sensible reforms, and built political capital for the day when he had the power to institute the kind of building and fire codes he knew the city needed.

That power came more quickly than even O'Hagan could have expected. In 1960, he was promoted to battalion chief, and a year later, to deputy chief in charge of Midtown Manhattan's 3rd Division. Then, in the fall of 1963, came the young chief's big shot, the test for chief of department—responsible for operational control of the job, second in command only to the fire commissioner. As with other promotions, each applicant's score on the chief of department's exam was averaged with an "experience score" based on seniority. Throughout his career, O'Hagan had always been one of, if not the, youngest and least-senior promotion applicants, but his test scores were always high enough to put him in the first batch of promotions. For the chief of department's exam, not only did O'Hagan have to be one of the top overall scorers, he had to be *the* top scorer, and he was giving up 9.75 out of 100 experience points to his chief competition, Chief James T. Ward, the best test-taker from the generation of firemen hired during the Depression, when jobs were scarce and a large contingent of college graduates, including a few Ivy Leaguers, joined the department.

A decade after the test was given, then Lieutenant Vincent Dunn came across a folder of old promotion tests, including O'Hagan's exam for chief of department, in the fire department library. Dunn was struck by how practical the nine-hour, eighteen-essay-question test was, with queries on some of the most vexing issues facing the department at the time— economizing without sacrificing protection, integrating new technology, cutting paperwork and red tape, increasing building inspections without diverting firefighting resources. But one question in particular—how to set up fire protection for the massive, Robert Moses–run World's Fair, to be held in Flushing Meadows in Queens—caught his eye.

The fair was a fire-protection nightmare: a square mile of cheap wooden structures, hastily wired electrical outlets, and serpentine extension cords. It was housed in a park with no population of its own and surrounded by thinly settled neighborhoods, and there was only one firehouse within a mile and a half of the site. This wasn't Flushing Meadows' first brush with fire problems: it had once served as an open-air incinerator for all of Brooklyn's garbage, "a valley of ashes," as F. Scott Fitzgerald described it in *The Great Gatsby*, "a fantastic farm where ashes grow like wheat into ridges and hills and grotesque gardens." In short, the essay question was a politically fraught topic with any number of plausible answers, from novel dispersal patterns of fire apparatus to a basic restating of what the department was planning to do: haphazardly deploy an engine and ladder to wait in a secluded corner of the fair, and hope for the best.

"At that time, I didn't know the first thing about writing," remembers Dunn, who has since gone on to write a graduate school thesis, three books, and a regular column for *Firehouse* magazine, "and I would really marvel at his writing. He would outline everything first in bullet points, then write it all out. . . . He started answering the World's Fair question and wrote for maybe two pages. Then, all of a sudden, he just scratched out those two pages and started over again in a whole new vein, and of course he wrote three or four pages after that. That was the way he thought—if he came up with a better solution to a problem, he'd fix it right then and there. And I'll tell you what, his plan for the fair was absolutely the way the department handled it."

When the scores were finally tabulated, it wasn't even close—the high experience-scorers like Chief Ward couldn't come within ten points of O'Hagan on the written exam. For John O'Hagan, a decade and a half of locking himself away at the firehouse to study instead of playing cards and breaking balls, holding study group sessions in his basement instead of relaxing or spending time with his family, had finally paid off.

But Fire Commissioner Martin Scott had no interest in letting an upstart reformer take operational control of the department. Ordinarily, the high-scorer was automatically appointed chief of department, but there was precedent in civil service law for a little leeway, a rarely invoked "one-in-three" rule that allowed a position to be filled with any of the top three scorers on an exam. The justification for the loophole was that a simple written test was not the sole measure of an applicant's value. "Five lucky Saturdays," the old chiefs would say, "and anyone could run the job." And in the 1963 competition for chief of department, Assistant Chief James T. Ward had come in third. O'Hagan was a dominant, controlling man, accustomed to stressful situations, able to command chaotic fire scenes with a few words and a cold glare. But the situation was out of his hands. He let word get out that if there was any attempt to pass him over, he would sue the city and the department, then put in for a few days' vacation time and holed up in his Bay Ridge home.

"He was almost apoplectic," remembers his daughter Catherine. "I can understand why, to come so close and fall just short." To calm his nerves, O'Hagan hung new wallpaper in his kitchen, a domestic-pastoral collage of coffee tins and salt and pepper shakers. "He hung every one of them upside down," Catherine remembers. "And that's the way it stayed until we sold the house" almost three decades later.

The case was settled when the department's two unions, the Uniformed Firemen's Association (UFA) and the Uniformed Fire Officers Association (UFOA) threatened to file a suit of their own, all the controversy helping convince Chief Ward to turn down Commissioner Scott's offer.

"The unions really saved his ass," says Captain Tom Henderson, who went on to become the president of the UFOA. "People liked Jimmy Ward. It wasn't so much that guys loved O'Hagan—guys in the Bronx didn't know who O'Hagan was, he'd never worked there—but they respected him and he was one of us, a young guy, smart as hell. But it was the precedent. You start bending rules and appointing chiefs and the whole civil service system, the tests, the promotions, all of it, goes right out the window."

On a chilly afternoon just a week before Christmas in 1964, a small promotion ceremony was held in the banquet room of Red Cross headquarters on Manhattan's Upper West Side. Midway through the pro forma speeches and incantations, a small child sitting in the audience broke free from her mother and older sister, bolted for the stage, scaled the steps with surprising alacrity, and jumped into her father's arms, two-year-old Susan O'Hagan becoming the youngest person to ever take part in an FDNY promotion ceremony, comfortably seated in the lap of her father, himself the youngest man ever raised to the position of chief of the Fire Department of New York.

ENTERING CONGRESS IN 1959, JOHN LINDSAY CONSIDERED himself the standard-bearer of New York City's century-old tradition of good-government reform. The movement tended to be fiscally conservative, socially liberal, and Republican-based, but its most defining traits were a progressive belief in the power of science and rationality to conquer society's ills, and steadfast opposition to Tammany Hall and the "urban mob" it represented. Since the mid-1800s, Democratic machines had run New York and nearly every other major American city. European cities had grown relatively slowly, with adequate time to build a professional government structure and fairly apolitical civil service, before seas of humanity were swept city-ward by the tides of the Industrial Revolution. Large American cities had no such opportunity. Boomtowns one and all, they operated not on codes of bureaucratic procedure but on the laws of the jungle—the fast buck and the fixed bid—and no American city grew larger or faster than New York. The only power the immigrant poor had in that free-for-all was their sheer numbers, and the votes those numbers translated into. The Democratic Party became their refuge, providing government jobs, Christmas turkeys, tenement apartments, burial money, whatever was needed to guarantee votes. Along with the machine's informal social welfare network came a great deal of leeway for corruption—particularly in the provision of jobs and awarding of valuable public works contracts. "The papers and some people are always ready to find wrong motives in what us statesmen do," Tammany man and State Senator George Washington Plunkitt, namesake of the George Washington Bridge, said in 1905. "If we bring about some big improvement that benefits the city and it just happens, as a sort of coincidence, that we make a few dollars out of the improvement, they say we are grafters."

New York's educated classes held a rather uncharitable view of that coincidental enrichment of Tammany politicians, in particular High Church Protestants (the so-called "Episcopacy"), who made their homes on the Upper East Side of Manhattan and sent their sons to boarding schools and Ivy League colleges. In short, John Lindsay's crowd. "Why is it," the idealistic young Princetonian Amory Blaine asks in F. Scott Fitzgerald's *This Side of Paradise*, "that the pick of the young Englishmen from Oxford and Cambridge go into politics and in the U.S.A. we leave it to the muckers?—raised in the ward, educated in the assembly and sent to Congress, fat-paunched bundles of corruption, devoid of 'both ideas and ideals' as the debaters used to say?"

But the divide between reformers and the machine went beyond the simple question of which social classes and ethnic groups would be in charge to a deeper disagreement over the basic philosophy of government. At its best, Tammany was an exemplar of what political scientist Charles Lindblom would call the "branch" approach to decision-making: an incremental, usually decentralized and bottom-up process of "continually building out from the current situation, step-by-step and by small degrees." Nearly every major aspect of New York City—its economy, population, ethnic mix, real estate market, transportation, and public health system—was in a constant state of flux, and Tammany's job was to stay out of the way when possible, provide services and deal with crises when needed, and remain flexible and responsive enough to keep the votes coming, practitioners of what Lindblom called "the science of muddling through."

Educated reformers, on the other hand, tended to favor what Lindblom called the "root" approach to decision-making: comprehensively analyzing a situation, determining the ideal course of action, and then charging forward with it, a generally centralized, top-down process of "starting from fundamentals anew each time, building on the past only as experience is embodied in a theory, and always prepared to start completely from the ground up." There are merits to both approaches, but the two sides were rarely comprehensible to one another, root-approach reformers seeing the machine's branch approach as cynical, plodding, and wasteful (not to mention corrupt) and the pragmatic Tammany chieftains writing the good-government types off as starry-eyed dilettantes too concerned with simplistic theories of what government and society *should* be to deal with the complicated realities of what the city itself actually *was*.

Throughout the nineteenth and early twentieth centuries, the Tammany–Reform rivalry formed a sort of dialectic, with the machine generally enjoying fifteen or twenty years of dominance before the inevitable hubris and corruption of unchallenged power caught up to it. When the populace was sufficiently indignant, the city's good-government groups would form something of a personality cult around a white-knight reformer, unite the disparate anti-Tammany elements (usually in a "Fusion" political party, as happened with the Whigs and the resigned firemen), and capture the mayoralty with the promise of saving the city. But the new reform administrations' comprehensive approach to governance rarely delivered tangible results, and the chastened Tammany Hall was usually able to tighten up the red tape and drum Sir Galahad out of office in the next election cycle.

The problem with the reformers' approach was that they didn't have the intelligence network necessary to truly understand the city and bureaucracy they were trying to control: Tammany had legions of ward bosses, precinct captains, street organizers, and civil servants collecting stories from their constituents and reporting back to the higher-ups. Reformers couldn't hope to build such a machine without becoming a "machine" themselves, but by the early twentieth century, a few new developments gave them the chance to build an information-gathering apparatus of a whole different sort, one based not on individually collected stories but mass-aggregated numbers.

Late-nineteenth-century inventions like the Burroughs adding machine and modern slide rule helped give birth to the new field of "management science." The brainchild of the original stopwatch-toting management consultant, efficiency expert F. W. Taylor, this new field gave rise to everything from the modern accounting techniques of Wall Street firms to the revolutionary new Ford assembly line. For good-government groups, management science promised to turn the city into an assemblage of numbers that could be easily understood by reform politicians and used to run the city. Public health, housing, and poverty data to better understand and help the poor. Economic data for spurring business development. Precise budget figures that would help reformers track the flow of city funds and root out corruption from the nooks and crannies of the bureaucracy—an honest system devised, as one New York reformer put it, "not so much to jail the grafters as to install business systems which will make grafting difficult."

It's no coincidence that the spread of management science during the 1910s accompanied the rise of Progressivism. For all the personal charisma of Progressive leaders like Teddy Roosevelt, Robert La Follette, and Woodrow Wilson, it was management science that provided the template for reformers across the country to introduce more honest, transparent systems of government (a "scalable solution," as a modern management expert might put it). In New York, these new budgeting tools and the crisis of the Depression ushered in a golden age of reform. When John Lindsay was eleven years old, the city elected liberal progressive Republican congressman Fiorello La Guardia—known as "the Little Flower," for the Italian translation of his first name, and his diminutive stature—as mayor after a series of Depression-era Tammany scandals. On his first day in office, the roly-poly La Guardia stood on the steps of City Hall in an enormous black hat and shook his tiny fist at the building's graceful French Renaissance–style marble façade, shouting *"È finita la cuccagna!"*—No more free lunch! For three terms he kept his promise, overhauling city budgets, reforming the civil service, eliminating do-nothing jobs, cutting salaries, and cleaning up the kickbacks and fixed deals that had become a staple of city government.

Just as La Guardia was reorganizing New York City along scientific principles, his great ally in Washington, former New York governor Franklin Delano Roosevelt, was doing the same for the federal government. Roosevelt's New Deal had turned Washington from a sleepy bureaucratic backwater to the nerve center of a rapidly expanding, activist federal government. FDR had to build that new government almost from scratch, and do so without huge sums of money being stolen or wasted, lest scandal discredit his entire program. That job fell to Roosevelt's "Brain Trust" of cabinet secretaries, undersecretaries, and administrators, most of them culled from the upper echelons of New York City's civil service system, good-government reform movement, and civic watchdog groups. "The New Deal made almost a fetish out of policing its own programs against potential corruption," Nobel Prize–winning economist Paul Krugman later wrote of their success. In enormous relief programs like the Works Progress Administration, FDR's New York City reformers and their statistical tools, Krugman continued, "proved so effective that a later Congressional investigation couldn't find a single serious irregularity it had missed."

JOHN LINDSAY OWED HIS MAYORALTY TO NUMBERS AND A narrative. The story came first.

In January of 1965, just a few weeks after John O'Hagan's promotion to chief of the fire department, the city's leading reform-Republican newspaper, the *Herald Tribune*, ran a series of articles under the title "A City in Crisis." Opening with the headline "New York, Greatest City in the World—And Everything Is Wrong with It," every day for six months the *Trib* ran a story detailing a different aspect—dirty streets, filthy air, crime, potholes, rudeness, narcotics, bad schools, the high cost of living—of what Congressman Lindsay had taken to calling "the urban crisis." It wasn't just the *Herald Tribune*; the (ironically, New York–based) publishing and media worlds made a virtual cottage industry of anti-Gotham screeds. That same year, reporter and future Nixon adviser Richard Whalen called New York "frowning, tight-lipped, short-tempered, the most nervous city in America . . . a city without grace," in his book *A City Destroying Itself: An Angry View of New York. Look* magazine ran a feature called "A Tough Day in New York," which described the city as "dangerously like an underdeveloped country . . . dirty, thirsty, tired, scared, old, worn, fouled and poor." Tom Wolfe thought New Yorkers were caught in the "behavioral sink" that befell lab rats forced into overcrowded cages.

A spiritual malaise had settled over Gotham, nowhere more so than in its politics. In the two decades since La Guardia had ruled City Hall, the patronage-starved Tammany Tiger had feasted, the city run by a trio of overlapping interests: Democratic clubhouses, a public works empire controlled by urban planner Robert Moses, and the powerful civil service and construction unions, which supported the Dems and made their living from Moses' projects. The result was the kind of corruption, inefficiency, and unaccountability that had landed Lindsay's reform idol La Guardia in the mayor's chair. Just months removed from his triumphant reelection in the midst of the 1964 Goldwater debacle, Lindsay was profoundly affected by the *Trib* series. He told friends he was having trouble sleeping at night, goaded by a guilty obligation to clean up his city. Declaring his candidacy for mayor in May of 1965, Lindsay's moral quest landed him on the front page of every paper in town and the covers of *Life*, *Look*, and *Newsweek* magazines, a white knight ready to save the distressed damsel of Gotham.

As central as New York's actual political problems were to the emerging consensus that New York was in crisis, there was another element to the story: the power of that story itself. The first great city of immigrants in world history, New York has always been an idea—of refuge, freedom, opportunity, new beginnings—as much as a physical place, and during the 1940s and 1950s that idea had dazzled. As radio and television spread, New York–based networks dominated airwaves around the country, but kept their headquarters, shows, and sensibilities attuned to city life. New York had the tallest buildings and richest residents; it was the banking, shipping, and manufacturing capital of the country, and—as the home of millions of foreign-born residents and the United Nations—the closest thing to a world capital since Babel. Even America's pastime was dominated by New York: in a ten-year span, the three New York baseball teams, the Giants, Yankees, and Brooklyn Dodgers, faced *each other* seven times in the World Series, with one of the three winning nine times, the lone exception coming when the Milwaukee Braves eked out a victory over the Yankees in 1957.

Not everyone appreciated the view. The city was shocked when the McCarthy period revealed a nascent antipathy for the liberal intellectualism and Eastern elite so at home along the Hudson. A backlash against New York, from both within and without, was slowly growing. The conventional Gotham tales of urban excitement and bootstrap success were fixating more and more on the city's already famous crime, noise, clashing ethnic groups, political corruption, and poverty—Horatio Alger, Jr., replaced by Hubert Selby, Jr.

The trend wasn't against just New York, but urban life in general. Before World War II, there were essentially two kinds of American communities: urban and rural. From the nation's founding, it had been unclear which of the two lifestyles would dominate—the philosophic agrarianism of Virginia-born aristocrat Thomas Jefferson or the frenzied innovation of urban capitalism espoused by Alexander Hamilton (the immigrant, bastard son of Scottish gentry who found fame and fortune in New York, where he penned one of his earliest works of political theory, *The Farmer Refuted*). The first half of the twentieth century, when cities grew from 40 to 60 percent of the country's population, seemed to vindicate Hamilton, but highways built with federal tax dollars and mortgages backed by federal guarantees and partially deductible from federal tax returns were about to create a third choice: suburbia. A nation once enthralled by the chaotic freedom of city life began preferring the isolated pleasures of stand-alone homes and fenced-in yards. It wasn't just that New York was changing; the lens through which America viewed it was changing as well.

In 1948, E. B. White's book-length essay *Here is New York* took note of the fact that the city was brutish and rude, "lonely," able to "destroy an individual." But White and America gave those sins a pass, the inevitable unpleasantness of a city so large, ambitious, and energetic. "By rights," White wrote, "New York should have destroyed itself long ago, from panic or fire or rioting or failure of some vital supply line in its circulatory system or from some deep labyrinthine short circuit." To White, what defined New York was not that it was vulnerable to these disasters but that it somehow managed to avoid them: "Mass hysteria is a terrible force, yet New Yorkers seem always to escape by some tiny margin: they sit in stalled subways without claustrophobia, they extricate themselves from panic situations by some lucky wisecrack, they meet confusion and congestion with patience and grit—a sort of perpetual muddling through." Yet the mere survival of New York and its citizens was no longer enough to satisfy the city's chroniclers. Once, the iconic pictures of New York had been the Chrysler Building in the sun, workmen taking a lunch break on the high steel, Alfred Eisenstaedt's photo of the V-J Day Kiss; slowly, that impression was morphing into the deserted coffee shops and bleak rooming houses of Edward Hopper paintings and the shadowy streetscapes of gritty noir films.

By the mid-1960s, this spiritual malaise was infecting New York's own sense of itself. When a 1964 *New York Times* article revealed that "for more than half an hour thirty-eight respectable, law-abiding citizens in Queens watched a killer stalk and stab a woman in three separate attacks in Kew Gardens," people's worst suspicions were confirmed, that city living—particularly New York City living—destroyed people's basic humanity toward one another. The slain woman, twenty-eight-year-old Kitty Genovese, became the defining symbol of a city so inured to suffering that people would not even alert the police to save her. "Nobody can say why the 38 did not lift the phone while Miss Genovese was being attacked, since they cannot say themselves," *Times* editor A. M. Rosenthal later wrote in a book about the murder. "It can be assumed, however, that their apathy was indeed one of the big-city variety. It is almost a matter of psychological survival, if one is surrounded and pressed by millions of people, to prevent them from constantly impinging on you, and the only way to do this is to ignore them as often as possible. Indifference to one's neighbor and his troubles is a conditioned reflex in life in New York as it is in other big cities." The story was an overnight sensation, an urban morality tale for the ages, picked up by newspapers, radio, and television stations across the country and becoming the inspiration for an episode of *Perry Mason*, an ABC TV movie, and, more recently, a subplot in the graphic novel *The Watchmen* and the cult film *The Boondock Saints*. It even engendered a psychological term, "Genovese syndrome," the tendency of people in large groups to not come to the aid of others because they assume someone else will.

John Lindsay was tailor-made to exploit the "City in Crisis" narrative: a glamorous, energetic campaigner who seemed capable of battling the city's malaise through sheer force of will, not only issuing his characteristic cries for honor and integrity in public office but also promising to bring back the verve and vigor of what he called "Fun City." The defining image of the election was a simple campaign poster of an enthusiastic, smiling Lindsay striding confidently down a dreary street as a pair of black children smile at him from the background. Above the picture was the unofficial motto of the campaign, borrowed from *Post* columnist Murray Kempton: "He is fresh and everyone else is tired."

Lindsay's message was simple: the city was in decline because it was run by a government "insensitive to its failings, arrogant in its power, contemptuous of challenge. A one-party rule that clings to patronage and pelf while the city's spirit crumbles." He blamed "tired management" for the city's problems, pledging to replace not only the mayor, three-term Democrat Robert F. Wagner, Jr., but the entire inefficient, unresponsive bureaucracy. Just like the Little Flower, Lindsay promised to reorganize and streamline city agencies, use new budget tools to root out corruption and inefficiency, improve the delivery of basic services, and foist accountability onto a bureaucracy governed by petty politics and insider interests.

"In the old days you communicated through the Democratic machine," says Lindsay's former chief of staff and longtime aide Jay Kriegel. "You used to go to Brownsville and get word to your district leader, who got word to City Hall. Well, if you weren't part of the Democratic club, you had no way to effect change at all. . . . [Lindsay held] the abiding assumption that you needed to confront these problems and . . . rationalize the system." Lindsay brought his characteristic energy and charisma to the campaign. He appeared on stage with Liza Minnelli, Sammy Davis, Jr., and Phyllis Diller. He walked through poor black neighborhoods in Brooklyn in the sweltering summer heat, and cooled off his athletic, six-foot-four frame at the Irish and Italian beach clubs of Queens and the Bronx. Even vacationing New Yorkers couldn't escape him, finding the candidate in the resort towns of the Catskills and Pocono Mountains, and on the beaches of Long Island. But despite his tireless campaigning, Lindsay was still a long shot to win. He was a WASP in a city dominated by Irish and Italian Catholics, Jews, blacks, and Puerto Ricans (and running against Jewish comptroller Abe Beame, a product of the Irish- and Italian-dominated Tammany Hall). He was Republican in a Democratic town. He even had a Republican rival, *National Review* founder and columnist William F. Buckley, who was running on the Conservative Party ticket. But for the Lindsay campaign, talk of scientific management and a rational, mathematical approach to problem-solving wasn't just campaign blather, it was a strategic edge. Lindsay's thirty-two-year-old chief strategist, Bob Price, was an obsessive electoral historian, and after studying recent returns from all of the city's five thousand or so election districts, he knew the pivotal neighborhoods and key demographics. Along with the "City in Crisis" narrative, it was Price's statistical breakdowns that had convinced Lindsay to run in the first place, and Price's own targeted, scientific polling kept the campaign bullish on its chances even as citywide newspaper polls showed Lindsay trailing Beame. In the days leading up to the election, every major paper predicted a decisive Beame victory, and hours after the polls closed, early results gave Beame a commanding lead of more than fifty thousand votes.

Still, Price stayed confident. He'd been keeping a close eye on thirty swing districts, and the numbers there told a different story. He made a call to *The New York Times* and persuaded his friend metro desk editor A. M. Rosenthal not to run a story declaring Beame the winner in the paper's bulldog edition, which hit newsstands around eleven p.m. (Most editors were still twice-shy about premature declarations of victory after the *Chicago Daily Tribune*'s "Dewey Defeats Truman" debacle in the 1948 presidential election.) At about eleven forty-five, Price received results from a precinct in the suburban Riverdale neighborhood of the Bronx that confirmed what his earlier numbers had indicated: middle-class Jewish Democrats had swung to Lindsay. It would be hours before the Beame camp finally realized what had happened, and conceded the race, but Price told Lindsay to wash up, change his shirt, and practice his acceptance speech.

The 23rd Street fire.
(Photo courtesy FDNY Photo Unit)

THREE

The Hangman's Trap

Monday, October 17, 1966, 8:00 p.m.

". . . by three fingers," Engine Co. 18's John Donovan said over the roar of pumper trucks, carefully studying his right hand. A few minutes before, it had gripped the nozzle of a fire hose and held his body above an inferno beneath the collapsed first floor of a Wonder Drug store on 23rd Street in Manhattan. Dazed but coherent, Donovan tried to explain the situation to Fire Commissioner Robert O. Lowery. "Some of my buddies pulled me out," he said, shaking his head. "And now my other buddies are still down there."

An hour earlier, Donovan had been on scofflaw duty, out ticketing cars parked in front of fire hydrants near his firehouse, Engine Co. 18 in Greenwich Village. When the company was called out on an alarm, Donovan raced back to check the house journal for the address of the call, jumped in his car, and headed for the corner of 23rd Street and Broadway. While Donovan drove to the scene, the men of Engine 18 entered the Wonder Drug store on 23rd Street with Ladder Co. 7. The bulk of the firefighting operations that night wasn't actually on 23rd Street, but a block south, on 22nd Street, in a building that was connected to the Wonder Drug building by a walkway on the third floor. There was a basement fire on the 22nd Street side, too hot and smoky for even Rescue Co. 1 to get water on it, and the crews on 23rd Street were supposed to check the connected building for signs of fire extension. They'd found a few small pockets of flame but not much, barely a pool-hall haze of smoke in the air. What they didn't know was that the basement on 22nd Street had been illegally extended forty feet beneath the 23rd Street building, where a blazing fire was eating away at the ceiling holding up the rear of the pharmacy. A wooden ceiling, which insulated the flames, kept them from heating the pharmacy's concrete floor above and thus alerting the men of Engine 18 and Ladder 7 to the fire below them.

Outside the Wonder Drug, John Donovan pulled up to the scene to find Engine 18's chauffeur—driver Manny Fernandez—connecting hoses to the pumper. Donovan asked him where the rest of the company was. "They're in there," Fernandez said, pointing at the front door of the Wonder Drug. With that, the flame-rotted wooden ceiling above the burning basement let out a brief sigh, and shrugged. The floor "fell like a hangman's trap," fire investigators said later, and ten of the twelve firemen in the back of the store went with it, the two left on solid ground blown backward and knocked unconscious by the explosion. The fireball that roared up through the collapsing floor blew out the windows of the pharmacy, and a fireman inside the doorway was shot out into the street like so much debris, landing face-first and skidding to a stop on the sidewalk by Donovan. Fernandez ran past them to the entrance, shouting, "Eighteen! Eighteen!" The only sounds he could hear over the roar of the fire were air-mask alarms, tripped when they're knocked from the tanks, to help locate fallen firemen.

The scene on the street turned to chaos, as panicky officers shouted orders at random and tried to figure out who was inside the store. Donovan grabbed the nozzle of a hose line and led a group back into the pharmacy in almost zero visibility, flashlight beams bouncing back uselessly off the black smoke. Inching forward, toward a flickering orange glow at the back of the store, he never saw the void in front of him.

"The walking was real slithery," Donovan said later. "You sort of slipped along, and then I just fell forward into it." As Donovan fell, he wrapped three fingers around the fire nozzle and held tight as the hose snapped taut in the hands of the men behind him. Someone grabbed him by the collar, an arm reached under his shoulder, and he was hauled, gasping and choking, to the street outside. He was barely even hurt, just a belly full of smoke and a pair of small burns on his left arm and ear.

As Donovan told his story to Fire Commissioner Lowery, he did so to a man who was completely unprepared for the scene in front of him. Appointed by the mayor, fire commissioners are often civilians with no firefighting experience. They handle the politics and the budgets, while the civil service–tested chief of department runs the everyday operations. Lowery was no civilian; he'd become a firefighter in 1941. But political connections in the Democratic clubhouses of Harlem quickly got him appointed as a fire marshal—part cop, part fireman, carrying a gun and investigating suspicious blazes (and, when needed, other firemen, marshals serving as the department's de facto internal affairs division). Cautious, dependable, and politically savvy, Lowery was the first commissioner appointed by Mayor-elect Lindsay after his victory, and the first black commissioner the FDNY had ever had, a good politician and an effective mediator between City Hall and the fire service. But he was out of his depth when it came to the battlefield tactics of handling a multiple-alarm blaze. Fire officers and even high-ranking chiefs were shouting panicky, contradictory orders at one another. Not sure what to do, firemen attacked the fire the best they knew how—some, like Donovan, nearly getting themselves killed in the process. No one even knew how many men were missing, although there was a rumor that the commanding officer on 23rd Street, Assistant Chief Thomas

Reilly—O'Hagan's replacement as the head of Manhattan's Third Division—had gone into the store with Engine 18 and hadn't come out.

Shortly after Donovan spoke with Commissioner Lowery, Mayor Lindsay arrived on the scene and wanted to see some of the action. His political hero, Fiorello La Guardia, had rushed to fires in the sidecar of a police motorcycle when he was mayor, storming into burning buildings in a long leather coat and enormous Stetson cowboy hat to conduct "personal inspections" of the fire scenes, once crawling through smoke and ash to kneel beside two firemen trapped beneath a collapsed wall and talk with them until help arrived. The formal evening wear Lindsay sometimes wore when called to a fire scene was less practical than La Guardia's getup, but Lowery usually outfitted the mayor in a fireman's heavy rubber turnout coat and white commissioner's helmet (a glossy, ostentatious bit of haberdashery that left the tall, elegant Lindsay sticking out like a manicured thumb on a bricklayer's hand) and sent him in to survey the action. Not understanding the extent of the fire on 23rd Street, Commissioner Lowery let Lindsay enter the building, where a second collapse nearly killed the poor mayor. Lindsay quickly made his way outside to talk to reporters, unnerved by the close call and the intensity of the blaze.

For all Lowery's trouble controlling the scene, it wasn't normally his responsibility. That job fell to John O'Hagan, a skilled commander with an encyclopedic knowledge of building layouts and a maestro's touch for organizing fire crews. In his chief's car he kept a handie-talkie radio and piles of building blueprints, searching for structural defects and relaying messages to chiefs on the scene as he rushed to fires. Arriving at a scene, he would pepper subordinates with detailed questions and deliver rapid-fire orders in a low, nasal voice that seemed to simultaneously snap men to attention and put them at ease: "Chief O'Hagan's in charge, just do what he says and you'll be fine. . . ." Except on the night of October 17, O'Hagan was out of town for meetings with the Chicago Fire Department. With operational control of the scene handed over to O'Hagan's appointed deputy, Chief Frank Love, Lowery joined the still-shaken mayor and spoke to the media with tears in his eyes.

WHENEVER HE WAS OFF DUTY OR OUT OF TOWN, CHIEF O'Hagan conscientiously checked in with headquarters, getting updates on the day's firefighting and leaving locations and phone numbers where he could be reached in an emergency. Yet it was his wife, Kaye, who had called him in the middle of the night to tell him about a story she'd heard on the radio. A building collapse, firemen missing. Calling in to headquarters, furious he hadn't been contacted, O'Hagan found out that the collapse was in the heart of his old command, the Third Division, and that his successor, Chief Reilly, was among the dozen missing men. The web of power in most cities is a tangled one, but fortunately for O'Hagan, the Chicago Fire Department, favored by Richard Daley's Democratic machine, had plenty of juice at O'Hare Airport. Within a few hours O'Hagan was on a plane, and by early morning he was at the scene. The chief had no way of knowing what had caused the collapse, though he had a pretty good idea about what had made headquarters not inform him.

Lowery had moles in O'Hagan's office—headquarter chiefs, known as staff chiefs, who were technically O'Hagan's subordinates but were often appointed by Lowery. Jealous of the reforming upstart, the old staff chiefs ridiculed him with a characteristic lack of discretion. Around headquarters, he became the college boy who always knew best, the get-ahead kid, angling for promotions, the "itinerant data diddler." O'Hagan's appearance played perfectly into the characterization. For a job defined by carrying victims and controlling a fire hose packed with hundreds of pounds of water pressure, he was not a large man. Newspapers put him at six feet tall and an "athletic 183 pounds," when he became chief, but most colleagues remember him as smaller on both counts. More than his size, it was his face—thin, youthful, with a fair complexion and delicate

features. The effect was complicated somewhat by a beard that grew to
five-o'clock-shadow length by lunchtime, and a chin oddly doubled for
a young man in good shape, but his youthful mien was enough. Among
the staff chiefs, he became "Little Lord Fauntleroy," the pubescent Earl of
Dorincourt from the nineteenth-century novel of manners (and later a
Mickey Rooney movie), a "figure in a black velvet suit, with a lace collar,
and with lovelocks waving about the handsome, manly little face, whose
eyes [had] a look of innocent good-fellowship."

For all their focus on O'Hagan's young face, the old chiefs ignored
the one aspect of it that truly reflected the man. When his temper flared,
he would crane his neck slightly and harden his face into a dead stare,
his left eye a deep, piercing blue, the right nearly all pupil—bottomless
black and ringed with a thin sliver of icy cobalt—thanks to a childhood
baseball accident. His countenance would remain frozen somewhere
between disbelief and fury, the only motion an almost manic fluttering
of his eyelids, as though he could blink back the rage like so many tears.
Sitting in the darkened living room of his Long Island home decades
later, a retired chief shakes his head and bites his lip at the memory of
O'Hagan's glare. "Deep down, he was the toughest man in that entire
department, and my God he'd kill you with those eyes," says the chief.
"Toward the end of his career, there were all kinds of controversies about
budget cuts, and the unions really went after him, I mean really hated
the guy. I remember I was at a funeral and everyone was being disbursed,
and as [O'Hagan's] car goes by, these union guys start hissing at him.
Sssssssss! Well, the car stops and O'Hagan gets out and just stares at them.
They all shut up! No one said a word to him."

It was common for politically appointed commissioners to use his staff
chiefs to spy on the chief of department, and Lowery's men were unusually
zealous in guarding the commissioner's authority, undercutting O'Hagan's
orders and diverting the flow of information from the chief's office to the
commissioner's. But not even O'Hagan could have imagined they'd keep
him in the dark about a deadly collapse and a dozen missing men.

THE MORNING AFTER THE FIRE, JOHN O'HAGAN WATCHED AS
six men from Ladder Co. 7 picked their way through the rubble outside
the Wonder Drug store on 23rd Street, carefully balancing a light metal
stretcher bearing a bundled gray blanket too large for its contents.
Twenty-nine year old Carl Lee of Ladder 7 was the twelfth and final
fireman pulled from the wreckage, and a thousand helmets were doffed
in a slow wave as his body broke through the crowd.

With the victims retrieved and the fire officially declared, it was
unclear who would take control of the scene. After playing the role of
Maverick Mayor the night before, John Lindsay had slipped back to Gracie
Mansion for a few hours of sleep before returning to the Wonder Drug in
the morning. Commissioner Lowery had stayed on 23rd Street all night.
The mayor or the commissioner could have called the men together
and said a few words for them and the press. But it was O'Hagan—late
to the scene, his authority under attack from the commissioner, his own
chiefs disloyal to him—who took command. He knew every man who
had died in the collapse, some of them, like Chief Reilly, for years, and
no one else was going to say the first words in their memory. O'Hagan
ordered the firemen milling about the scene to form up across the street,
in Madison Square Park. They marched past the Eternal Light flagpole,
dedicated to the dead of World War I, and in clean rows of rubber boots
and turnout coats formed a hollow square, with O'Hagan at its center.
He called for hats off, and a thousand heads bowed.

"This is the saddest day in the one-hundred-year history of the Fire
Department," he began. "They never had a chance. I know that we all
died a little in there." He said a few more words and finished by asking
everyone to join him "in a moment of silent prayer, for the repose of
their souls." He bowed his head for a long minute before walking off to
oversee the cleanup crews across the street and discuss arrangements for
the twelve widows and thirty-six children of the dead.

LOOKING BACK ON IT DECADES LATER, FIREMEN WOULD come to see the fire on 23rd Street as a line of demarcation. For the fire department itself, it was the moment when, after all the bureaucratic infighting and attempts to undermine him, John O'Hagan finally began to assert true control over the department on his way to becoming the most influential fire chief in America.

But firemen also saw the collapse as a moment of transition for the city and country. Since the end of World War II, it had been boom times in New York and the country at large, two decades of relative peace and unprecedented prosperity anchored by what writer Tom Wolfe called America's "magic economy." People worried about nuclear war, Soviet spheres of influence, and, increasingly, civil rights and women's lib, but the one thing nearly everyone took for granted was that the economy would continue to grow and the standard of living rise.

New York City was at the very vanguard of that success. Politically, the new mayor was promising to introduce to city government the same kind of whiz-bang statistical methods that had brought unprecedented success to American industry, and while Lindsay himself didn't know it yet, young civil servants like O'Hagan were chasing the same goal. Economically, New York was America's flagship city, not just its entertainment and banking capital but its manufacturing and shipping capital as well, with more industrial jobs than the next two largest American cities combined. New York's white ethnic groups—Jewish, Irish, Italian, and Slavic, most of them a generation or more removed from the Old Country—were breaking out of the ghetto and into the rapidly expanding middle class. The GI Bill helped them pay for college and secure tax-deductible mortgages, and they could finally buy the cars and televisions and other consumer accoutrements of the American Dream. With more money, cars, highways, and mortgages, some of that white working class was moving out to the suburbs, replaced by an influx of Puerto Ricans and Southern blacks. But the trend was nothing new for a city of immigrants, and there was little reason to believe that New York would not employ and urbanize these new arrivals, just as it had done for the Irish who flooded New York after the Potato Famine, Jews fleeing the pogroms of czarist Russia, and Italians and Eastern Europeans escaping poverty and political upheaval. Acceptance and prosperity would come slowly for blacks and Puerto Ricans, just as it had for the other groups, but in 1966, in the midst of seemingly unending economic growth, the Great Society, the War on Poverty, and the Civil Rights Movement, there was no reason to believe it would not come.

New York firefighters, traditionally Irish and increasingly Italian, with a smattering of Germans and Jews, were experiencing this spreading prosperity not just in their personal lives but on the job as well. "Fires," sociologist and New York senator Daniel Patrick Moynihan would later write, "are, in fact, a 'leading indicator'" of a society's health, and the statistics all looked good. Despite a population increase, the total number of fires in New York held steady through the 1950s, and civilian deaths decreased. In 1960, the fire mortality rate for the nation at-large was a shade under forty-five deaths per million people. New York's was a third of that.

And then the magic stopped. Like a candle snubbed in the dark, the change was so sudden it left people blinking, postwar Pax Americana replaced in an instant by the social turmoil and stagnant economy of the late 1960s and the 1970s. In New York, the changes came first in the fire department. "You see, fires, if you will pardon my language," says retired captain Vincent Julius, the former president of the Vulcan Society of black firemen, "are the asshole of civilization—everything that happens in a society comes out in the form of fire. Fires may be a chemical phenomenon, but they are also a sociological problem. And during the War Years, we saw all those problems."

More than most people in city government, O'Hagan had an inkling of what was to come—a handful of troubling statistics and trends that punctuated the unremitting optimism of the early 1960s. The 23rd Street fire had revealed weaknesses—bad information about the burning building and number of missing men, confused fire crews, a disorganized response to the collapse—that needed to be fixed if the fire department was going to face the new challenges, and O'Hagan knew he was the only man in a position to fix them. His short speech in Madison Square Park became the clarion call. The *Daily News*, the city's largest-circulation paper, gave the first public indication of O'Hagan's rise, running his words—"WE ALL DIED A LITTLE IN THERE"—in 300-point Linotype on the front page the next day (*The New York Times* quoted him in a less ostentatious sub-headline). The more important shift, though, was in the department itself and the minds of its members. "After that speech," remembers one retired fireman, his sentiments echoed by scores of his colleagues, O'Hagan's allies and enemies alike, "we would have followed that man into hell."

THE PUBLIC REACTION TO THE COLLAPSE WAS NOT THAT OF a normal tragedy, forgotten in a news cycle or two. Four days after the fire, tens of thousands of people lined Fifth Avenue for the official funeral procession. Thousands of firemen made the trip from as far as Canada, California, and Alaska. Pope Paul VI sent a message in memory of the men, and his representative to the United States, Archbishop Egidio Vagnozzi, the son of a Roman firefighter himself, gave the funeral homily for six of the men at St. Patrick's Cathedral.* For weeks, the newspapers

---

*St. Pat's, a number of nervous firemen had noted during preparations for the funeral, was a firetrap, with nothing to keep a blaze from climbing up the walls to the roof and into the cathedral spires, which firemen couldn't reach with a tower ladder from outside or climb to from the inside. Two years later, for Robert Kennedy's wake, the department posted two firemen around the clock on a rickety catwalk above the altar. "Heave a Molotov cocktail into the triforium and you'd burn the whole place down," says one fire officer who spent a night above the slain senator's body. "There were no fire plans for that place. The only way to put out a fire would be sprinklers, but that costs money, and the cardinal had a lot of juice in the department, so no one even suggested that. They had us go underneath the altar, where the cardinals are buried, and up this spiral staircase forty, fifty feet easy, then out on catwalks about five feet wide. There's a ceiling below the catwalk, but step on it and you'd go right through. So we used some rope to haul six lengths of hose up to the catwalk, so that if there was a fire all you'd have to do was toss the hose down and connect it to a hydrant for a makeshift standpipe system. I spent the night up

printed stories on the unnecessary dangers firemen faced and ran them under bold headlines: "Science Has Neglected the Heroic Firefighter"; "Protecting the Fireman"; "City's Cost-Cutting Imperils Firemen"; "TOP FIRE PROBLEM: WOOD STRUCTURES."

John O'Hagan knew that in the calls for action following a crisis, those with a plan rise to prominence. Fortunately, he had those plans in spades, his desk filled with three-by-five index cards covered in ideas for reforms and innovations he'd thought up over the years. At headquarters, O'Hagan became a man possessed. He drew up a proposal to create a federally funded fire prevention agency, and President Lyndon Johnson actually signed off on it. He convinced reporters to write articles about pet concerns of his that had nothing to do with the 23rd Street collapse, in particular the dangerous new generation of steel-and-glass high-rises made possible by the city's lax fire codes. He handled arrangements for the families of the victims and worked with the department's unions and fraternal organizations to plan fund-raisers for them. He fired off memos, sent teams of investigators to pore through the rubble, called staff chiefs to the carpet for keeping him in the dark about the fire, even got into a scuffle with one chief who had the temerity to disagree with him.

On the job, O'Hagan maintained his usual reserve, but at home the strain of the twelve deaths showed. "Twenty-third Street was absolutely devastating for him," says O'Hagan's daughter Catherine. "He kept in touch with the families for years afterwards, it really stayed with him."

"Before Twenty-third Street, the department would never investigate how a fire had been handled," says Chief Vincent Dunn, who fought the 23rd Street fire as a young lieutenant and helped investigate the collapse. "If guys died and there needed to be an investigation, it was usually a

---

there with one guy who brought up a gallon of red wine with him. Well, he ran out of the stuff and would've started into a second bottle if he'd had one, spent the night puking and farting and shitting in his pants, all this at Kennedy's funeral. As far as I know, those hoses are still up there on the catwalk."

whitewash. It was tough, investigating and criticizing guys who had just lost friends, saying they were to blame for it. No one wanted to point fingers. But O'Hagan saw it as an issue of accountability and education; you needed to study these mistakes and learn from them."

Seizing on the memory of the post-collapse chaos on 23rd Street, O'Hagan codified his own techniques for managing complex fire scenes and turned them into standard operating procedures (SOPs, in firemen's military parlance) for the entire department. Previously, the chief in charge of a scene would choose a somewhat arbitrary spot for a command post (usually just in front of wherever his chauffeur found a spot to park) and a crowded, confusing phalanx of officers, aides, and firemen would cluster around. O'Hagan ordered that a formal staging area be set up outside the "collapse zone," where a crumbling building could potentially land. He ordered all chiefs to keep an updated command board—usually a plastic tablet with a grease pencil—for mapping fires and keeping track of which units were assigned where. Commanding officers had to radio back to headquarters with regular updates on the progress of the fire and solicit advice from O'Hagan or any other ranking chief taking an interest. For different building types (old-law tenements, private dwellings, high-rises, factories, etc.) specific procedures and protocols were formalized.

O'Hagan's new SOPs were the same kind of procedures the chief had seen used, and sometimes ignored, in combat. Military history tends to focus on daring, counterintuitive maneuvers by genius generals: Robert E. Lee dividing his heavily outnumbered troops at Chancellorsville; Erwin Rommel and Heinz Guderian blitzkrieging forty years of trench-warfare doctrine into obsolescence at the Battle of France; Douglas MacArthur's amphibious assault through the rapid tides and heavy fortifications of Korea's Bay of Incheon. But competence saves more lives than creativity, and for every successful break with convention, there are countless cases where lapses in protocol have doomed armies to failure. O'Hagan knew that the handful of chiefs who could keep track of the myriad factors at a fire scene and make decisions from the gut with the skill of a MacArthur didn't need SOPs. But he also knew that most men's guts have shit for brains and they needed the proper parameters to operate within.

And it wasn't just his own methods that O'Hagan turned into protocol. Dozens of chiefs had developed successful methods for dealing with unique situations, but the techniques remained limited to the officers who devised them and the men they worked with. O'Hagan sought the innovators out and encouraged them to write training manuals for probey classes and articles for the department magazine, WNYF (With New York Firemen), and give presentations to big firefighting organizations like the International Association of Fire Chiefs (Vice President: John T. O'Hagan). The same went for new firefighting equipment. In 1948, FDNY Deputy Chief Hugh Halligan designed a tool that combined the pair of ten-pound iron prying tools, carried by every company, into a single steel bar that weighed less than either; he registered a patent, and began manufacturing them.* Angry that Halligan was profiting from the new tool, the FDNY refused to buy it, but individual FDNY companies and departments around the country snapped up the tools as fast as Halligan and a host of knock-off companies ("Hooligans" to the firefighting purist) could produce them, quickly making Halligan tools the most common firefighting tools in the world.

When he came to power, O'Hagan lifted the ban on Halligans and encouraged other firehouse tinkerers to come forward with their inventions. After nearly being blinded by a falling beam, Brooklyn fireman Lester Bourke created an eye-shield that O'Hagan made standard on all new helmets. For high-rise fires too hot to get water on, one company came up with a U-shaped pipe that could be hung out a window from the floor above the fire and slung back through the window below to put water on the flames. Another firefighter came up with an early version of the "jaws of life" metal-cutting saw.

For the kind of gear you couldn't make with a soldering iron, O'Hagan

---

*The tools were generally strung together with a rope and carried by the strongest man in the company; this gave birth to the term "Iron Man."

set up partnerships with leading technology companies. He turned the FDNY into the first computerized fire department in the country, partnering with IBM to build a computer system that tracked fire report data to discover hidden fire patterns and point up dangerous trends. The chief worked with Howard Hughes' aircraft company to develop an infrared sensor to detect fire behind walls, with NASA to make lighter, more practical air-masks, and with Mack Trucks to develop a new super-pumper engine that could spray ten thousand gallons per minute with enough pressure to knock down a brick wall. *Polytechnic Engineer* magazine printed a glowing profile on the chief and his department, calling New York "foremost" among American cities in developing and adopting new life-saving technology. "When he became chief, his first thing was innovation, to increase the knowledge about firefighting," says Chief Elmer Chapman.* "Until that time we were pretty parochial and stayed within the job. We didn't go outside and see what other people were doing. That was why he got us hooked up with [these companies], got guys to write, to go back to school, to go to conferences and join the national organizations."

Even those who clashed with O'Hagan, often bitterly, gave the man credit for the improvements he brought to the FDNY and the countless fire departments that followed his lead. "The innovation all came from O'Hagan," says Jimmy Boyle, a former president of the firemen's union. "All of these things that we really take for granted now. There were guys who hated O'Hagan, I mean hated him with a passion, but many of them

---

*Along with the technical improvements, O'Hagan encouraged his chiefs to take business classes, enter MBA programs, and read books on organizational theory. His favorite writer was management guru Peter Drucker, who coined the terms "management by objective"—a concept on which O'Hagan would base his career—and "knowledge worker." Drucker's books, like his study of General Motors, *The Concept of the Corporation*, became required reading around the department. O'Hagan was "not a typical civil servant," says Chief Vincent Dunn, who worked for him at headquarters. "He truly believed in efficiency, management. He had every chief in the department reading Peter Drucker. . . . All this in the fire department! This was revolutionary stuff."

looking back on it eventually realized how much good he did, too. He really saw the need to professionalize the job, and he did it."

Slowly but surely, O'Hagan was beginning to dominate the department, beyond even what he could directly control by himself. He had an eye for talent and took scores of like-minded young officers under his wing at headquarters, then sent them out to quietly colonize different fire divisions, even the commissioner's office. He used engineers from the high-flying technology companies he worked with as advisers, so whenever there was a disagreement with the commissioner's office or City Hall over budgets or a technical matter, O'Hagan had a cadre of fast-talking, impressively credentialed experts who could be called on to settle the dispute—invariably, in the chief's favor.

O'Hagan's greatest ambition went beyond new technology and the day-to-day running of the department. There was a revolution under way in American business, a management style that relied not on industry-specific expertise or the unquantifiable intuition of a few maverick leaders, but on statistical analysis and tight financial and managerial controls. A professionalized, objective way of doing business that O'Hagan thought could be applied not only to the FDNY but to bureaucracies everywhere. The new statistical approach promised ways of looking at the fundamental, until then unanswerable, questions of firefighting: how much fire protection a city needed, how many companies, how many men, where they should be placed, when they should be on duty. Traditionally, firehouse locations were chosen based on which neighborhoods *seemed* to need another firehouse, or firehouses were placed in the districts of powerful city councilmen and prominent Tammany bosses. Companies were staffed with the same manpower all day, every day. The refusal to adapt led to all kinds of wasteful policies—units that mostly fought Staten Island brushfires in the summer but stayed open all winter, Wall Street companies working all night when there wasn't a soul to be found for twenty blocks—but no one knew how to change them. Now, O'Hagan realized, he might be able to answer those questions, bring a rational, analytic approach to fighting fires.

It wasn't just abstract issues that the chief needed statistical help with. Some troubling numbers were beginning to come into his office from the Morrisania and Hunts Point neighborhoods of the South Bronx. The once thriving industrial districts had fallen prey to job loss, white flight, overcrowding, and rising fire rates. A few days before O'Hagan was sworn in as chief in December of 1964, a captain in Morrisania's Engine Co. 82 had walked into the firehouse kitchen and announced, to everyone's shock, that the company had just gone on its unprecedented four-thousandth run of the year. By 1966, Engine Co. 82 was going on more than six thousand runs, and the fires were spreading.

O'Hagan's goal of reshaping the civil service far outstripped his mandate as the second in command of a single municipal department, but the chief had never fallen short of an overambitious dream before. He would plant seeds in the young chiefs' minds, get them reading books on management theory and taking business school courses, and once again bide his time until the circumstances were right. And while Fire Commissioner Lowery had little interest in such ambitious reforms, his boss, Mayor Lindsay, was staking his mayoralty on them, quietly overhauling his own budget bureau and soon, Lindsay hoped, reorganizing the entire bureaucracy along the same rational, statistically based lines that O'Hagan envisioned for the fire department.

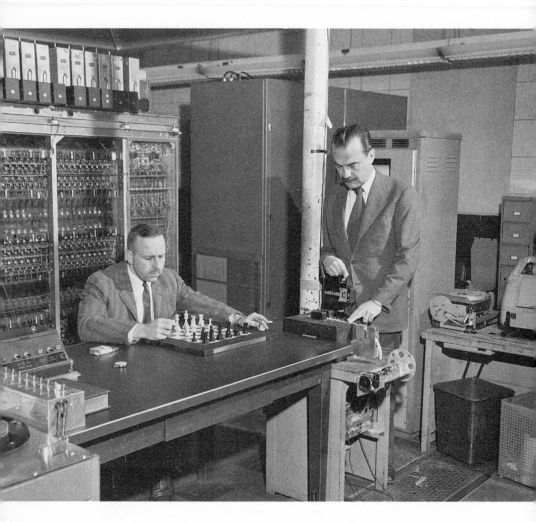

*The RAND Whiz Kids. RAND's Paul Stein and Nicholas Metropolis in front of
the MANIAC I computer, designed by RAND's John von Neumann in conjunction
with Los Alamos laboratory for the calculations to build the hydrogen bomb.*
(Photo courtesy Los Alamos National Laboratory)

FOUR

Of Whiz Kids and Think Tanks

They believed that they could create a better world, and have control over this process of re-creating the world, through their science and their mathematics.

—SAMUEL COHEN, RAND CORPORATION

If people do not believe that mathematics is simple, it is only because they do not realize how complicated life is.

—JOHN VON NEUMANN

The new statistical approach to problem-solving that Lindsay and O'Hagan wanted to bring to city governance could in some ways trace its roots to the management science of the Progressive Era, but it held a much more direct link to techniques born out of necessity during the war that had so shaped Mayor Lindsay and Chief O'Hagan as young men. There's generally a lot more to the winning and losing of a war than is taught in grade-school history class, and during World War II it was mathematics that proved essential to the Allied victory.

The story of that unheralded weapon begins in 1941, with two Texans sitting in an office in the headquarters of the War Department, the squat, stolid old Munitions Building across from the Washington Monument. When Robert Lovett was appointed assistant secretary of war in the months leading up to Pearl Harbor, he found the military desperately outmoded after two decades of isolationism and ten years of the Depression. Lovett, the son of the chairman of the Union Pacific

Railroad, was a decorated World War I pilot and a wealthy Wall Street power broker, and his area of expertise, the Army Air Force,* couldn't even tell him how many pilots and planes it had, never mind how many it would need and how quickly they would be needed to fight a two-theater war. Its organization chart, Lovett was fond of saying, "resembles nothing in the world so much as a bowl of spaghetti."

Lovett needed men with the numerical skills of a Wall Street accountant and the fortitude to stand up to the blustery generals who prowled the War Department. His search led him to Charles "Tex" Thornton, a New Deal number-cruncher who'd arrived in D.C. seven years earlier in true Horatio Alger splendor, hopping off a Greyhound bus with nothing but the suit on his back and the remnants of a $50 loan from his hometown bank in Haskell, Texas, in his wallet. After friendly introductions, Thornton turned the tables on Lovett and started asking him the questions. "Mr. Secretary," Tex said, "we're putting a tremendous effort into enemy intelligence. But how are we doing at friendly intelligence—reliable information about us?" Lovett had found his man.

Put in charge of a small group of statistical planners, Thornton got a crash course in the confusion and jealous politicking of the War Department. The Air Force laid claim to more than a dozen statistical agencies whose sole function seemed to be to create a barrage of arbitrary figures and then bicker over the discrepancies. Commanding General Henry "Hap" Arnold was in the habit of asking four different agencies for the same information, choosing the closest pair, and splitting the difference. At one point, Tex tracked down the author of a War Department plan that called for training twelve thousand pilots a month and asked him how the number had been arrived at. "It was pulled out of thin air," he told Tex. Did the figure have any relation to plans for procuring aircraft or any other expansion programs? "None at all," came the reply. "If there is a relation, it's purely coincidental."

---

*At the time, a sleepy backwater of the Army, too small to be designated its own branch of the military.

The entire War Department was in a similar state, but no one seemed in any particular hurry to do anything about it. When Japan attacked Pearl Harbor in December, Lovett and Thornton knew they needed more than a few National Guardsmen with slide rules to bring order and efficiency to the war effort. The situation called for a statistical analysis bureau with enough independence and prestige to wring legitimate numbers out of the military's tightfisted bureaucracy. Hot-tempered Tex could provide the independence, but the college dropout needed prestige. He decided to borrow it from Harvard University.

During World War I, the Harvard Business School had all but dissolved as students decamped for Europe and professors for Washington, but Dean Wallace D. Donham was determined to keep the school afloat during World War II. Tex arrived at Donham's office four months after Pearl Harbor with a plan to do just that, turning HBS into a training academy for soldiers in his newly formed Statistical Control group. Tex wanted to do for the American war effort what Donham and HBS had been trying to do for American business for decades, each of them "charting the birth and evolution," wrote business journalist John Byrne, "of an idea with profound consequences: that measurement, through numbers and facts, could make America a mighty power, a global empire built on the ability to hold a yardstick up to nature."

Talking as though the academy was a brick-and-mortar institution and not just an image in his own mind, Tex recruited professors (particularly young ones, with draft numbers low enough that they might actually have to fight) with stories about the origins of Stat Control, how disorganized the military really was, and how much influence they could have over it. "Knowledge is power," Thornton told the wide-eyed academics, "and in this chaos, we're going to be the only people with knowledge. Everyone else will be guessing."

HBS's Charles River campus was converted into Tex's academy, training top scorers on the Army's Officer Candidate School tests in the basics of acquiring and interpreting statistics to more efficiently manage the war. Already among the brightest soldiers, Stat Control officers received rigorous training that gave them the ability to read columns of data like a novel and the aura of infallibility that an easy facility with numbers—hard *facts*—can confer. Students moved directly from Harvard to the front lines—by statistician's standards, anyway—deployed around the world to transform arcane data into the backbone of American military might.

Stat Control proved an immediate success. Just one of Thornton's sixty-six units was able to cut the number of planes grounded for repairs by 75 percent, saving $1 billion and freeing up five thousand aircraft for critical bombing runs over Germany. For the procurement of bombs and ammunition, in 1943 alone Tex's group saved the Air Force the equivalent of a year's combat pay for 3 million pilots. One of Stat Control's most vexing problems was how to prioritize the infinite combinations of soldiers, weapons, supplies, and replacement parts that needed to be shipped to the front lines. Such "linear programming problems" were virtually unsolvable until a young Air Force officer named George Dantzig came along. The son of mathematician Tobias Dantzig, he was something of a legend even before the war. In his first year at Berkeley, George solved what he thought were homework assignments, but in fact were two of the great unsolved problems in statistics. Over time, the details of the story changed and it was misattributed to a handful of famous mathematicians (and a recondite janitor in the movie *Good Will Hunting*), but Dantzig was the source. He devised the "Simplex Method," which gave Stat Control a rational way to prioritize transportation and shipping problems, and which is still used in an estimated 10 to 25 percent of all scientific computations.

Of all the bright bulbs in Stat Control, none burned as brilliantly as Robert Strange McNamara, a reedy twenty-five-year-old Berkeley grad and Harvard accounting professor (the youngest in HBS history) already wearing the wire-rimmed glasses and Brylcreemed coif that would become his trademark. McNamara's strength lay not just in his capacity for absorbing vast quantities of charts and numbers, but also in his uncanny ability to pull useful ideas and conclusions from them.

At one point, nearly 20 percent of all bombers that took off for Germany aborted without dropping a single bomb. McNamara analyzed mission reports to isolate the problem but found only a patternless hodgepodge of electrical outages, sick pilots, radio failures, iced-over wings. The real reason for the aborts, he realized, was fear. There was a 4 percent loss rate on bombing routes, and a combat tour was twenty-five routes. Bomber crews could crunch numbers too.

McNamara's report caught the eye of Air Force Colonel Curtis "Bombs Away" LeMay (the cigar-chomping, monosyllabic model for General Buck Turgidson in *Dr. Strangelove*). Before their next mission, LeMay told his pilots that he would be flying the lead bomber himself, and would court-martial the crew of any plane that didn't reach the target. The abort rate plummeted overnight. The coolly intellectual McNamara and irascible LeMay formed an unlikely alliance when they were sent to the Pacific. Analyzing the new B-29 "Superfortress" bomber—which could fly nearly three times as high as B-17s and B-24s, well above Japanese antiaircraft guns and fighter planes—McNamara found that the inaccuracy of bombing from such high altitudes outweighed the substantial savings of lives and planes. With McNamara's studies in hand, in 1945 (now General) LeMay revamped the missions, loaded the planes with incendiary bombs and flew them five thousand feet above the wooden cities of Japan. On a single night, LeMay's men dropped 3.5 million pounds of bombs on Tokyo, destroying fifty square miles of the city and burning to death a hundred thousand Japanese civilians. From Tokyo, the firebombers moved on to Nagoya, Osaka, Yokohama, and dozens of other Japanese cities. Low on the list of major Japanese urban areas before the war, Hiroshima and Nagasaki became nuclear targets only because they were the largest cities left standing.

As the end of the war approached, so did decommissioning, and, most Stat Control officers assumed, a return to whatever course their civilian lives had been on. But Thornton had other plans. Six weeks after Emperor Hirohito surrendered, he read an article in *Life* magazine about the sad state of the Ford Motor Company. Henry Ford's modern assembly line had been a stroke of genius four decades earlier, but by 1945, his ham-fisted refusal to modernize left the company on the verge of collapse. Ford didn't trust any balance sheet that couldn't be scrawled on the back of an envelope, refusing to even create an accounting department until the Internal Revenue Service forced him to. In forty-four years of operation, Ford had never had a single internal audit. When an outside team of accountants were hired to do one in 1945, they spent a year sifting through the records and quit in defeat. The disorganization was shredding the company's bottom line, dropping its share of the U.S. auto market from 60 percent at the end of World War I to 20 percent by the start of World War II. "U.S. industrial history," said the *Life* article, "can show no other example of corporate recession on so prolonged and grand a scale."

Tex fired off a brief memo to Henry Ford, Jr., about what Stat Control had done for the Air Force and, within a few months, Thornton, McNamara, and eight of the brightest, most ambitious Stat Control officers—Tex had offered Henry only a package deal: he could have them all or he could have none—were roaming the halls of Ford's Dearborn, Michigan, headquarters. As they inquired into the workings of various departments, suspicious Ford managers began grumbling about these new data-diddling "Quiz Kids" and, later, "Whiz Kids," an appellation the group quickly latched on to. What they found as they dug deeper into Ford was even more shocking than the stories Tex had told them about the Air Force bureaucracy in Stat Control's founding days. In Ford's accounts-payable department, stacks of receipts were kept on wooden sleds. When a bill arrived, accountants rearranged the sleds until they found the proper pile, dug around in it for the corresponding receipt, then pinned them together and sent out a check, usually a few months late. To figure out how much money the company owed, they stacked up all the bills, measured them with a ruler, and through a formula of unknown provenance turned feet into dollars.

Ford had no organization chart, barely even had different job titles in its executive ranks, because old Henry thought titles were "almost equivalent to a badge bearing the legend: This man has nothing to do but regard himself as important and all others as inferior." One day Tex asked an office secretary to type a few letters for him, and later a man showed up in his office asking for the afternoon off to go to a doctor's appointment. Tex said sure, but why was he asking *his* permission? "Well," the man stammered, "I saw you giving my secretary orders, so I figured you must be my boss, too." That man who had no idea who his boss was, Tex told his Whiz Kids, controlled a Ford division that employed seven thousand people.

The work proved more daunting than any of the Whiz Kids had initially assumed, with a handful of the original ten resigning, one committing suicide after the failure of the Edsel, and Thornton himself, after sparring with Henry Ford's number-two man, being forced out.* But their system paid off. Accounting was brought into line, quality-control procedures introduced, and new cars like the Ford Falcon, built for consumers who wanted smaller, more practical automobiles—a segment of the American populace thought nonexistent until data from McNamara's careful market research revealed otherwise—created profits the company hadn't seen since the first days of the Model T.

The Whiz Kids and their nifty statistical methods became perfect fodder for myth-making journalists, who wrote feature-length paeans to the men who had somehow tamed the unruly auto business and its mechanic-culture boardrooms with columns of numbers and bar graphs on overhead projectors. It marked a fundamental shift in American business culture, away from industry-specific knowledge—the days when auto execs worked on their own cars and the head of a paper company likely started out working in a pulp mill—to generalized management skills. In capitalist iconography, Gilded Age robber barons and enterprising inventors like Edison and Ford had faded into the past; swashbuckling

---

*Thornton went on to take over Howard Hughes' struggling aircraft company and turn it into a defense industry giant, then founded Litton Industries, the world's first modern business conglomerate, and became one of the richest men in America.

corporate raiders and billionaire Internet kings were still decades away. In the middle of the American Century, it was the corporate analyst, the management consultant, the clean-cut efficiency expert—with a Wharton diploma on his wall and stacks of inventory charts, profit margins, and sales projections on his desk—who captured the American business imagination. He didn't need to know cars or steel or chemicals so long as he knew *numbers*.

"Just as the student now feels technique more vital than content," sociologist William H. Whyte wrote in *The Organization Man*, "so the trainee believes managing an end in itself, an expertise relatively independent of the content of what is being managed." Interviewing Ford men for his book, Whyte realized that the shift the Whiz Kids had fostered in business went beyond the corporate world, for "blood brother to the business trainee off to join Du Pont is the seminary student who will end up in the church hierarchy . . . the physics Ph.D. in a government laboratory, the intellectual on the foundation-sponsored team project." These Organization Men were perhaps "bloodless, colorless nonentities," as one Ford executive put it, but with their numbers, credentials, and confident articulation, they were pressing their way to the top. "It is from their ranks that are coming most of the first and second echelons of our leadership," Whyte wrote, "and it is their values which will set the American temper." Appearing in *Fortune* features and on the covers of *Business Week*, *Newsweek*, and *Time*, Bob McNamara and the Whiz Kids were the perfect models. By 1960, their ascension was official. In November, young Henry promoted McNamara to president of the company, the first man not named Ford to run the family business.

WHILE THE MILITARY VETERAN WHIZ KIDS WERE RESHAPING American business and academia, a group of academics was reshaping American military policy. From the moment the first atomic device was dropped on Hiroshima, it was clear that conventional military doctrine no longer applied, but what the new doctrines would be, no one was quite sure. For most intellectuals and even military brass, pondering how to wage and win a nuclear war amounted to plotting apocalypse, "thinking the unthinkable." But where most blanched, one group saw an opportunity to eliminate the deadly irrationality of war and finally bring the logic of math and science to bear on the most pressing security issues of the Cold War: the researchers of the Air Force's official think tank, the RAND Corporation.

The Stat Control Whiz Kids may have been the most heralded World War II statistical analysts, but they weren't alone. A group of British military analysts gave the techniques a name, "operations research," and another team did for the U.S. Navy's defense against German U-boats what McNamara and Stat Control did for LeMay and the Air Force. Simple adjustments, like changing the flight patterns for Navy aircraft on seek-and-destroy missions and altering the settings on the depth charges they dropped on U-boats, increased success rates more than fivefold. Some German crews plucked from the sea asked their captors about the powerful new underwater über-bomb they assumed the Americans were using.

For all the Navy's success with operations research, it was still the Army Air Force that was most interested in the confluence of science and warfare, in particular, the man who just a few years earlier couldn't get a straight answer on how many pilots he had: General Hap Arnold. Arnold was desperate to create a permanent team of top-level scientists to "investigate all the possibilities and desirabilities for postwar and future war's development." The need for high-level security clearance meant a university could not house his "defense intellectuals," private industry would lead to too many conflicts of interest, and low civil-service pay precluded an operation run by the military. So Arnold and his old fishing buddy Donald Douglas, the founder of Douglas Aircraft, created a private think-tank that would operate out of Douglas headquarters in Santa Monica, California, but answer to the Air Force. Douglas Aircraft's Frank Collbohm volunteered to run the think tank until a permanent director could be found, and Douglas' chief engineer, Arthur Raymond, came up with a name, derived from the group's "research and development" mission: RAND.

By 1948, RAND had outgrown its Douglas Aircraft britches to become a unique hybrid in the burgeoning think-tank world: an independent nonprofit corporation, but one that was reliant on the Air Force for all of its contracts. In its early years, RAND worked on purely technical matters, like rocket thrust and designs for a potential "world-circling spaceship." That technical success bred a technical culture dominated by the hardest of hard scientists: engineers, physicists, and applied mathematicians who disdained the artsy "essay tradition" of military strategists. But that all changed when the head of the mathematics division became intrigued by a new theory of economic strategy.

In 1928, a cherub-faced Hungarian academic named John von Neumann found himself sitting in on a poker game. Not much of a gambler himself, von Neumann realized that while a player's goal was always to maximize his winnings and minimize his losses, his strategy varied depending on the actions of his opponents *and* what he expected his opponents' reactions would be to his own moves. A smart player doesn't just think "I should do X," he'll go further: "If I do X, then he'll do Y, then that will force me to do Z, then he'll respond by . . ."

A child prodigy who entertained family friends by memorizing entire pages from the phone book when he was six years old, at the time of the fateful poker game von Neumann was the youngest assistant professor at the University of Berlin. His academic interests tended toward pure mathematics and physics, theoretical, abstract matters untainted by concerns about unpredictable human behavior. But his poker observation brought him into the world of practical mathematics, and proved a bit like the apple that supposedly fell on Isaac Newton's head. Von Neumann wasn't the first thinker to see that strategic thinking was important, any more than Newton was the first person to realize things fell to the ground. For years economists had understood the significance of the strategizing that goes on between pairs and small groups of people in human and economic relations, but they had never been able to understand and predict the actual results of that strategizing. Just as Newton invented calculus to describe gravity, von Neumann developed a series of formulas that formally plotted and quantified how the strategizing worked. Von Neumann called his discovery the theory of games, or "game theory." In 1928, he published a paper on his findings that caused a small stir in European academic circles, but he retreated to more abstract concerns, leaving game theory an unfulfilled promise until 1944, when he and Princeton colleague Oskar Morgenstern wrote their *Theory of Games and Economic Behavior*, an instant sensation that garnered a front-page headline in *The New York Times*.

Game theory struck a powerful chord with the head of RAND's mathematics division, John Williams, a three-hundred-pound pool shark, occasional sports journalist (he wrote an article on professional wrestling for the first issue of *Sports Illustrated*), and probably the first man to adapt radar to automobiles when he built a "fuzz buster" for his souped-up Jaguar sports coupe. Williams was as committed a mathematician as could be found at RAND, but he thought game theory had almost limitless potential, able to explain just about any kind of rational strategizing between people. It opened up previously unquantifiable fields like sociology, psychology, and, of the most interest to RAND, military and political strategy, to statistical analysis, turning decisions traditionally made by instinct and sentiment into matters for scientific inquiry.

The classic example of using game theory to explain strategic interactions is a scenario developed at RAND called the "prisoner's dilemma." It comes in a variety of forms, but in its most basic iteration, two people are arrested for the same crime, but the police don't have enough evidence to prosecute either of them. They are put in different cells with no way of communicating, and given the same offer: If they both keep quiet, they will be charged with a lesser crime and released after six months. If one betrays the other, the betrayer will walk free and the betrayed will spend ten years in prison. If they both betray each other, they will each spend five years in prison. When you look at the problem from the perspective of the two prisoners collectively, the rational choice is for both to keep quiet; not only will neither have to live with the shame of being a rat, but more important, they will serve only a single year in prison, combined. If one or both betray, they will serve ten years, combined. However, if each prisoner is purely self-interested—or worries that his partner is—the rational decision will be to snitch. If his friend doesn't betray him, he will walk free instead of serving six months. If his friend betrays him as well, he'll do five years in prison instead of ten. Either way, he is better off betraying his partner. True to form at RAND, the dilemma can be diagrammed and the rationality of snitching shown mathematically.

John Williams convinced von Neumann to join RAND as a part-time consultant, but Williams saw that, for game theory to be applied to the real world, experts from the very fields that he hoped game theory would turn on their heads needed to be consulted. Even with a game as simple as the prisoner's dilemma, more needed to be understood about human motivation to accurately weigh the value of different choices. People didn't necessarily see a five-year jail sentence as precisely twelve times as burdensome as a six-month sentence, or five years twice as desirable as ten. How would the guilt of betrayal affect different people? Would a potential betrayer fear retribution when the betrayed was set free? Williams proposed creating two new RAND divisions, economics and social science, that could give precise weightings to different motives and values, helping turn people's sentiments into numbers (what economists sometimes call "utility functions") that could be plugged into game theory calculations. The hard scientists scoffed at Williams' idea, but Frank Collbohm, who had stayed on as RAND's president, respected Williams and gave his assent.

At the same time, a close friend of Williams' at RAND, Edwin Paxson, was also trying to rationalize and quantify decision-making. The "operations research" of World War II was spreading to American industry and academia, but the future Nobel winners at RAND thought it lacked the heady panache that befitted their intellectual status. Operations researchers were in some ways just glorified bean-counters, finding the most efficient ways to use a particular set of weapons to achieve a predetermined goal. Paxson opened the field up by flipping the question around, starting with a mission that needed to be accomplished, then working backward to determine what kind of weapons could be used (or invented) to best accomplish it—in effect, turning efficiency experts into military planners and weapons designers. Because he used the new method to analyze weapons *systems*, he called it "systems analysis."

Paxson and von Neumann not only created systems analysis and game theory, but also lent the fields the credibility of their genius. Von Neumann was one of the great intellects of the twentieth century, a brilliant mathematician, physicist, and computer scientist. He and Albert Einstein came to the United States in 1933 as two of the six "demi-gods," the original appointees to the Princeton Institute for Advanced Study, which was set up in large part to help Jewish intellectuals leave the Third Reich. Once in America, von Neumann became a key figure in the development of the nuclear and hydrogen bombs, and designed the first modern digital computer. Paxson wasn't nearly as illustrious, but within RAND he was legend, a hard-drinking, chain-smoking workaholic and the most celebrated participant in RAND's notorious "Murder Boards," a sort of trial-run peer review in which RAND analysts presented their work to the skeptical ears and withering criticisms of their colleagues (one RAND analyst actually fainted during a round of questioning from Paxson). In short, no one was going to accuse John von Neumann, Edwin Paxson, or the fields they created of being part of the "essay tradition."

Through Paxson and von Neumann, game theory and systems analysis gained early traction at RAND, but the two fields came to be personified by a third man, Albert Wohlstetter.* He had been a bookish teenager

---

*Wohlstetter would be a founding father of another intellectual field, neoconservatism, at least in its foreign-policy incarnation. Much has been made of the influence that University of Chicago political philosopher Leo Strauss had on students who were influential neocons later in life, but it was in fact Wohlstetter—who taught at Chicago after leaving RAND—who proved more influential, both philosophically and personally. He worked closely with Ph.D. candidates

from a well-to-do New York family, and his intellect was shaped by the writings of mathematician and logician Bertrand Russell and his notion that logic and rationality were the foundations of not only mathematics but philosophy, art, and, ideally, society. During the Depression, Wohlstetter was a student at two of the country's most politically active campuses, City College and Columbia University in New York, yet his politics were influenced less by breadlines and strike-breakers than by the elegant aesthetics of formal logic. Reading Karl Marx, John Maynard Keynes, and free-market economist Alfred Marshall, he reformulated their arguments as mathematical proofs and evaluated them for their logical consistency (he found Keynes sorely lacking, Marshall fairly plausible, and Marx somewhere in between). To the idealistic young Wohlstetter, the intellectual compromises of practical mathematics held all the appeal housepainting has for an abstract artist, but he was able to carve out a niche for himself at the War Production Board during World War II, using probability analysis to improve quality control on products that were too inconvenient to test individually, like lightbulb filaments.

Joining the RAND social science division in 1951, Wohlstetter gravitated to game theory and systems analysis, the chance to take problems of strategy and tactics and reformulate them as logical proofs and mathematical models, just as Bertrand Russell had done with philosophy and young Wohlstetter himself had done with economics. His first major project with RAND was a seemingly dull study on the location of Strategic Air Command (SAC) bases. SAC was an Air Force outfit responsible for the United States' entire nuclear arsenal and the linchpin of Mutual Nuclear Deterrence—a theory developed at RAND that had become official military doctrine—which posited that neither the United States nor Russia would use nuclear weapons so long as each feared the other's

---

Zalmay Khalilzad and Paul Wolfowitz (under whose mathematician father Wohlstetter had studied at Columbia), shepherded the career of a young Richard Perle (who was a childhood friend of Wohlstetter's daughter), and gave Wolfowitz and Perle their first taste of government life when he hired them for a project he was working on with hawkish Senator Henry "Scoop" Jackson.

ability to retaliate in kind. Studying SAC locations and radar warning systems, Wohlstetter realized that the bases were vulnerable to a surprise attack by the Soviet Air Force. As big an advantage as America held in the number of nukes and the planes to deliver them, a well-coordinated first strike by the Soviets could effectively destroy SAC's ability to retaliate, and with it the whole notion of deterrence.

It was a shocking conclusion, but one Wohlstetter was able to support quantitatively with game theory and systems analysis. He devised various scenarios for a Soviet attack, used a systems analysis computer program to isolate myriad factors—what percentage of Soviet bombers were likely to make it through America's air defense shield, which air bases they were likely to attack, how many American planes and bombs would survive—and determined America's ability, or rather inability, to launch a large counterstrike.

The results were damning, but Wohlstetter's whole project rested on an assumption that American foreign policy experts and the Air Force itself considered outlandish at best: an unprovoked Soviet attack. To this criticism, Wohlstetter argued that the Soviets might attack even if they weren't inclined to, because the logic of the Cold War made it the rational choice. He used the analogy of a Western gun duel where neither gunfighter wants to be the aggressor, "but they each might find themselves in the position where they had to draw first in order to survive—and this would be a rational act if they found themselves in that position." Knowing how vulnerable the United States was to a first strike, the Soviets might launch one, or become convinced that America—fearful of its own vulnerability—would attack first, thus compelling the Soviets to preempt them. It was classic game theory, the prisoner's dilemma writ large, and just as with his analysis of the results of a surprise attack, Wohlstetter had carefully constructed game-theoretic models to support his claims.

Published in 1953, Wohlstetter's report argued for a complete rethinking of American assumptions about nuclear and Cold War strategy, and sent off shockwaves within RAND and the Air Force. RAND colleagues marveled not only at the breadth and scale of the report but at the precision with which Wohlstetter had computed it: every conceivable scenario of attack and retaliation accounted for numerically, spun into elegant equations, and run through the modeling system countless times; game theory and systems analysis consolidated into mathematical models so complex they would have been impossible for state-of-the-art computers to handle just a few years ago.

Initially, Air Force brass wrote off Wohlstetter and his findings, most of them simply because they weren't about to be lectured on strategy by a foppish intellectual who'd spent the war counting lightbulb filaments. And the highest-ranking generals, like SAC commander Curtis LeMay, knew that the assumption the report rested on—a preemptive Soviet strike—was, in fact, impossible: the United States was illegally using its U-2 spy planes to monitor Soviet airstrips, and was prepared to act if needed. "If I see that the Russians are amassing their planes for an attack, I'm going to knock the shit out of them before they take off the ground," LeMay later said, at suggestions of a Soviet first strike. Told that wasn't the president's policy, LeMay—who was fond of saying that on some Mondays he didn't trust himself, never mind the president—roared back, "I don't care. It's my policy. That's what I'm going to do."

But Air Force officers eventually changed their tune on Wohlstetter's report. Not because they thought it was accurate but because they realized it was useful. In a few short years, the Air Force had gone from a subdivision of the Army to a near-equal in budget and influence, all because it was the sole military branch in charge of nuclear weapons. The Department of Defense (and the Army and Navy, which competed for the same DoD funds) was skeptical of any Air Force calls for more money, but Wohlstetter's report provided a quantitative, scientific argument for just that. The only way to properly deter the Soviets, the Air Force argued, was to have so many bombs and bombers spread around the country that it would be impossible to take them all out with a first strike. Buttressed by Wohlstetter's facts and figures, they found sympathetic ears in Thornton's old Air Force boss, outgoing Secretary of Defense

Robert Lovett, and his replacement, General Motors CEO Charles Wilson, two businessmen well aware of the importance of statistical analysis.

As Air Force funding increased, a sizable chunk of the money was spent on the think tank that had been so essential in arguing for the new largesse, and most of the new research projects were systems analysis– and game theory–based projects on nuclear strategy, not the traditional hard science RAND was founded on. Among the slew of young economists and mathematics Ph.D.'s hired to fill out RAND's expanding economics and social science divisions, a bit of a personality cult began to develop around Wohlstetter, who was quickly replacing Edwin Paxson as RAND's top systems analyst. To the young pocket-protector set, Wohlstetter seemed the pinnacle of style and worldly sophistication. His office was decorated all in black, with silk wallpaper and futuristic furniture designed by Charles Eames. He and his wife, Roberta (also a RAND analyst), threw fashionable dinner parties at their modernist home in bohemian Laurel Canyon, where the mathematicians could mingle with artists and intellectuals, like Wohlstetter's good friend Le Corbusier, and listen to Albert expound with scholarly omniscience on the great issues of the day over fine wine and Roberta's gourmet meals.*

Some of the more sober-minded RAND analysts, particularly in the engineering and physics divisions, saw Wohlstetter as a patronizing dilettante overly enamored with his own ideas, and laughed at his adoring acolytes, suddenly so interested in modern art and vintage Bordeaux. But from the board of directors on down, everyone benefitted from the lavish contracts Wohlstetter and the economics and social science divisions brought in. RAND's culture was shifting from the technical to the strategic, and systems analysis and game theory were fast becoming "the RAND Method" for approaching almost any kind of problem.

---

*Wohlstetter's tendency to miss fatal flaws—like the impossibility of a Soviet sneak attack—extended to his party planning as well. Hosting a gathering after he and Roberta moved into a new apartment, Wohlstetter served a delicious meal and excellent wine, but forgot to buy chairs for the guests.

JUST AS ROBERT McNAMARA AND THE WHIZ KIDS HAD TAKEN power from car jocks and given it to accountants and MBAs, Wohlstetter and RAND's systems analysts were soon wielding more influence over American defense strategy than any five-star general or chief of staff. In 1960, the Whiz Kids' and RAND's simultaneous revolutions came full circle. In November, John F. Kennedy, who had been receiving secret policy briefings and speech drafts from RAND analysts like Wohlstetter for months, won the presidency, in large part because of his calls for a stronger military. In particular, he won because of a perceived "missile gap" the Soviets had opened up on the United States during the Eisenhower–Nixon administration. As it turned out, the missile gap was a complete fabrication, the result of faulty Air Force intelligence and some runaway systems analysis on the part of RAND, intended to force the Department of Defense to spend more on the Air Force's intercontinental ballistic missile program.

Robert Lovett turned down Kennedy's offer to return to be secretary of defense, citing poor health, but suggested that Kennedy call on his old Stat Control hand, Robert McNamara. Just five weeks after becoming president of Ford, McNamara resigned to take the job, accepting only on condition that he could hire whomever he chose and would have Kennedy's unwavering support to impose his rationalist approach on the Pentagon. McNamara wanted to do for the Defense Department what he had for Ford, but knew that with the fickleness of politicians and voters, he had little time to accomplish in D.C. what had taken fifteen years in Detroit. Well acquainted with RAND's techniques and friendly with a number of its analysts, McNamara looted RAND's cost analysis division for talent to install a new Planning, Programming, Budgeting System (PPBS)—the brainchild of RAND analyst Charlie Hitch—that was essentially an advanced version of the financial controls he had instituted at Ford. From RAND's economics and mathematics division, he hired scores of systems analysts and game theorists to work on tactical issues:

the broader questions of how to prevent and, failing that, fight and win nuclear and conventional wars.

As McNamara and Thornton had taught their Stat Control pupils, when few people speak the language of numbers, those who are fluent carry the day. In Washington, D.C., political cunning and strategic brilliance were commonplace, but McNamara's raw analytic ability was something few had seen, and it quickly made him the leading light in Kennedy's "best and brightest" cabinet. He became known as the "human computer," an "IBM machine with legs," disarming hostile congressmen and skeptical reporters just as he had so many auto men: by confidently and articulately crafting an air of omniscience, and being prepared to unleash a mind-numbing barrage of charts and statistics to prove his points. McNamara's brilliance became the talk of Capitol Hill, like the time he sat, all but silent, through a seven-hour debriefing on overseas supply lines—slide after slide whirring by on an overhead projector—then suddenly told the presenter to stop. "This slide," he said, "number 869, contradicts slide 11." Slide 11 was dug up, and McNamara was right.

The bright young things McNamara hired from RAND developed the same reputation as their rabbi, and quickly became known as his new generation of "Whiz Kids." When Kennedy asked the secretary of defense or one of his aides how likely a new weapon system or battle plan was to work, there weren't any wordy vacillations or mutterings about there being a "good" or "decent" chance for success; it was all "55 percent likelihood, Mr. President . . . 23 percent chance of success, sir." Kennedy liked not only their brilliance but also their savvy, their use of statistics and slide rules as leverage against the inveterate bureaucrats and gruff generals they squared off with.

Lyndon Johnson was even more impressed than Kennedy by "that fellow from Ford with the Stacomb in his hair." When he became president after Kennedy's assassination in 1963, Johnson ordered all federal departments to adopt PPBS and the "McNamara Management Revolution," dispatching Whiz Kid budget analysts to the bureaucracy like colonizing missionaries from the Church of Rationality. When Johnson unveiled his plans for the Great Society and the War on Poverty, it was the Whiz Kids who were put in charge. They had rationalized business, the military, and warfare itself; now they would do the same for welfare, housing, education, and health care.

Back at RAND, the board of directors was proud that their men and methods were exerting such influence on Washington, but they wanted a larger role for the think tank itself. After running RAND for twenty years, Frank Collbohm was stepping down, and in July of 1966 the RAND board named Henry Rowen its new president. A former RAND analyst, Wohlstetter acolyte, PPBS architect, McNamara aide, and assistant director of the federal budget bureau in charge of transferring PPBS from the Pentagon to social welfare agencies, Rowen was chosen in large measure because of his connections within the federal government. His overarching goal was to create an "urban RAND" to guide America's social policy with the same mathematical precision as its defense policy. Johnson's War on Poverty was promising the kind of federal funds rarely seen outside the Defense Department, and there was a sudden sense of urgency for understanding America's social and economic issues.

Thanks in part to RAND's nuclear strategizing, a full-scale conflict with the Soviet Union appeared unlikely. The new trend in the Cold War would be proxy wars—some far-flung, like Vietnam, but others perhaps much closer to home. On August 11, 1965, a routine traffic stop of a black motorist by a white police officer in the Los Angeles slum of Watts escalated into a three-day riot that ended with thirty-four people dead, 3,758 arrested, nearly $200 million in property damage, and the poverty and increasingly violent frustration of rapidly expanding black urban ghettoes finally on full display. When rioting broke out in a handful of New York neighborhoods, economist Barbara Ward warned a symposium of the New York City Planning Commission that "unless someone comes up with some jolly good solutions, the problem facing cities may become more lethal than the bomb." Renowned psychologist Kenneth Clark noted that "the dark ghettoes now represent a nuclear stockpile which can annihilate the very foundations of America," and one German journalist wrote that the future of the United States depended less on its military might than "whether in the long run human life will remain possible in big cities, whether black and white will learn to live with each other." With riots in cities like Minneapolis; Detroit; Dayton, Ohio; and Cambridge, Maryland, erupting in 1967, and the "long, hot summer" of 1968 on the horizon, urban civil war (not to mention spiraling street-crime statistics) was becoming a serious threat to national security.

Rowen and his analysts were convinced that the "RAND Method" was *the* tool for getting to the bottom of the problem and, when Lyndon Johnson's War on Poverty made unprecedented sums of money available for social welfare research, RAND's board of directors realized it could be the think tank's greatest boon since the nuclear strategy vacuum, a chance to diversify beyond the Air Force, which was still virtually RAND's sole patron. Rowen met repeatedly with Joseph Califano, a former McNamara deputy now serving as Lyndon Johnson's chief domestic adviser, to push for the creation of an "Urban RAND" to study poverty, crime, urban planning, education, health care—any and every social issue that came to the fore. Califano liked the idea so much he stole it, creating the Urban Institute, putting a former RAND analyst in charge, and pushing federal agencies to hire his new think tank instead of RAND. Rowen remained confident, though, that all RAND needed was a test case—the domestic equivalent of Wohlstetter's SAC vulnerability study—to make its mark.

O'Hagan meets the media in Bushwick, Brooklyn.
(Photo courtesy FDNY Photo Unit)

FIVE

Enter the Poet

There are lies, damned lies, and statistics.

—Benjamin Disraeli

January 1967, three months after the 23rd Street collapse

Striding through the glass-paneled doors of fire department headquarters, Steve Isenberg checked in at the front desk and was quickly ushered to a door bearing the stenciled legend ROBERT O. LOWERY, FIRE COMMISSIONER. Six-foot-four and solidly built, the young Lindsay administration budget aide did his best to look calm and confident in his only suit, a navy-blue number that he wore with dark suspenders and, on cold days, a brown fedora—the fake-it-till-you-make-it garb of an inexperienced twenty-six-year-old holding down a very adult job.

Isenberg had a touch of the butterflies, perhaps, but from excited anticipation as much as nerves: just a week into his new position as the budget bureau liaison to the fire department, and already meeting the commissioner. With degrees in English literature from Berkeley and Oxford, and no quantitative training since high school math class, Isenberg had worried about his qualifications for the position. Originally, he'd been hired to work on education ("At least I'd actually been on the inside of an educational institution before"), but his first day on the job he was told that he'd be working with the fire department.

After settling in and familiarizing himself with past FDNY budget reports, Isenberg called over to the fire department and arranged a meeting with Commissioner Lowery. Isenberg hung up and noticed a budget bureau colleague sitting nearby with a look of exasperation on her face. In her budget bureau job for months, she hadn't spoken with so much as a deputy commissioner, and here the English major ("the poet," Mayor Lindsay took to calling him) was arranging meetings with a full-fledged commissioner in his first week on the job. "That's the [great] thing about ignorance," says Isenberg. "I thought I'd just go in and have an informal chat with the commissioner."

The budget bureau and fire department were both housed in the Municipal Building, a forty-floor granite grace note separating the huddled tenements of the Lower East Side from the soaring Beaux-Arts and glass-and-steel skyscrapers of Lower Manhattan. A crown jewel of the City Beautiful period—when the architectural reform movement was bent on combating the corruption and poverty of Gilded Age urban life with massive, Roman Imperial–style public edifices—the "Muni" had an interior no less intent on overawing than its exterior: endless heel-clicking marble hallways, enormous arched doorways, heavy-hanging brass chandeliers, even the men's room urinals huge and somehow portentous.

Going up a few flights of stairs from the budget bureau to fire headquarters, Isenberg expected a short meeting that would doubtless be little more than a social call, he and Lowery exchanging pleasantries and a smattering of shop talk, feeling each other out. Entering the commissioner's office, a dimly lit room made darker still by the trappings of executive power—dark wood, thick leather, plush carpeting—Isenberg found himself facing the broad side of an enormous rectangular table, a seat at the head for Lowery, one at the foot for himself, and between them, seated like something out of *Twelve Angry Men*, Isenberg thought, a dozen or so brass-burdened uniforms, the crème de la crème of the FDNY. The butterflies perked up a bit.

———

A FEW MONTHS EARLIER, ISENBERG HAD BEEN SWEATING through a Washington, D.C., summer, working for Lyndon Johnson's War on Poverty. For years, Isenberg had felt the tug of Kennedy's "what you can do for your country" call to the young and the talented, and, after grad school, had answered it. Young and intellectually ambitious, he found D.C. staid and provincial, a rift between what Daniel Patrick Moynihan later called "the New York mind and the Washington mind," the difference between "the bookstores, the restaurants, the ferocity, even vulgarity, of the teeming cultural life of the great metropolis, as against the somehow embarrassing efforts to keep alive in Washington one-each, a modern art gallery, a symphony orchestra, a repertory theater."

"They had one movie theater that only played [the surf documentary] *The Endless Summer*," says Isenberg. "I didn't like the war, didn't like Johnson, and I knew I was more of a New York person than Washington." Through friends, Isenberg heard about the liberal Republican congressman who had just become mayor of New York, and was able to land an interview with Lindsay's budget director, Fred Hayes. Looking to install a municipal version of Robert McNamara's PPBS, Lindsay had originally offered the budget job to Henry Rowen, who turned him down to become the president of RAND. Rowen had a colleague, though, whom he held in high esteem, a former urban renewal and War on Poverty administrator and rising star in the federal budget bureau named Frederick O'Reilly Hayes. Hayes had the look of a young Dave Brubeck in Organization Man garb: all cheeks, hair, and glasses. Equal parts Harvard-educated reformer and tousled Irish civil servant, Hayes was a vital bridge in the federal budget bureau between the idealistic New York intellectuals who had designed the War on Poverty and the D.C. bureaucrats who administered it, a man unusually adept at overcoming what Moynihan called "the contrast between ideas and information, between brilliance and endurance, between innovation and preservation."

A top official in the Community Action Program when Lindsay

approached him with the budget job, Hayes didn't want to leave the
Johnson administration to work for a Republican rival (Lindsay was
one of the first vocal opponents of the Vietnam War in Congress and
a potential threat to Johnson in the 1968 election), but he decided to
mull it over, and picked up a copy of political scientists Wall Sayre and
Herbert Kaufman's *Governing New York City*, to learn more about the
job. "What they wrote," said Hayes' aide David Grossman, "was that
the budget director is the most powerful official in New York. Fred
felt that sounded pretty good." Hayes took the job in August of 1966,
and on his first day lived up to his Washington reputation as one of the
"toughest budget men in the United States," according to one reporter,
by remaining calmly "unruffled . . . [amid] the high-decibel hurly-burly
of the corridors and offices at City Hall."

Hayes brought a rigorous approach to budget-making, with no tolerance for imprecise measurements of effectiveness. It was not enough
to say the sanitation department was doing a good job because the
streets looked clean, he needed to know the precise tonnage hauled,
the percentage of trucks lying idle for repairs, which divisions hauled
the most trash per man-hour expended or dollar spent, and why the
others lagged behind. He staffed his bureau with young analysts who
developed a vast array of quantitative tools to more precisely gauge the
city's effectiveness at providing basic services, and improve the system
where it lagged.

Hayes' way of doing business was a complete departure from the
old favor-based traditions of the Democratic clubhouse. In that system,
municipal commissioners ran their departments, and when problems
arose—dirty streets on the Lower East Side, noisy dance halls in Hell's
Kitchen—residents would complain to their local ward boss, who,
depending on his level of influence with Tammany and the department
concerned, got it fixed. The name of the game was stasis: departments
were left alone until a problem arose, and then they muddled through
the task of fixing it with as little disruption as possible. For insiders, the
system worked beautifully, but outsiders were shut out of the decision-

making process. Perhaps more important, the bureaucracy in recent years had become insular, corrupt, and more concerned with maintaining its own existence than providing services to the public.

"The entrenched principle of established bureaucracy was that city government had the nature of the ocean," says Edward K. Hamilton, who later took over as Lindsay's budget director when Hayes retired after three years on the job. "That is to say, it is a giant thing that will move as it is going to move, and you [the municipal employee] are simply a cork. You move as you do and float as best you can—usually by getting paid as much as possible. But none of that has anything to do with changing the flow of the ocean, because the assumption is that it's not something you can do anything about."

Lindsay had run directly against the complacent clubhouse, calling for a management style "of total supervision," and Hayes' systematic approach to analyzing the bureaucracy fit the mayor's reform campaign slogans perfectly. "All New Yorkers," the mayor said after hiring the new budget director, "can look toward Fred Hayes as a man who will see to it that every dollar spent in the management of their government will return a dollar's worth of service." Hayes' most ambitious goal was to move the budget bureau's mandate beyond mere accounting. Conventionally, a budget office doesn't determine goals for a government or company, create programs to achieve those goals, or even allocate funding for them. The accountants' job is simply to make sure different departments and programs spend their money wisely. If not, the bureau wields its power, the "negative power" of denying requests for more funding. A good budget director could transform this negative power into some semblance of positive policy-making authority through funding or not funding certain programs, but generally that's as far as a budget bureau's influence reaches. The McNamara-style system that Hayes had overseen in the federal budget did away with those boundaries, giving budget staffers a direct role in setting goals and designing programs. The reformed budget bureau's job was to focus on what O'Hagan's favorite business writer, Peter Drucker, called management by objective: defining a department's goals, designing specific programs to meet those goals, accurately measuring the relationship between "inputs" (i.e., money spent) and "outputs" (items produced or services rendered) to determine the relationship between the two, and finding ways to make the system more efficient. Some observers wrote off management by objective as an ivory-tower term for common sense, but it went a long way toward eliminating the artificial boundaries dividing the planning, implementation, and funding of programs. The reorganized New York Bureau of Planning and Budget became the first of its kind in municipal governance, the domestic-policy equivalent of Edwin Paxson's transformation of the bean-counting of operations research into the weapons-planning of systems analysis. The revolution was almost complete—from the military, to American business, to federal and now local government, the management scientists and efficiency experts were in control.

Excited by Lindsay, Hayes, and their new style of management, Isenberg went to New York to interview for an opening as the budget bureau's liaison to the education department in the fall of 1966. The education aspect of the job Isenberg figured he could handle, but he was nervous about his lack of analytic know-how or government experience. "I barely knew the difference between a budget bureau and a mayor's office," says Isenberg, "but Fred was the very best kind of government professional, a really discursive and eclectic intellect. . . . He and I had this three-hour conversation about *The Road to Wigan Pier*, about Charles Dickens, and it really put me at ease. . . . I made one more trip to see him and he took me to this divey kind of bar where you could drink twenty-cent beers . . . to talk about the job, and he explained his idea that all you needed sometimes was 'brains, balls, and ignorance.'"

With enough intelligence and gumption, Hayes was saying, experience wasn't a necessity, could even be a hindrance, clouding a manager's mind with tired traditions, all those trees you'd learned to identify mucking up your view of the forest. This view that business management wasn't industry-specific but skill-set–specific (quantitative skill-sets, in

particular), was fundamental to the emerging Organization Man view
of the world, where twenty-five-year-old MBAs and green eyeshade–
wearing accountants were given the authority to make decisions
about bombing runs and product rollouts. It was the same philosophy
McNamara (who saw cars as nothing more than a means for conveyance
from Point A to Point B, and had never experienced war beyond Luftwaffe
raids during his Stat Control days in London) had applied at Ford and
the Pentagon, and the same philosophy that was leading to the explosive
growth of management consulting companies like McKinsey & Co.,
Bain, the Boston Consulting Group, and Booz Allen Hamilton, during
the same period. Hayes left his bureau's traditional budget-examiners
largely alone, but wanted fresh-minded outsiders to handle the planning
aspects; he hired Isenberg and dozens of other young budget analysts,
many of whom had little experience with accounting and budget-
making, but all of them idealistic and formidably intelligent. Hayes
had a remarkable eye for finding talent, and Lindsay eventually filled
the core of his administration with budget-bureau analysts. Isenberg
himself went on to work as Lindsay's chief of staff while simultaneously
attending Yale Law School. "He would show up to Yale every couple of
months for exams," says colleague Charles Morris, who also did double
duty at the University of Pennsylvania law school and the budget bureau.
"He never went to classes but his test scores were all [high]; the professors
didn't know what to do about him."

"In the federal government, there has always been a loud trumpet call
heard by the young and the smart," says Isenberg. "That wasn't true of
New York City government, but Fred and John Lindsay made it true. It
was not unlike the clarion call of John Kennedy in 1960 . . . it wasn't that
we thought *anything* was possible, but we really thought in terms of what
we *should* do in government, not what we *shouldn't* do."

Confident in Lindsay, Hayes, and their vision for a new kind of
budgeting and government system, Isenberg reported for his first day
of work only to find that he was assigned to the fire department, not
education.

"They've got twelve thousand men and officers, a $250 million budget, and I don't know if anyone has ever looked at what they do in a fresh way," Hayes explained to the nervous young analyst. "All your life you've learned and been taught to define and solve problems in terms of words. You're working in a budget bureau now, you'll have to learn numbers." After a few days spent studying the numbers from previous fire budgets, Isenberg made his call to the commissioner.

THE FIRE DEPARTMENT BRASS ASSEMBLED IN LOWERY'S office looked on quizzically as Isenberg introduced himself. Municipal Building veterans had slowly inured themselves to the influx of strange new employees who'd answered Lindsay's "clarion call." Volkswagens with California and D.C. plates peppered nearby parking lots, young longhairs and Ivy League prepsters paced the halls. However, the three uniformed services—fire, police, sanitation—had remained relatively untouched by the trend. Isenberg was equally befuddled by his greeting committee, but also realized that Lowery had unintentionally tipped him off about how much power he actually had. If Isenberg were an insignificant functionary, Lowery would have met with him alone or not at all—but for someone with the power of budget behind him, the commissioner needed backup. Sensing this, Isenberg relaxed and tried to put the chiefs at ease too, asking them very basic questions about the department to get them talking about what they knew best. How many fire companies and firemen were there? What's the difference between ladder and engine companies? Did certain sections of the city have bigger fire problems than others?

"As they started talking, they became more and more comfortable," says Isenberg. "And I started to realize what a social X-ray [the fire department] can be. There are a million ways to slice up a city, by the size and age of buildings, by race, by income, the whole demographic list. But suddenly, when you start looking at neighborhoods in terms of fires or false alarm rates, it really tells you a lot about a place."

Fascinated by the variation in fire rates from neighborhood to neighborhood and year to year, Isenberg found out that the department built only a few new firehouses every year. With well over two hundred firehouses in the city, he realized that a firehouse had to last fifty years, maybe longer.

"That's interesting," he said. "If the fire pattern is always changing, how do you know where to build a new house?"

The room was silent for a moment until one of Lowery's politically appointed deputy commissioners piped up.

"Well, that's easy," he said.

"Well, it doesn't sound easy to me, it actually sounds rather complicated," said Isenberg, slightly confused.

"No, no," the deputy commissioner said, "you just build it sixty feet from the corner."

Four decades later, Isenberg still shakes his head incredulously as he tells the story. "But he wasn't joking!" he says, laughing. "The guy just didn't get it. I put my fist down and I said, 'You're a lot of really brave and competent men, but it seems that on some things you've been doing the same thing since the year of the white mice,' . . . I'd heard somebody say that, it means 'since the days of the Bible,' that kind of thing. So they kind of laughed at what I said, but were slightly chilled."

Wrapping up the meeting cordially, Isenberg left the office and headed for the budget bureau.

"I'm probably fifty feet outside the door," says Isenberg, "and I heard a voice behind me, 'Isenberg, you have a minute?' It was Chief O'Hagan. So we go into his office and sit down and he says to me, 'Isenberg'—I'll never forget this—'Isenberg, are you for real?' I said, 'What do you mean, chief?' and he said, 'Are you *for real*?' I said I sure as hell hope so, and he said, 'Because if you're for real, you're the man of my dreams.'"

JOHN O'HAGAN'S LUCK COULDN'T HAVE BEEN BETTER. THE 23rd Street collapse had served its purpose, given him the chance to institute some long-needed reforms and consolidate his power. It had come at a hell of a cost but that was the nature of the job, and at least the twelve deaths had led to changes that would save the lives of others. But it had been three months since the collapse and things were settling back to normal, the slow-slog bureaucratic trench war O'Hagan had been fighting for years returning to its lingering pace—until Isenberg showed up.

After their meeting, Isenberg says, "I reported all this right to Fred and he sensed right away that O'Hagan was absolutely amenable to having a highly analytical system put in place. No one had ever looked at the fire department this way before and he saw the opportunity. It's a bad pun but [O'Hagan] wanted the analytic firepower to become a modern manager. . . . All of this happened, I think, in a very unlikely place. In other words, when you're looking at things on the scale of welfare and human resources and health systems, there were going to be people who wanted to look at large-scale systemic problems. You go into the traditional uniformed services and you don't think it's going to happen. I think all the stars became aligned."

With the mayor's office now aware that they had an unexpected ally in the quest to reform and rationalize municipal services, Isenberg doubled down in his crash course on systems analysis and firefighting.

"John went out of his way for me," says Isenberg. "I was able to go out and ride with [FDNY] chiefs. I went into some of the worst neighborhoods and it gave me a sense of the reality. [Commissioner] Bob Lowery was a cautious man, he called the mayor and said, 'There's a young man in the budget bureau, he wants to go out to the Bronx and ride with some chiefs.' Lindsay said something like, 'You mean the poet?' That's what he said about me, having the two degrees in English. He said, 'Bob, you mean somebody in the budget bureau actually wants to get off their ass and see something outside the building? For God's sake, let him go.' "

Isenberg and O'Hagan began collaborating on new ideas for study-ing and quantifying the fire department's complex operations. For the chief, the most ambitious questions were how to predict fire patterns and alarm rates, and when and where to open fire companies to most efficiently respond to those fires. The implications were enormous. Succeed in predicting something as complicated as fire patterns and you could adapt the system to predict crime rates, public health problems, real estate values, economic development, almost every conceivable trend City Hall was in the business of following and responding to. With accurate predictions, city (not to mention state and federal) government could move beyond the reactionary muddling through of public policy—getting caught off-guard by trends and jury-rigging responses to them—to a proactive approach to governing, spotting problems, and heading them off before they even developed.

Isenberg and O'Hagan brainstormed new ways to approach the problem and pitched ideas to the budget bureau and mayor's office, holding individual meetings with the federal department of Housing and Urban Development (HUD), private consulting companies, and fire experts at the National Academy of Sciences. But as smart and confident as the poet and the chief were, they knew they didn't have the kind of quantitative expertise needed for such an ambitious undertaking. Fortunately, Fred Hayes had been working on a hush-hush project to bring in a new team of outside consultants, an entire department that would tackle the city's problems with systems analysis and computer models, and the fire department was shaping up to be the best candidate for a trial run.

Brooklyn is burning.
(Photo courtesy FDNY Photo Unit)

SIX

The Fire Next Door

Past may be prologue, but which past?

—HENRY HU

January 8, 1968, one year after Isenberg
and O'Hagan's first meeting

Standing behind a lectern under the glare of television lights in City Hall's Blue Room, John Lindsay's face broke into a warm, broad smile. The Blue Room was used for press conferences and official pronouncements and had once been the private office of Fiorello La Guardia. As the first serious Fusion mayoral candidate since the Little Flower, Lindsay had borrowed La Guardia's line that there wasn't a Democratic or Republican way to pick up the garbage. And as mayor, Lindsay had La Guardia's portrait and desk moved into his own office, and adopted his hobby of racing to multiple-alarm blazes and other emergencies.

Lindsay was rarely favored by the comparison. There may not have been a Republican or Democratic way to pick up garbage, but with seven sanitation commissioners quitting on him in four years and a weeklong strike that left more than 200 million pounds of vermin-infested garbage rotting in the streets (and public health officials warning of a possible typhoid outbreak), there didn't seem to be much of a Lindsay way, either. To historian Robert Caro, Lindsay's appropriation of La Guardia's desk was a fitting symbol for the administration: "During La Guardia press conferences, the man behind it had dominated the room; so unable was Lindsay to control the photographers he was constantly summoning to his office that during one picture session, less than a week after the desk had been moved in, several climbed onto it and it caved in."

But at this press conference Lindsay had news of an accomplishment truly worthy of the pint-sized reformer who had stalked the room three decades before: the creation of the New York City–RAND Institute, a joint endeavor of the city and the think tank that would study the fire, police, health, and housing departments, and expand to other departments from there. Standing next to his original pick for budget director, RAND president Henry Rowen, the mayor hailed the revolutionary "partnership adventure" as the culmination of his plans to reshape the municipal bureaucracy along rational, scientific lines, with RAND promising to complete the "introduction into city agencies of the kind of streamlined, modern management that Robert McNamara applied in the Pentagon with such success in the past seven years."

Lindsay didn't necessarily have the clearest understanding of what exactly all the RAND wunderkinds would be up to. When Rowen mentioned that the Institute would be employing a meteorologist, a what'll-they-think-of-next grin flashed across the mayor's face and he asked the RAND president why. "We'll explain that later," Rowen said as the press chuckled along with Lindsay.

For all the praise Lindsay and Rowen lavished on each other and their new partnership, the formation of the institute was a sigh of relief as much as a celebration. It had been a difficult two years for both Lindsay and RAND, the project a would-be savior for each. Losing out on an urban RAND hadn't just been a lost opportunity to gain in size and influence: it was a serious blow to the think tank's long-term plans for survival. Under intense pressure from Congress to cut the cost of outside consultants, in 1966 the Air Force started pressuring RAND to roll back its high fees, "first-class" expense-account policy, and the flexible, undefined nature of its contracts. RAND was shocked. The fee structure and flexibility of its contracts were the lifeblood of the think tank, providing the extra funds that allowed researchers to devote time to the kind of open-ended side projects that yielded RAND's biggest discoveries, like Wohlstetter's SAC basing study and most of the breakthroughs in game theory and nuclear strategy. It was what attracted so many bright minds to Santa Monica in the first place: the opportunity to do cutting-edge research without the commercial pressures of a company or the teaching requirements of academia. RAND was a bit more flexible on its "first class" policy, but scrimping on the cost of hotels and airfare for the preeminent thinkers on the most important national security issues of the day seemed like pound-foolish penny wisdom.

Despite their expertise on strategic posturing and game-theoretic negotiations, RAND botched the contract talks. A new deal was eventually worked out, but the Air Force negotiated significantly lower fees and intimated that the "objective" nature of RAND's reports might have to go too; the brass was tired of paying good money to have their plans shot down. This second issue was a much bigger threat to RAND than any budget cuts. The whole point of RAND's work was to remove personal bias from decision-making, basing it on hard science and inarguable numbers rather than political concerns. The think tank needed to diversify its clientele if it was going to remain viable, and the New York City–RAND Institute was its last, best chance. The think tank's contract with the city—with RAND fronting some of the money itself—reflected that need.

The Lindsay administration was in similar straits. The mayor had utilized his white-knight image and the city's ennui masterfully to win the 1965 election, but the campaign had created higher hopes than he could deliver. As outgoing mayor Robert Wagner had said, "One of John Lindsay's handicaps is that he was the greatest mayor the city ever had before he took office." Lindsay did manage to quickly balance the city's budget—Wagner had to borrow $255 million for his last budget. But by many other measures, New York was in worse shape after two years of Lindsay than it was before.

Lindsay's first day in office began with a strike by transit workers that shut down the city's subways and buses for nearly two weeks, and resulted in a contract that cost the city tens of millions of dollars in higher wages and pension benefits. Lindsay owed his election in large part to his progressive stand on civil rights, winning black, Puerto Rican, and liberal white districts on pledges to confront racism, bring minority concerns to City Hall, and fight the crushing poverty of inner-city neighborhoods. His first initiative on race was a proposed Civilian Complaint Review Board, to look into police brutality complaints. It was a bold proposal, characteristic of Lindsay's uncompromising commitment to civil rights, but was perhaps a strategic blunder. Conservative political scientist Aaron Wildavsky called the issue a negative-sum game, one in which "everyone's feelings are exacerbated and the conflict continues at a new height of hostility. . . . The game begins with a publicity campaign focusing on fascist police, various atrocities, and other lurid events. The police and their friends counter with an equally illuminating defense: nothing is wrong that a little get-tough campaign would not cure. The game ends with a ballot in which white voters are asked to choose between their friendly neighborhood policeman and the specter of black violence."

Lindsay's proposal lost at the polls, leaving civil rights activists disillusioned, black neighborhoods feeling further alienated from the white power structure, Lindsay's already tenuous relationship with civil servants on life support, and many of the city's working-class whites convinced that the mayor cared only about poor minorities and rich liberals. On two other racially tinged issues—crime and jobs—the results were equally disheartening. Lindsay had promised that "no issue in this campaign is more important than the problem of rising crime." One of candidate Lindsay's flyers warned that "in our city there is a murder every 14 hours, a reported rape every six hours; a reported assault every 12 minutes; a reported theft every three minutes." Mayor Lindsay saw the murder rate rise 18 percent in his first two years in office.

Arguing that the city's economy was stagnant, candidate Lindsay had criticized the large welfare rolls, which rose to more than 500,000 people under Wagner. Mayor Lindsay oversaw an even sharper increase, with welfare enrollment more than doubling during his first term.

The crime and welfare increases had more to do with decades of bad urban and economic planning than with the recently elected mayor. But even Lindsay's hallmark issue of reforming the bureaucracy was having trouble getting traction. There was no shortage of ideas that seemed great on paper: Consolidating the city's myriad departments into a handful of streamlined "super-agencies." A new "war-games room" at City Hall devoted solely to "issue mapping," described by one reporter as "an attempt to use systems analysis to provide Lindsay with up-to-date data on city problems." But the new initiatives faced more resistance from canny, entrenched bureaucrats than Lindsay had ever expected, and many of the programs proved impractical in the real world. Some departments seemed too busy reforming themselves to actually reap any of the productivity gains that were the whole point of the reform in the first place. As one former Lindsay aide told historian Vincent Cannato, a Tammany mayor "knew the city and how it works to a 'T.' He knew the first name of the guy you had to call to get a pothole filled on a particular block out in Brooklyn . . . [or] knew the clubhouse pol or the power broker . . . who was responsible for getting that pothole-filler his job in the first place. But Lindsay—he only knew his own assistant. And his assistant—he only knew Lindsay. And nobody knew the pothole-filler or how to reach him." It's a perhaps unfair sentiment—Lindsay would never have been elected if that clubhouse system was actually working as well as some liked to think—but it reflected a growing consensus on the new mayor's management skills.

PUBLIC POLICY HAS ALWAYS BEEN A BIT OF A GUESSING game. The connection between how much money is spent on the police department (never mind how it's divvied up among training, communications, equipment, manpower, etc.) and how safe the streets are is much more difficult to determine than the relationship between, say, how much a car costs to produce and how profitable it is, or what combination of rocket thrust and depleted uranium it would take to level Moscow. As Fred Hayes had told Steve Isenberg about the fire department on his first day on the job, the budget bureau generally wrote out big checks, crossed their fingers, and hoped the money was well spent. Because they didn't understand how to conduct a murder investigation or manage an emergency room, there was only so much that accountants could tell a commissioner about running his department. In the Tammany days, that didn't matter—the accountants and commissioners were all members of the same machine, and when it functioned properly, that machine kept them in line. But as the "City in Crisis" sentiment had shown, the public didn't think the old system was functioning properly at all, and in a pique of "Throw the bums out" anger, in 1965 elected not a pragmatic gradualist but a moralizing crusader. While he'd won the tight three-man race with only 43 percent of the vote, Lindsay thought he had a moral mandate not to compromise but to wage an all-out assault on the unresponsive bureaucracy. The new NYC-RAND Institute would be his secret weapon, an administrative Excalibur for the dragon-slaying mayor.

Lindsay could never be expected to master the intricacies of the bureaucracy like a clubhouse savant, but RAND promised to rationalize the system so he didn't have to. Just as it had done with warfare, RAND's systems analysis would reduce the myriad complications of the bureaucracy into easily defined variables. Once the facts were gathered and the relationship between inputs and outputs determined, new policies could be tested on a computer model to see which worked best, and like NASA engineers manipulating the movement of a rocket, the mayor's office could control a department by tweaking the budget or making a few scientifically determined shifts in priorities. To make sure clubhouse stalwarts didn't gum up the new system, RAND would develop metrics to see who was doing his job and who wasn't, and hold people accountable for their performance right on down the line—from Lindsay to his assistants and commissioners to middle managers and the rank-and-file.

It may sound a bit Panglossian in hindsight, but the notion that advanced computer models—freed from partisan concerns and able to process enormous quantities of data instantaneously—would soon be making public-policy decisions was almost a foregone conclusion in many government circles. President Johnson was deploying PPBS modelers throughout the federal government. McNamara's Whiz Kids were using computers to predict Vietcong attacks and decide where to move troops and drop bombs. In a speech before the American Academy of Political and Social Sciences, influential defense intellectual C. West Churchman predicted that by 1990, decision-making technology would outstrip the minds of high-level thinkers and policy-makers, and presidents would consult computers for advice on how to fight wars and manage the economy.

For John Lindsay's administration, the most pressing issue was the urban crisis that had gotten the mayor elected, specifically the racial and economic tensions on the verge of boiling over in cities like New York. Lindsay was willing to stake his reputation on the belief that the "techniques that are going to put a man on the Moon," as Vice President Hubert Humphrey once said, "are going to be exactly the techniques that we are going to need to clean up our cities." With the NYC-RAND Institute, Lindsay was about to take the first major step toward putting the might of Cold War military science to use in the lives of ordinary Americans—something they would no doubt appreciate in future presidential primaries.

Both Lindsay and RAND knew that the young institute faced at least two major obstacles. First, city bureaucrats were likely to see RAND as interlopers sent by the mayor's office, and would be loathe to give over any power, even advisory power, in their municipal fiefdoms. Second, designing public policies was a far more complicated matter than designing weapons systems, and predicting outcomes harder still. They saw these as operational problems, though—incidental obstacles that could be overcome with enough careful coalition-building and precise research. What Lindsay and RAND were not prepared for was a more existential flaw in the assumption that the institute—and, in many ways, the entire Lindsay administration—was based on: that New York was, in fact, a "City in Crisis," at least in the way the *Herald Tribune* series had shown it.

Almost the entire "City in Crisis" series could have been summed up with a single sentence: "Every facility is inadequate—the hospitals and schools and playgrounds are overcrowded, the express highways are feverish, the unimproved highways and bridges are bottlenecks; there is not enough air and not enough light, and there is usually either too much heat or too little." But that sentence was written by E. B. White in his 1948 paean to the city, when both he and most other critics were willing to give New York a pass for its inevitable troubles. A compelling case could be made that the city was actually doing pretty well, particularly by New York's topsy-turvy historical standards. Despite Lindsay's campaign crime statistics, New York was one of the safest big cities in the country; fire rates, that "leading social indicator," had been steady for years. So why had the *Trib* series found such resonance?

On November 23, 1951, Princeton defeated Dartmouth in a rough, penalty-filled football game in which both starting quarterbacks left with injuries—one with a concussion and broken nose, the other a broken leg. After the game, a pair of research psychologists showed replays to students and asked them to count all the penalties they saw, and Princeton students reported "seeing" the Dartmouth team commit twice as many penalties as Dartmouth students saw. The results aren't news to anyone who's ever watched a game at a bar in a rival town, but the study hints at an often overlooked fact. Given the incredible amount of data we take in when analyzing complicated situations like a long, hard-fought football game (or the state of a city), our brains have to find some organizing principle to understand it all, usually a storyline that turns seemingly disconnected events into a coherent narrative, like, say, "Dartmouth is full of cheats." The problem is that our perception of the facts is colored by which side, which storyline, we have already bought into. Whether it's using out-of-context crime stats to support a narrative like "The city is in decline," or "seeing" a rival team play dirty, the same process of subtle bias is at work. After decades as a media darling, it was time for New York's comeuppance, with every unconnected and unavoidable nuisance of city life seen as damning evidence of decay. The most glaring example of the "crisis narrative" overshadowing reality is that great parable of urban morality, the Kitty Genovese murder. In the *Times* formulation, thirty-eight people spent a half-hour watching as a woman was stalked, stabbed, and killed in three separate attacks, and not one of them so much as picked up a phone to call the police. But through an exhaustive examination of investigative records, court documents, and interviews with surviving witnesses, over the last ten years Queens attorney Joseph De May, Jr., has pieced together a far more complicated picture of the murder.

Returning home just after three a.m. on the coldest night of the year, Genovese was stabbed from behind outside her apartment building by a serial rapist and suspected necrophiliac, Winston Moseley. Genovese's screams roused sleeping neighbors, whose windows were shut against the cold, and at least one of them shouted down to the street, scaring Moseley off. Only two people saw the initial attack, and one of them thought Moseley had only punched or shoved Genovese. When Genovese got up and walked into her apartment building without a word, most onlookers assumed that it was just another lovers' quarrel that had spilled over from a rowdy bar down the block. At least one person did, in fact, call the police to report an assault, but officers never arrived. Meanwhile, Genovese entered her apartment building through a back door and collapsed in the hallway. Ten minutes later, Moseley entered the building, killed Genovese, and attempted to rape her. An upstairs neighbor, whose door faced a stairwell that led to the hallway, was aware of this second attack (although it's not known exactly what he heard or saw) but had been drinking heavily and was afraid to call the police, although he did eventually persuade a neighbor to call.

The *Times* claimed three attacks, thirty-eight *eye*witnesses, and zero calls to the police. In fact, there were two attacks, three people who actually saw them (only one of whom really understood what was happening), and multiple calls to the police, who didn't respond until Genovese was already dead. There were a few more *ear*-witnesses, but most of them thought it was a drunken scuffle, not a murder in progress. "I don't know where that came from, the thirty-eight," said Queens prosecutor Charles Skoller, who handled the case. "I didn't count thirty-eight."

"Yeah, people heard something. You can question how a few people behaved. But this wasn't 38 people watching a woman be slaughtered for 35 minutes and saying, 'Oh, I don't want to be involved,'" said Mr. De May. "We didn't have what the *Herald Tribune*, I think, described at the time as being a scene reminiscent of the Roman Colosseum with the Romans watching the Christians being slaughtered while they cheered them on."

But the complex reality of the Genovese case didn't matter in the mid-1960s, only public perception, the simplified media morality tales that fed it, and the way that perception drove the search for ever more evidence of a city in crisis. All of this is not to say that New York City in the mid-1960s was not in a precarious position, but the challenges the city faced were very different from the "crisis" proclaimed by the press and the Lindsay camp. The city was not simply in the *midst* of a moderate downturn brought on by a few years of corrupt and inefficient government; it was on the *verge* of a much deeper crisis, one with roots that stretched back for decades.

People certainly sensed this deeper decline—they could see it in the working-class neighborhoods and factories that were disappearing, the flight of middle-class whites to the suburbs, crime statistics that were just beginning to creep up, the disconnect between the power brokers that ran the city and the city itself—and this unease contributed to the popularity of the crisis narrative and Lindsay's election. But, preoccupied with the exaggerated downturn, virtually no one in the power structure spotted the warning signs of the approaching precipice. The evidence of that downturn was harder to find, but the clearest clues came in the fire department.

A FEW HOURS AFTER LINDSAY AND ROWEN'S PRESS CONFER-
ence announcing the formation of NYC-RAND, twenty-nine-year-old
Juan Diaz was watching television with his family in their apartment in
the Williamsburg section of Brooklyn when he noticed smoke seeping
under the door from the hallway. Diaz led his wife and children to his
brother-in-law's apartment on the fourth floor and tried to open a window to the fire escape, but found it frozen shut.

Outside on the street, dozens of people streamed into the freezing
night air while parents trapped inside screamed for help, holding young
children out windows at arm's-length to shield them from the smoke
and flames. Then they started dropping them. "They came too fast and
it was too dark to see them all," said police officer Ralph Salerno, who
reached the scene in time to help catch what he guessed were twenty or
so children. "Some of them," he said, "hit the ground."

Diaz led his family out into the hallway, and made his way through the
panicked crowd to the top of the building, where he jumped safely to the
roof of a small house next door. When he reached the ground, he realized
that he'd somehow lost his family. He made a dash for Ladder 108 and
tried to climb back into the tenement, but was grabbed by firefighters.
Diaz's second cousin Noel Castro watched from the street. "Poor Johnny
thought his wife and kids were with him until he got down," said Castro.
"He kept trying to fight his way up the firemen's ladder, screaming, 'My
family—they're going to die.' Johnny went *loco* for a while, watching the
flames shooting out of his apartment."

The fire department battled high winds, temperatures hovering
around zero, and low water-pressure from frozen hydrants to eventually
bring the seven-alarm blaze under control, rescuing close to a hundred
people. It was "the worst apartment fire there has been in New York in the
last eight or ten years," Commissioner Lowery said the next morning, "a
miracle" so many people were rescued. Juan Diaz's family wasn't among
them. His wife Concepcion, their five children, Diaz's brother-in-law

Francisco Mojica, his wife Juanita, their four children, and the children's grandmother Victoria Moreno all died. From an extended family of nine children and five adults, Diaz was the only survivor. He wandered aimlessly in front of the smoking, ice-encrusted building for hours, saying, *"Todos muertos, todos muertos"*—everyone dead—over and over.

The following day, a fire crew on its way to a call in Harlem spotted another blaze and radioed it in. Started by a space heater used in a frigid apartment, the second fire left thirty-four families homeless. Before it was put out, another four-alarm fire broke out twenty blocks to the north, and companies from across the city had to be called to the scene. Just across the Harlem River that night, a fifteen-year-old boy saved nine of his cousins from a roaring Bronx apartment fire. The day after that, two four-alarm fires broke out simultaneously in the West Bronx. Less than an hour after they were extinguished, a fire started by a hair dryer claimed three buildings in the Soundview section of the Bronx. When two ladder companies cut a hole in the roof of one of the buildings, a backdraft blew it apart, injuring seven truckies but somehow killing no one. It took six alarms—nearly forty pieces of equipment and 170 firemen—to knock the blaze down.

Later that night, in the northern Manhattan neighborhood of Washington Heights, a fire started by a defective oil burner killed one man and spread to three buildings, taking four alarms to put down. All told, there were seven multiple-alarm fires in northern Manhattan and the nearby Bronx in less than forty-eight hours. Including the Williamsburg blaze, fourteen people, among them nine children, were killed and roughly five hundred people left homeless by eight multiple-alarm blazes over four of the coldest days on record in New York.

It was the culmination of a deadly trend that had started earlier in the winter. Two months before, a fire had killed a twenty-five-year-old woman, her two children, and a niece and nephew. A month after that, the Lower East Side apartment of Regina and Charles Schiebel caught fire, and Charles was unable to open the wooden shutters he'd installed the previous year after one of their children fell from an open window and died. Charles, Regina, and their two oldest children survived with severe burns, but the three youngest children, all under the age of seven, died from smoke inhalation. Earlier that same day, five young cousins left alone in a Brooklyn apartment died in a fire. Out buying groceries, the mother of three of them ran back to the building when she heard the approaching sirens. Firefighters found her trying to fight her way up a smoke-filled stairwell screaming, "My kids! My kids!"

What all these fires shared was location: some of the poorest black and Puerto Rican neighborhoods in the city—Manhattan's Lower East Side, Harlem, Washington Heights, Brooklyn's Williamsburg and Bushwick, and a previously differentiated assemblage of neighborhoods coming to be known collectively as the "South Bronx." The declining fire numbers of the late 1950s and early 1960s had masked a small but growing fire problem in New York's ghettoes that had doubled the number of civilian fire deaths to more than 300 in a few years. It was a threat that Chief O'Hagan was uncharacteristically unsuited to face. Named chief of department at the age of only thirty-nine, O'Hagan was the youngest chief in department history, but he may have also been the most experienced thirty-nine-year-old the department had ever seen. He'd worked in engine, ladder, and elite rescue companies, winning commendations and battling fires in everything from aging lofts and warehouses to ultramodern high-rises.

But if there was any aspect of the job that O'Hagan wasn't an expert on, it was "ghetto firefighting"—fighting fires in the crowded row houses and aging tenements of poor, usually black and Puerto Rican neighborhoods. Ghetto fires caused a disproportionate number of civilian and firefighter deaths, but they held none of the intellectual challenges O'Hagan sought. The physics of fire and smoke-flow in tenement build-ings was well understood (particularly after O'Hagan and a group of scientists staged a series of experimental fires in an abandoned building in Bushwick), as were the weaknesses and strengths of the building con-struction. Even the physical demands were predictable, if extreme.

There was a personal element as well. From the time he joined the department, O'Hagan was drawn to high-rise houses and elite rescue squads—they fought some of the biggest, toughest fires, but went on fewer runs, which left him more time to study and get ahead. Ghetto firehouses had a different feel to them: the danger and camaraderie were a little closer, the men rowdier, less concerned with rising through the ranks than with fighting as many risky blazes as they could.

"I started fighting fires at twenty-two," says Mike Benning, who worked on the Lower East Side in the 1960s and 1970s, "and I'll tell you what, if you wanted to create an adrenaline junkie, you take a twenty-two-year-old and have him fighting four or five fires every night. It was dangerous, you'd get sick, you'd get lost in the smoke in an apartment. . . . Maybe you'd have to tear up the linoleum on the floor to find the old wood beneath it and see which way the seams ran to find the door out. All those little tricks to stay alive, it was really something else, excitement-wise."

If John O'Hagan and the new generation of get-ahead test-takers he came up with were at one end of the spectrum of "professionalism" (in the by-the-book, buttoned-down sense), most ghetto firefighters seemed to be at the other. O'Hagan was a military man and he liked a military operation—uniforms pressed, shoes shined, the rig fresh-washed and gleaming. Most busy houses in the Bronx had so little time between fires that the rigs went unwashed, and bunk rooms and kitchens were left messy. Shoes were shined and the uniforms stayed pressed, but they were left inside lockers: no sense in changing clothes when you'd have to change right back in fifteen minutes. O'Hagan didn't bear any ill will toward ghetto fire companies, but he didn't hold them in particularly high esteem either, certainly not the regard he had for specially trained rescue crews or the companies in high-rise districts whose officers could match wits with architects and engineers. Some of O'Hagan's deputies had more experience in the ghetto, but most of his top aides were from the same mold as he, and the unspoken assumption they held was that any jamoke could put out tenement fires and bust balls in some raucous firehouse in the South Bronx, the real pros were in Manhattan.

"When I transferred from the Bronx to a midtown company, my eyes were really opened, politically. All the important guys all went through there, the guys with real influence, especially through the Third Division," says Captain Tom Henderson. "And the attitude of midtown officers was that guys from the Bronx didn't know what the hell they were doing—and in some ways they were right, it took a little while to learn that kind of Manhattan firefighting. In the Bronx, the door opened and you rushed in. You couldn't do that in Manhattan [high-rises], you might not come back out. And midtown guys had to fight some tenement fires too and they knew how to handle those, so they looked down at guys working in the ghetto. The difference was, in Manhattan you caught one, maybe two calls a night, put them out, and you were done. Of *course* apartment fires seem easy when that's all you do. In the Bronx, you'd be chasing calls all night, maybe thirty of them in a fifteen-hour shift. On top of that, the equipment didn't work in those neighborhoods. The rigs were always breaking down, getting flat tires. Open a hydrant in Manhattan and water came out; in the Bronx you take the top off a hydrant and you'd find a cat some kid shoved down there."

And so a blind spot, a rare hole in the chief's own experience and in the perspectives of the men he surrounded himself with, allowed O'Hagan to downplay the alarming trend in ghetto fires, just as a similar blind spot was allowing Mayor Lindsay and RAND to overlook the broader economic and social collapse underlying those fires. Virtually no one in city government, the media, academia, or New York's renowned good-government groups saw what was coming. Certainly no one was predicting that in ten short years New York would lose nearly a million jobs and a similar number of residents. That the homes of hundreds of thousands of people would burn to the ground, turning vibrant neighborhoods into rubble-strewn wastelands. In fact, most pundits and policy-makers had it backward: while they complained of a city grown too crowded, disorganized, muddled, mixed-up, and dirty, the real decline was rooted in those very same complaints and an earlier generation of reformers' attempts to impose order, cleanliness, and rationality on unruly Gotham. They did so by reimagining and reshaping the physical city itself, and with it the urban landscape of America.

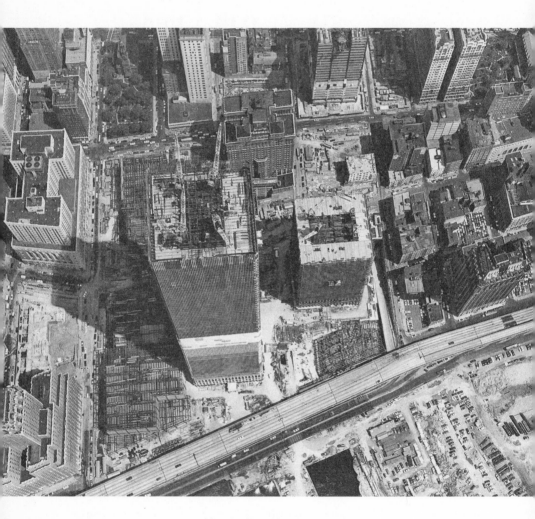

The World Trade Center rises.
(Photo courtesy FDNY Photo Unit)

SEVEN

How the Other Half Thinks

You say what is a city? Well, a city is many things, but one of the things that a city is is a home to its people. If you think of the great cities of history, Athens is glory, you say Rome is grandeur or power, Paris is culture. What is New York? New York is a home. New York's great gift to the world was that peoples from all over the world could come here, they could create their own communities, their own neighborhoods, so people felt a sense of community, a sense of belonging, a sense of neighborhood. That's really the basis of human endeavor. If people feel they belong they can go on to other things. Now, all of a sudden, that was going to be harder for New York than ever before, because at this crucial moment in the city's history, the city loses its way. Whereas before neighborhoods were created, now neighborhoods are destroyed.

—Robert Caro

New York, né New Amsterdam, had the "good fortune," reporter and author Pete Hamill once remarked, of being "started by a company, the Dutch West India Company, not by a religious sect, not by a king, but by a company." Unlike Puritan New England or aristocratic Virginia, New York's sole reason for being was the unbounded pursuit of money. This founding ethos brought with it a number of noble attributes, in particular a willingness to take in anyone that was good for business. Within a few years of its founding, there were eighteen languages spoken on the streets of the city, and it was home to the only Jewish congregation in North America. But it was the pursuit of wealth that allowed such tolerance, just as it allowed slavery (but let masters seeking a better return on their investment train slaves as skilled craftsmen and offer them freedom in return for hard work). New Amsterdam's rigid director-general, Peter Stuyvesant, acceded to the pervasive freedom of the city by creating "free market days," on which food prices, normally fixed by the government, were lifted and the laws of supply and demand allowed to take hold. The creative capitalism wouldn't even stop for war. When British ships sailed into the harbor in 1664, Stuyvesant was presented with a petition of surrender signed by ninety-three of the town's most prominent men (including his own son). They didn't care who was in charge, so long as they be allowed to go about their business, and Stuyvesant begrudgingly agreed.

The attitude prevailed through the Colonial and Federal periods, and as the industrial era brought even more economic opportunity to New York, it continued to welcome immigrants by the millions—Chinese, Jews, blacks from the American South and West Indies, Italians, Irish, Poles, Russians, Romanians, Armenians, Turks—as many as twelve thousand a day, one and a quarter million per year. "Every four years," wrote one chronicler, "New York adds to itself a city the size of Boston or St. Louis. It is the largest Jewish city in the world, the largest Irish city, one of the largest German cities. More than 700,000 Russians call it home, and it houses more Italians than Rome. New York is the great whirlpool of the races."

With a calm port, connection to the Midwest Grain Belt (via the 1832 opening of the Erie Canal), extensive manufacturing base, and almost limitless supply of cheap labor, by the late nineteenth century New York was the world's greatest economic engine. But that very same success also planted the seeds of a shift in the city's founding ethos, a move away from unfettered freedom toward a more regulated, government-controlled economy. The cause of that shift was slums. The worst of them, on Manhattan's Lower East Side, housed as many as 2,200 people per block, packed into dark, airless, four- and five-story walk-up tenements run by landlords intent on obtaining whatever profits and avoiding whatever expenses they could. Barely one in three children made it to his fifth birthday in the worst neighborhoods; they died in droves from diarrhea, malnutrition, diphtheria, cholera, and the "Captain of all these Men of Death," as writer John Bunyan once called it, tuberculosis, the source of the Lower East Side's dreaded "Lung District" nickname.

The city's educated classes showed sporadic interest in "the problem of the slums," but that concern was crystallized by the 1890 publication of *How the Other Half Lives*, a small book of photos and essays by police reporter Jacob Riis. With newly invented flash-powder photography and a pithy first-person reporting style, the once penniless Danish immigrant catalogued for the first time the desperate plight of the new arrivals, quickly becoming a best-selling author and one of the most sought-after speakers in the country.

While the use of flashbulbs was the most famous formal innovation of Riis' book, just as important was the unique way he wed intensive crime, housing, and health data to his sensationalistic stories and photos. Riis was no longer simply telling a sad story about a handful of malnourished children from "Jewtown," or a few frightening thugs and beggars lingering around "Bandit's Roost," he was talking about "37,316 tenements" whose "population is over 1,250,000." Neighborhoods that "throw off a scum of forty thousand human wrecks to the island asylums and workhouses year by year . . . a standing army of paupers, criminals and sick poor," who cost the government "$7,156,112.94" in 1889 alone. Previously, a brief tour of the Five Points or a charitable donation would have sufficed to ease the consciences of those (wealthy, progressive) New Yorkers concerned with the plight of the poor. But Riis' statistics overwhelmed his readers, made the scattershot work of private charities seem insufficient to the task.

The city's leading reformer, U.S. Civil Service Commissioner Theodore Roosevelt, read the book with such interest that he called upon Riis at home, the once impoverished immigrant quickly becoming a close confidant of the future president. When TR became New York's police commissioner, Riis prevailed upon him to shut the brutal police department lodging houses, where Riis himself had been forced to take shelter when he first arrived in America, and to close down hundreds of illegal rookeries (old mansions and warehouses hastily converted into housing) each year. Working with the growing ranks of middle-class housing reformers, Riis convinced the city to engage in some of the country's first experiments in "slum clearance": widening crowded city streets and tearing down tenements to build small parks. The high point of the movement came in 1901, when Riis, Roosevelt, and a small group of progressives were able to push the first serious tenement-house regulations through Albany, requiring that all new residential buildings have ventilation, enough light to read by, and at least one water closet for every two families.

Riis was far ahead of his time when it came to understanding the causes of social ills. Most contemporary thinkers still clung to versions of "Social Darwinism," the idea that poverty was something people brought entirely upon themselves, the result only of their weakness, laziness, and, as eugenicists (including TR) claimed, genetic inferiority. By showing the terrible conditions under which so many impoverished children and immigrants were forced to live, Riis helped popularize a notion that is now all but taken for granted: that people's surroundings affect their behavior and economic lot in life.

Yet Riis' insight had its limits. The single, more humane lodging house that Commissioner Roosevelt built was unable to handle the scores of homeless people that relied on the many police department lodges he closed, forcing many onto the streets. Because they housed only those who couldn't afford a better place to sleep, the thousands of rookeries Riis and Roosevelt closed resulted in a virtual refugee crisis on the Lower East Side, pushing more people into already overcrowded tenements and Bowery flophouses (usually located above a storefront gin mill). Riis blamed the surge on saloonkeepers plying the poor with cheap drink and shelter, but they had been doing that for decades; it was Riis' misguided attempts at improving housing conditions that actually drove the crisis. The most disastrous results came from slum clearance. One of the largest projects was Columbus Park, carved out of the Five Points slum in 1897 at the cost of ten thousand people's homes.* The New York City Parks Department's write-up of the park says that "Riis remarked of the park that it is 'little less than a revolution' to see the slum housing go down, while 'in its place come trees and grass and flowers; for its dark hovels light and sunshine and air.'" An improved setting, no doubt, but for whom, exactly?

The irony of Riis' oversight was that it sprang from the same source as his activism: his own brushes with poverty as a young immigrant. A well-educated, middle-class Protestant Dane who read and spoke some English when he arrived in New York, Riis possessed none of the internal *causes* of poverty—physical or mental infirmity, a lack of marketable skills, language barrier, belonging to a race or religious group that faced prejudice. Riis was much better acquainted with the external *results* of poverty that he did briefly suffer: having to live in degrading and dangerous tenements and lodging houses. For Riis, simply removing these trappings of penury was enough to let his internal strengths come to the fore, but the conclusion that his experience led him to—that if you get rid of slums, you get rid of poverty—proved disastrous when translated into public policy.

AROUND THE SAME TIME THAT THE HOMES OF THE POOR WERE being exposed to the patronizing pity of the upper classes, so were their jobs. On the afternoon of March 25, 1911, a small fire broke out on the upper floors of a ten-story industrial building on the corner of Washington Place and Greene Street. Within fifteen minutes, 146 women and girls in the employ of the Triangle Shirtwaist company ("shirtwaist" was the contemporary moniker for a woman's blouse) on the eighth floor

---

*Depicted in Martin Scorsese's *Gangs of New York*, the Points was the city's most notorious slum, but also a hotbed of immigrant businesses and even artistic innovation: caricaturing and challenging one another, Irish and black dancers and musicians invented tap dancing there. In just a few years, reformers were able to clear the entire Five Points slum; it is now the site of a pair of small parks, an assemblage of courthouses, and a prison.

of the building were dead. Dozens succumbed to smoke inhalation, but most died falling from a broken fire escape or hurling themselves down the shaft of a broken elevator and out of windows, many of the falling bodies impaled on the spikes of a wrought-iron fence that surrounded the building.

Public outrage at the Triangle Fire forced Tammany Hall to put its two best men, State Senate leader (and father of the future mayor) Robert F. Wagner, Sr., and State Assembly leader Al Smith, in charge of an investigation. The inquiry turned the pair of Tammany loyalists into unlikely allies of the reform movement, and they eventually pushed through Albany more than fifty separate reform bills that established building and fire codes, child-labor restrictions, wage protections, and limited working hours, the first labor laws of their kind in America. It was a fundamental shift in the role that American government played in people's lives. No longer would government simply provide the laws and security needed for a capitalist economy to flourish: it would guarantee citizens, even noncitizen immigrants, basic protections from the harsh living and working conditions that capitalist economy often engendered. "The New Deal," said Frances Perkins, who served on the Triangle investigation committee with Smith and Wagner, and later became the first female cabinet member as FDR's secretary of labor, "began on March 25, 1911. The day the Triangle factory burned."

In some ways, the Progressive Era's housing, labor, and industrial regulations were a violation of New York's founding principles of freedom and unfettered business. They were a minimal violation, a begrudging intrusion by the government to curb the worst excesses of free-market capitalism, but this humble foray gave birth to a much more powerful and coercive kind of government intervention. One that, like Riis' book, derived much of its influence from the power of numbers.

THE DOMINANT POLITICAL PARADIGM OF MOST AMERICAN industrial cities—the branch approach of (usually Democratic) political machines—developed not in isolation but as a reflection of the cities themselves. Aside from Washington, D.C., most cities grew like branches, in fits and starts and by the dictates of the market, with businesses springing up and fading away as economic opportunities waxed and waned. The field of urban planning developed in opposition to this unplanned development. Planners favored a comprehensive root-approach to citymaking: scientifically analyzing an area, determining the ideal pattern of housing, industry, and transportation, and then charging forward with it.*

The root approach is, of course, necessary for the kinds of large-scale projects that big cities often need—no one was going to take part in a decentralized, uncoordinated effort to dig the Erie Canal or fill in the marsh that is now Boston's Back Bay. The trouble with the root approach is that it's extremely vulnerable to bad ideas. Given the hasty, often unexamined nature of the branch approach, bad ideas are perhaps more common than with the comprehensive planning of the root approach— just think of the number of businesses that open on the wrong block, only to close up shop shortly thereafter. But there's a safety mechanism in that failure: the shop owner sees the error of his ways and closes before he wastes even more time and money. Because the root approach presumes to have considered all possible options before proceeding, there is no equivalent rethinking, and bad ideas are given a much longer lifespan.

Unfortunately, the young field of urban planning fell under the sway of a number of bad ideas. In America, the reigning urban theorists of the early twentieth century were self-described "Decentrists," like Catherine Bauer, Lewis Mumford, and Clarence Stein, who believed cities should

---

*Root-approach urban planning doesn't always have to come from the government. The most recent example would be the gated communities and sprawling exurban developments hastily thrown together in the waning days of the early 2000s real estate bubble, but the process is nothing new. Manhattan's Harlem was built in a similar fashion, with developers snatching up land and erecting luxury apartment buildings and brownstone townhouses only to see a credit-and-housing bubble burst, forcing developers and landlords to rent to Italians, Jews, and, eventually, blacks and Puerto Ricans.

be less dense, with housing and commerce allocated scientifically through-out whole regions. This belief was based largely on their negative reaction to the crowding, poverty, pollution, and noxious smells of dense cities that writers like Riis and Charles Dickens had been decrying for decades. Mumford called Midtown Manhattan "solidified chaos"; to Bauer, urban centers were "a foreground of noise, dirt, beggars, souvenirs, and shrill competitive advertising"; and to Stein, cities were nothing but "a cha-otic accident . . . the summation of the haphazard, antagonistic whims of many self-centered, ill-advised individuals."*

The trouble with this negative view of the dense metropolis is that, like Amory Blaine's take on machine politics, it is the view of the bewildered outsider. To the Tammany ward boss, the parish priest, or the local businessman, the chaotic ebb and flow of the streets made perfect sense. It took years for anyone in the planning world to describe the beauty and logic of a bustling city street, but the eloquent Jane Jacobs was up to the task. "Under the seeming disorder of the old city is a marvelous order," she wrote in 1961. "This order is all composed of movement and change, and although it is life, not art, we may fancifully call it the art form of the city and liken it to the dance—not to a simple-minded precision dance with everyone kicking up at the same time, twirling in unison, and bowing off en masse, but to an intricate ballet in which the individual dancers and ensembles all have distinctive parts which miraculously reinforce each other and compose an orderly whole."

And New York's great economic strength was that from street to street, year to year, even day to day, the dance was in flux, constantly changing and adapting. New patterns of immigration, technological innovations, macroeconomic shifts—these things could not be planned for, but with a flexible economy they could be dealt with, muddled through, as dancers

---

*Stein's critique of the city reads like a critique of the free marketplace and the power it confers on ordinary, "ill-advised" people to shape the world around them. As Irving Kristol would write of a later generation of liberal reformers, early urban planners were perhaps "suspicious of, and hostile to, the market precisely because the market is so vulgarly democratic."

were suddenly added or taken away. Chased from the Russian Empire by violent pogroms, hundreds of thousands of Eastern European Jews— many of them skilled in needlework and willing to work for incredibly low wages—immigrated to New York in the late 1800s. So a canny New York businessman might convert an old factory into a garment-manufacturing sweatshop. Observing the new workers closely, a clever street peddler would see the hungry workers forced to walk ten blocks to the nearest kosher deli for lunch. With a little pluck and determination, he'd learn the rules for handling kosher meat, load up his cart from that deli each day, and sell fresh sandwiches to garment workers all too happy to pay an extra penny to rest their feet at lunchtime. Newsboys from the Yiddish papers would soon flock to the street, and while an Irish pub not frequented by the newcomers might go out of business, a Jewish bakery or butcher would quickly replace it.

In Gotham, the urban planning movement's distaste for sporadic development, density, tenements, and industry coalesced in the Regional Plan Association of New York and Its Environs, a group of well-heeled reformers and businessmen committed to cleaning up, reorganizing, and decentralizing the city along rational lines. In the scientific tradition of Progressive reformers, the RPA collected extensive data on the city's housing and economy. "Some of the poorest people live in conveniently located slums on high-priced land," read the group's 1929 "Master Plan" for New York City. "In the very heart of this 'commercial' city on Manhattan Island south of 59th street, the inspectors in 1922 found nearly 420,000 workers employed in factories. . . . A stone's throw from the stock exchange the air is filled with the aroma of roasting coffee; a few hundred feet from Times Square with the stench of slaughterhouses. . . . Such a situation outrages one's sense of order. Everything seems misplaced. One yearns to rearrange things to put things where they belong."

With the Wall Street boom of the 1920s swelling the ranks of New York's white-collar workforce, the RPA assumed that there was an almost unlimited need for more office space and luxury apartments, and that the "conveniently located," slums, factories, warehouses, docks, and

slaughterhouses that operated a mere "stone's throw" from Wall Street—
needed to make way for them.

The only thing stopping the RPA from putting things "where they
belong" was the fact that all this teeming confusion was the basis of the
city's economy. But scouring the statistics, the RPA found a glimmer of
hope: certain industries, because of the high price of land and changes in
their customer base, were beginning to relocate outside the city. The trend
was small, and more than compensated for by the arrival and growth of
other manufacturing and industrial concerns, but the planners of the
RPA—so eager to find evidence that would justify their dreams for a new
metropolis—saw the thin trickle as an inexorable exodus of industry.
Not content to simply point out a trend (and one of dubious validity,
at that), they argued that New York should hasten the alleged retreat of
noisome factories and their immigrant laborers by using new zoning
regulations to outlaw industry from huge swaths of the city.

Since it was the *Regional* Plan Association, the report suggested
that Manhattan's malodorous factories and dingy tenements be zoned
out of existence and dispersed to the outer boroughs, Long Island, and
New Jersey. The great Port of New York, one of the largest, deepest,
and calmest in the world and the city's raison d'etre since its founding,
could be pushed across the Hudson to Elizabeth, New Jersey. Linking
the suddenly white-collar central city and industrial outer boroughs
would be the central player of the RPA's 1929 plan, the automobile, with
graceful bridges and smooth-flowing highways running along the edges
and through the very heart of Manhattan, the central city pumping the
lifeblood of cars and people and information outward through a ring of
arterial highways.

The leaders of the RPA—counting representatives of the Rockefeller,
Morgan, and Roosevelt families (FDR's uncle Frederic Delano was chair-
man), the New York and Penn Central railroads, First National City
Bank, Equitable Trust, and real estate magnates like William Sloane
Coffin, Cord Meyer, and the Pratt family—weren't driven by mere civic
duty, but economic interest as well. Landlords could charge nearly ten

times as much rent for an office as for factory space, and those offices could stretch over a thousand feet into the air, not the five or ten stories that most industrial lofts topped out at. The Morgan- and Vanderbilt-controlled New York Central Railroad, which owned the land along the industrial Hudson, could lease it out for river-view offices and apartments (as will happen once the Hudson Yards project on the far West Side of Manhattan is finally completed). The Pennsylvania Railroad, which ran through New Jersey, would be the beneficiary of the new port traffic coming into Elizabeth. And the industry and population dispersed from the central city would fill up the hinterlands of Long Island and the outer boroughs, where developers like the Pratts, Cord Meyer, and the Penn Central–controlled Long Island Rail Road owned massive tracts of land. With the Depression coming fast on the heels of the RPA's 1929 plan, industrial New York wasn't going to be done in any time soon, but RPA members were content to bide their time and let their aims slowly morph into conventional wisdom among their fellow planners and Gotham power brokers. That transition came surprisingly quickly.

AT ABOUT THE SAME TIME THAT PRESIDENTS TEDDY Roosevelt and Woodrow Wilson were bringing scientific Progressivism to the country at large, the most cutting-edge work was being done in New York by a young civil-service expert named Robert Moses. In 1915, he created the world's first comprehensive scheme for scientifically quantifying and grading every aspect of every civil-service job in New York City's fifty-thousand-strong workforce. The system removed "personal and political pressure" from the civil service and replaced it with statistics, hard facts about who should be hired, promoted, and given a pay raise. It also deprived Tammany of its most effective tool for garnering votes: giving cushy jobs and easy promotions to those most adept at rounding those votes up. Moses' elaborate system was swiftly defeated by the wily political operators of the machine, who nearly destroyed his young career. All but exiled from New York government, he was forced to while away in the administrative hinterlands of places like Pennsylvania and Long Island City (in Cleveland he was turned down for a job as a glorified clerk). But with a touch of "If you can't beat 'em, join 'em" humility, Moses took a job working for Tammany's most progressive chieftain, Governor Al Smith (one of the leaders of the Triangle investigation), and earned himself a reputation as that rarest of creatures, a reformer who could actually Get Things Done. Having learned the hard way that idealism was no match for political cunning, Moses deftly manipulated the levers of power to install parts of his scientific hiring-and-promotion system in the state bureaucracy, create the country's first state park system, and build the world's first series of public limited-access roads (what we now think of as "highways") to connect the masses to those parks—most magnificently, a serene strip of white-sand beach just miles from the New York City line, which on a sunny summer's day holds more people than the city of Pittsburgh: Jones Beach on Long Island. And it was only the beginning of the era of Robert Moses, the hero of New York reformers and envy of planners and builders the country over.

During the Roaring Twenties, Tammany Hall had, like the city itself, gone on "the greatest, the gaudiest spree in history," as F. Scott Fitzgerald put it. The final and most dashing of Tammany's Jazz Age bandleaders was a Puckish former vaudeville song-and-dance man, Mayor James J. Walker, who conducted the city's affairs from a private room at the Central Park Casino. When he did deign to come to City Hall, it was usually just to ask his secretary if there were any checks in the mail, sweeping the great piles of correspondence from his desk if the reply was in the negative.

More than simply skimming off the top, the corruption of Walker and Tammany all but ground the business of the city to a halt. His police commissioner was on the mafia payroll and the boys in blue spent as much time extorting bribes from honest citizens as pursuing criminals. Car ownership tripled in New York City from 1915 to 1920, and took off even more spectacularly thereafter—yet during the 1920s the city didn't build a single mile of arterial road. For three decades, planners had been talking about building a Henry Hudson Bridge connecting the Bronx and northern Manhattan, all to no avail. Work on the Triborough Bridge—a nexus of bridges and approach roads emanating from Randall's Island in the East River to connect Manhattan, Queens, and the Bronx—had been started and stopped so many times that New Yorkers had taken to calling it "The Bridge to Nowhere." Even the great public works the city had already built had fallen into an almost comical state of disrepair. It was nearly impossible to discern the dregs of the Tammany Machine employed by the Parks Department from the rummies they napped next to on park benches. The cages in the Central Park Zoo were so unsound that a small fire or industrious animal could have easily loosed the most dangerous beasts (although it's unclear whether the mangy, senile lion or rickets-stricken puma would have pursued freedom). Instead of fixing the cages, Tammany issued shotguns to the guards.

The public took a "Boys will be boys" attitude toward the mayor and his cohorts until the Depression left everyone wondering just where all their tax dollars were going. After nearly a decade of Al Smith's progressive governance, and with Franklin Delano Roosevelt now at the helm, New York *State* was uniquely prepared for the social service demands of the Depression, but most of the city funds intended for the poor and jobless were funneled instead into Tammany's coffers. After Walker was forced to testify that he'd accepted nearly a million dollars in "beneficences" from city contractors over the years, he saved himself and Tammany the ignominy of being ousted from office by resigning and sailing off into the sun on an Italian ocean liner. Tammany claimed it had no influence over Walker's replacement, John Patrick "Boo Boo" O'Brien, but the façade fell quickly when the new mayor told reporters he wasn't sure who his new police commissioner would be, because "They haven't told me yet."

It was a golden opportunity for a Fusion reform mayor, coming this time in the personage of roly-poly Republican congressman Fiorello H. La Guardia. Well aware of the inability of reform administrations to understand and control the city's complex administrative machinery, La Guardia turned to Moses—whose civil-service reforms had already been adopted by the state and were slowly seeping into city government—to fix the city's ailing public works department.

Over the next decade, Moses' public works consumed more New Deal dollars than any city or state in the country. And unlike La Guardia, who stepped down as mayor after three terms, Moses' power continued to grow, his career spanning the political lifetime of five mayors and a half-dozen governors.* New York is a city of islands: Manhattan, Staten Island, and Long Island (which houses Queens and Brooklyn on its westernmost edge), carved out of the continent by glaciers during the last great Ice Age. Like his namesake, Moses led the masses across that water, building seven tunnels and bridges to stitch together what nature had torn asunder. The Depression-era construction of just one of those bridges, the Triborough, necessitated the reopening of cement factories from Maine to Mississippi, and the clearing of an entire forest in Oregon. He built every highway, expressway, and limited-access road in New York City and most of Long Island, 627 miles of roads in and around the metropolis. At the southwest corner of Central Park, he built a coliseum; ten blocks away, a seat of high culture, sixteen acres of opera, theater, ballet, and music at Lincoln Center; in Queens, he built a World's Fair and a sixty-thousand-seat stadium that played host to the Mets, the Jets, the Beatles, and the pope; along the East River, he erected the headquarters of the United Nations. And it wasn't just the monumental but the mundane as well: thousands of vest-pocket parks, swimming pools, public baths, baseball diamonds, ice rinks, and courts for handball, basketball, hopscotch, and roller skating, the little niceties that make New York livable.

But Moses wasn't some autonomous actor, building and bulldozing as he saw fit. He was simply the most effective practitioner of what had

---

*When Lindsay tried to fire Moses shortly after his election, he learned he didn't even have the authority to do so (the canny old planner had personally written most of the eye-crossingly complex legislation that forbade it), but not before Moses humiliated the young mayor for his ignorance in front of state legislators and television crews at an Albany hearing. Moses finally met his match a few years later, however, forced into a begrudging retirement by Governor Nelson Rockefeller.

come to be a virtual consensus among bankers, politicians, and planners: that cities should be managed and built with comprehensive plans from the top down, with cars and glistening, government-subsidized high-rise office and residential towers taking precedence over all else. In fact, for all his originality and genius, Moses' projects were often derivative in their location and design, and depended on broader historical and legislative trends for the money and authority to build them.

For cars, Moses copied the 1929 RPA Plan's sketches for a series of arterial and central-city highways almost to the block, and relied on legislation, like the Interstate Highways Act, for much of the funding. The scope of the housing developments built by Moses and New York's Housing Authority (which built all of the city's low-income housing projects and was heavily influenced, though never fully controlled, by the Master Builder) were made possible by a pair of federal laws. The first was the United States Housing Act of 1937, the country's first public housing law and the brainchild of New York's housing-reform movement (it was popularly known as the "Wagner Act," after its leading proponent, New York senator Robert F. Wagner, Sr., the Tammany stalwart who, along with Al Smith, was responsible for the Triangle investigation and reforms). Within a few decades, public housing projects littered cities across America, housing more than half a million people in New York City alone. Moses' preferred legislation was the Housing Act of 1949, which let cities use federal dollars to condemn and clear "slum properties" and sell the land to private developers at a substantial discount.

In terms of design, Moses' and the Housing Authority's projects were fairly derivative as well, borrowing from the architectural and planning world's leading light, a comically bespectacled, Fascist-favored Swiss architect and urban planner who wrote and designed under a pseudonym thought by some historians to mean "the crow-like one," Le Corbusier. Le Corbusier dreamed of an abstracted future city with none of the gritty imprints of the past, the "Radiant City" with gleaming towers dropped symmetrically in sprawling grass parklands and connected by the highway and the car. "Suppose we are entering the city by way of the Great Park," he wrote. "Our fast car takes the special elevated motor track between the majestic skyscrapers: as we approach nearer, there is seen the repetition against the sky of the twenty-four skyscrapers; to our left and right, on the outskirts of each particular area, are the municipal and administrative buildings; and enclosing the space are the museums and university buildings. The whole city is a park." The most striking feature of Le Corbusier's Radiant City is really more of an absence: there are no people. It's not just that they are invisible from the "elevated motor track," it's that people have had no impact on this prefabricated world: they have set up no stores along its highways, painted no billboards advertising them, reshaped and repurposed nothing to make their physical surroundings—built and doled out by some anonymous bureaucracy—their own. That is because people are merely abstractions in Le Corbusier's vision, placid inhabitants of the fixed and unchanging Radiant City that he has bestowed upon them. Unlike actual cities, where factories become warehouses become artists' studios become loft apartments as people's wants and needs change, in the Radiant City, everything has been thought of, nothing need be changed. It is the root approach and the discomfort with the "vulgar democracy" of the free market hinted at by earlier planners brought to its logical, dictatorial conclusion.

The city fathers of Paris laughed off Le Corbusier's proposals to level the City of Light north of the Seine. Even Mussolini thought his plans to sack some of Italy's ancient metropolises too radical. It was in New York that Le Corbusier received his most enthusiastic support, and in Robert Moses his most determined disciple.

In the two decades following World War II, Moses and the Housing Authority used the latest trends in architecture and planning, and the enormous government funds suddenly available for top-down, root-approach public works projects, to devastating effect. For in the zero-sum game of urban development, each new highway, housing development, and public park meant the equal and opposite declension of some other aspect of the city—and in Moses' case, that meant the tenement neighborhoods, bustling markets, smoking factories, and thriving industrial districts of working-class New York. Reflecting Jacob Riis' assumption that clearing slums removed poverty, the Wagner Act that helped fund public housing projects required the city to demolish at least one unit of slum housing for each unit of public housing created. How such legislation was supposed to address the housing shortages that created slum conditions in the first place is unclear, but New York's Housing Authority used the act to bulldoze thousands of tenements, mom-and-pop stores, small manufacturers, and industrial concerns that housed and employed the already impoverished.

Moses was even more prolific, overseeing the destruction of hundreds of thousands of people's homes to build highways, parks, luxury housing, and office towers. All told, the city spent billions of dollars to tear down the houses of roughly a million of its own residents, and the jobs of hundreds of thousands more. Debates have long raged as to why exactly Moses was willing to go to such lengths to enact his vision of a gleaming, postindustrial New York. He's often seen as the bogeyman of twentieth-century urban development, a reputation his personality did nothing to diminish: he built his Long Island parkways with overpasses too low for buses, preventing the carless masses from reaching his pristine parks and beaches. He held almost no regard for public opinion or the concerns of those displaced by his projects, telling one interviewer that the man on the street "doesn't know what's in his own interest. He isn't smart enough to visualize what you're going to do." He rarely built pools, playgrounds, or parks in, or even near, neighborhoods with a sizable black or Puerto Rican population. In two instances, he ordered the heaters kept off in pools that black children were beginning to patronize, convinced that blacks would not swim in cold water. To avoid displacing an ailing bus depot owned by powerful members of the Bronx Democratic organization, he rerouted his Cross Bronx Expressway through a solid mile of apartment buildings,

evicting thousands of people and spending millions of dollars to condemn and clear the land. When asked about the evicted residents' protests, Moses said, "I don't think they were too bad. It was a political thing
that stirred up the animals there."

But for all the personal criticism heaped upon Moses, there is perhaps
less to be learned from understanding *why* he built and bulldozed as
he did than from *how* he was allowed to do so. Moses was, after all, a
builder, and like Nietzsche's explanation of why bankers and brokers buy
and sell as they do (like stones rolling down a hill, from the sheer force
of gravity), building at all costs was both in Moses' nature and his job
description. As for the people displaced, this was the same man whose
early career revolved around turning civil servants into mathematically
evaluable production units. His job was to view people as a statistical
problem to be dealt with, units of citizenry to be housed and transported
and given recreation. If destroying the homes and jobs of some of them
was necessary to better house and transport and entertain the (generally
wealthier, more politically influential) rest, so be it.

Such hard-driving, accomplish-at-all-costs types are a necessity in
government, essential to kick-starting the bureaucracy from its usual
stasis and inertia. But the type of person able to all but create the state park
and highway systems from scratch does not come with an off switch—
he must be constrained by the power structure he operates within.
Fortunately for Moses, but unfortunately for the city he dominated,
that power structure shared his vision of the City Efficient: a highway-
laced, high-rise-filled post-industrial city built by the prescripts of
mathematically rational, top-down, root-approach planners. The old
city, with its bustling port, smoking factories, stinking slaughterhouses,
pushcart peddlers, and crowded tenements was just that: old. *New* New
York was to be all glass and steel, towers and parks, office buildings and
luxury condos. Moses and the assorted architects, planners, politicians,
and businessmen who shared his view of the future believed they were
on the winning side of history, and, as the Master Builder himself used to
say, "If the ends don't justify the means, what does?"

———

UNDER NORMAL CIRCUMSTANCES, THERE WOULD HAVE BEEN
a conspicuous obstruction to Moses and his allies' plans for New York.
Not intended for canvas or paper or celluloid, their vision needed to be
imposed upon the real world, and required spending vast sums of money
to bulldoze real places, displace real people, and destroy real jobs. In New
York, that meant votes, and it meant Tammany, the implacable obstacle
to dreams of better government, better housing, better anything, it
seemed, for decades. Unlike the reformers before him, though, Moses
knew the shortest route to Tammany's heart.

Public works has always been the richest source of money and power
in New York City—during his heyday, Boss Tweed held the same job as
Moses—but the Master Builder wielded it as no other man had. By the
end of World War II, La Guardia and the era of reform were done and
Tammany was back in power, but during La Guardia's reign, Moses had
mastered the art of what Tammany's George Washington Plunkitt had
dubbed "legal graft." If a politician was opposed to a new highway being
built through his district, he could usually be made more amenable if
the law firm where he was a partner was hired to write up the necessary
land acquisition contracts. Or if his biggest donor, a local real estate broker,
was charged with acquiring the land. Or perhaps a real estate development
company in which he held a secret stake could be made privy to
blueprints of the highway, a Rosetta Stone to nearby property values,
before they were publicly released. Controlling nearly every major public
construction project in New York for decades, Moses dispensed billions
of dollars in contracts to powerful insiders who owed him favors in
return. By the time the Democrats took City Hall back from La Guardia
and the reformers in 1946, they were so thoroughly enmeshed in the web
of money and power Moses had spun that they were as eager as anyone
to continue clearing and building.

Moses dealt with the more conservative business community—
which would typically have been up in arms about spending billions of

government dollars to interfere with the functioning of the free market—
just as he did Tammany, by buying them off. (In one instance, Moses
paid the Kennedy family a previously unheard-of $62.88 per square foot
for run-down property near what would become Lincoln Center, evicted
the residents, cleared the land, and sold it for $7.00 per square foot to the
Rockefeller family's designated developers.) While ethically questionable,
Moses' methods weren't technically illegal, and they reached so deeply
into the city's power structure that anyone with the authority to actually
challenge Moses would be committing professional suicide, and might
even end up implicating himself in the process. Whether Republican or
Democrat, nearly every major political figure and institution in New York
had some stake in Moses' projects. The candidates and clubhouses who
grew fat on his contracts. The banks that financed his projects at profitable
interest rates. The contractors, architects, engineering firms, lawyers,
PR consultants, labor unions, and mob-run construction companies
that built them. The Catholic Church, whose parishioners were the base
of those unions and which itself received prime real estate deals from
Moses (like Fordham University's Lincoln Center campus). For those
who wanted to maintain their power, and perhaps make a few dollars
in the process, the system was the ideal means. Perhaps Moses did not
possess the autocratic power of an emperor, but he didn't need to: he was
the effective manager of a game that all the powerful players prospered
from and had no inclination to disrupt. He ruled not by decree but with
cash-greased consensus.*

With the decks stacked against the tenement neighborhoods and
industrial districts that were the lifeblood of the great immigrant city
and its economy, the hand played out predictably. While Moses was never
able to build a highway across Manhattan, hundreds of thousands were

---

*The system also guaranteed loyalty to Moses himself. Should some politician decide to buck
the Master Builder, there was always the matter of those questionable contracts he'd benefited
from (none of which could be traced to Moses, of course); wouldn't it be a shame if the papers
got wind of those.

evicted to make way for those he cut across the outer boroughs. By 1957, Moses and the Empire State had spent more than twice as much money from the Housing Act of 1949's Title I "slum clearance" fund as the rest of the country *combined*, leveling the homes of hundreds of thousands more New Yorkers in the process, many of them not in slums but exactly the kind of integrated, stepping-stone neighborhoods the city was in dire need of.

SLUM CLEARANCE AFFECTED CITIES ACROSS THE COUNTRY, but industrial clearance was unique to New York. No other city in the country had the audacity to plow under its own economy, and, in fact, most industrial American cities have subsidized and supported their dying industries to a fault. But New York was unlike other cities for two key reasons. First, the boldness of its civic leaders' vision of a postindustrial future, and their willingness to fight for it. And second, unlike most industrial cities, New York was not a one-horse town, with a single industry that would lobby for subsidies, or at the very least fight against its own destruction. New York had the largest, most competitive, most diverse industrial economy in the world. It held more manufacturing jobs than the next two largest American cities *combined*, and spread them out in dozens of industries that were constantly growing, adapting, and attracting bright new entrepreneurial minds. New York was the world's largest garment manufacturer, but it was also a leading food processor, beer distiller, and producer of everything from electrical parts and finished jewelry to cardboard boxes, furniture, and musical instruments. But the single most influential industry was what some economists call the F.I.R.E. industry: finance, insurance, and real estate, all of them eager to expand into the city's waterfront docks, rail yards, factories, and "conveniently located slums." (Ironically, while New York's industrial diversity weakened its lobbying power, it would have made it uniquely suited to surviving the automation and globalization that have doomed other American industrial cities.)

Moses' slum clearance and highways program was the largest single destroyer of industrial jobs, but it went far beyond him. Even during the Depression, the La Guardia–appointed reformers on the City Planning Commission declared that if the free market wasn't going to drive out factories that no longer conformed to their vision of the city, government coercion would, barring industry from vast swaths of the city. Housing projects cleared small stores and factories and banned industrial and commercial uses from the sites. Commercial vehicles were banned from some streets and avenues and many of Moses' highways, expressways, and bridges. The Planning Commission even proposed clearing all industry from the East River south of 125th Street, barring heavy manufacturing from midtown Manhattan, and in 1939 drew up plans to clear the entire Lower East Side south of 23rd Street, the project scuttled only after commissioners realized it would require bulldozing a power plant responsible for keeping the city lit.

America's "magic economy" and New York City's central role in it kept the city's job market, even its industrial job market, strong through the 1950s. But by the 1960s the city's systematic dismantling of its own industrial economy had reached a tipping point. In 1961, a new zoning law prohibited manufacturing from large swaths of the outer boroughs and all but a few small sections of Manhattan. That same year, New York Governor Nelson Rockefeller, his brother David (the head of Chase Bank), and the Port of New York Authority took possession of sixteen acres of the most expensive real estate in the world in Lower Manhattan, cleared thirty thousand jobs from the site, took it off the city's real estate tax rolls, and built the World Trade Center. The Trade Center, though, did more than replace a successful industrial area with what turned out to be an unsuccessful office complex on welfare; it carved out the literal and symbolic heart of industrial New York—the Manhattan port—effectively moving it to Elizabeth, New Jersey, just as the RPA's 1929 plan had suggested three decades earlier. By the Port Authority's own estimate, half a million jobs were directly dependent on the cheap, convenient shipping the port offered, and like a pebble tossed in a pond, each lost job caused ripples outward through New York's deeply entwined industries. From 1968 to 1977, 600,000 industrial jobs disappeared from the city, with New York *losing* as many industrial jobs in ten years as the entire city of Detroit *held* at its peak. It took Motown, that great exemplar of American industrial decline, nearly three decades to lose half of its industrial jobs. It took New York just one.

New York wasn't the only city losing blue-collar jobs. Automation was replacing manpower with machines. The suburbs and nonunionized South offered cheaper land and labor. After a half-century of blowing one another's economies to smithereens, European countries were finally putting their industrial capabilities to use, and a modernized Japan was on the rise. But instead of simply allowing the free market to run its course, New York's planners, politicians, and power brokers cut the city's industrial economy off at the knees in the hopes of spurring a postindustrial rebirth that never quite came, even the World Trade Center towers sitting largely empty for decades.*

SLUM AND INDUSTRIAL CLEARANCE CAME AT A PECULIARLY sensitive moment in the city's history. A flood tide of new arrivals not seen since the end of the nineteenth century was coming to Gotham, not boats full of European immigrants but trains bearing Southern blacks chased northward by Jim Crow and the mechanization of cotton picking, and planeloads of Puerto Ricans, fleeing their own desperately poor homeland.

By 1952, Moses' biographer Robert Caro noted, almost 800,000 people, about 10 percent of the city's population, was black or Hispanic

---

*Despite massive job losses, early drafts of Lindsay's 1969 Master Plan for the city were still calling for the dispersal of industrial jobs: "In the long run, New York does not want to retain the low-skill, low-wage segment of its industrial mix," one draft read. "The displacement of manufacturing activity in the CBD [Central Business District] is the complement to the expansion of office construction which results in more intensive land use, higher investments, and more jobs than manufacturing activities they replaced."

(that number would nearly triple by 1970). "If the city was to prosper," he wrote, "it would have to offer the newcomers the same chance it had offered their forerunners: . . . neighborhoods which would serve as urbanizing and staging areas. And it would have to provide urbanizing and staging areas that were integrated. If it did not, if these newcomers to New York were forced to live in ghettos, compounded with their resentment at their inability to provide a decent place for their children to live would be an alienation from the society which had isolated them. These people—who were making up more and more of the city—would be an alienated, hostile, hating force within it."

Slum and highway clearance not only isolated blacks and Hispanics, it chased away whites. Much has been made of the "white flight" that robbed New York and other American cities of a large portion of their stable, middle-class population following World War II. While Moses' projects displaced a disproportionate number of black and Puerto Rican families, he and the city housing authority bulldozed the homes of roughly half a million white New Yorkers and the jobs of hundreds of thousands more, just as federally tax-deductible mortgages and Moses' own government-subsidized roads were making the suburbs an inexpensive, readily accessible option. Most took him up on the offer.

And so, the ghettoes of New York, torn apart by slum clearance, scarred by unemployment, pushed into isolation and decline, turned into the tinderbox that was soon lit by the War Years. The leap from slum and industrial clearance to social collapse and fire is a twisting and inexact path, a series of perhaps tendentious suppositions, incomplete statistics, and circumstantial cases. But chasing the white middle class to the suburbs, destroying integrated "staging areas" when they were most desperately needed, and leveling the blue-collar jobs that had allowed previous groups to pay for and adapt to urban life, had an untold effect on the city's neighborhoods and economy. And nowhere can that connection between misguided, root-approach urban and economic planning and the War Years be seen more clearly than in the South Bronx.

The World Series fire immortalized by Howard Cosell.
(Photo courtesy Harvey Eisner)

EIGHT

Red Lines and White Flight

On the method I call "Haussmann" . . . I mean the practice, which has now become general, of making breaches in working-class quarters of our big cities, especially in those that are centrally situated . . . the result is everywhere the same: the most scandalous alleys and lanes disappear, to the accompaniment of lavish self-glorification by the bourgeoisie on account of this tremendous success—but they appear at once somewhere else, and often in the immediate neighborhood.

—FRIEDRICH ENGELS

Sometimes I think the United States embarked on urban renewal out of some kind of elaborate guilt trip over bombing so many places in the course of the Second World War. Because we saw that by clearing these sites, suddenly the bombs made it possible for new kinds of developments and a way to modernize cities. How to tackle the problems here? We really used the same techniques; we declared whole areas, after some kind of "study" of the declining demographics, susceptible to demolition, just simply moved people out.

—ROBERT A. M. STERN

The South Bronx has never been a place, only a situation. Before the 1940s, the designation was almost unknown, the borough broken into the east and west by the Bronx River, and further divvied up into neighborhoods named after whatever rural village they had grown out of. When the subway and commuter railroads opened the city's northernmost borough to the masses in the early 1900s, it quickly became a showcase for New York's middle class. It didn't have the glitz of Manhattan or the history of Brooklyn, but the Bronx was the proud home of thousands of first- and second-generation immigrant families, mostly Irish and Jewish, who were finally able to move up and out of the Lower East Side Lung District.

It was an earnest, hardworking place, but tinged with an air of upward mobility and bourgeois sophistication. The Bronx's main drag was and still is the Grand Concourse—a wide thoroughfare lined with shade trees and prosperous Art Deco apartment buildings, which runs north-south along the Harlem River—sometimes referred to as the "Champs-Élysées of the Bronx," with tongue inserted only slightly into cheek. Just a few blocks from the Concourse, at 161st Street, sat the original Yankee Stadium, and a few blocks from there were the borough's finest hotel, the Concourse Plaza, and the majestic flagship of the Loews movie theater chain, the Paradise. At the center of the borough were the Bronx Zoo and the Botanical Gardens, with Freedomland amusement park, "The World's Largest Entertainment Center," farther to the north, and Orchard Beach and quaint seaside City Island on the borough's eastern edge, along the shores of Long Island Sound.

In the 1940s sociologists noticed something strange in the otherwise idyllic Bronx: a small pocket of poverty at the southern tip of the borough. Crowded out of nearby Spanish Harlem, Puerto Rican families were taking advantage of the low rents and industrial jobs in the largely Irish neighborhoods of Port Morris and Mott Haven. Not sure what to name the impoverished area, people started calling it the "South Bronx."

Like Southern blacks before them, the hundreds of thousands of Puerto Ricans coming to New York after World War II were at first seen as a replacement for the cheap labor that the city lost after federal immigration restrictions were passed in 1924, and often garnered flattering comparisons to the similarly rural Irish immigrants who had come to the city a century earlier. The arrival of an impoverished immigrant group, particularly one with a different skin color and language, has always created problems in New York neighborhoods, but in the Bronx it combined with the most thorough job of Robert Moses–backed slum clearance and highway-building anywhere in the city.

The first stage was public housing. Unlike Brooklyn and Manhattan, the more recently settled Bronx didn't have any old-law tenement slums. But the neighborhood did have the high population density and mix of factories and residences that planners associated with slums, and a growing nonwhite population to boot. By the mid-1950s, Brooklyn and Manhattan had seen enough of the results of slum clearance and public housing projects to not want any more. That left the Bronx, where Housing Authority director Warren Moscow found a willing, if less than ecstatic, partner in Borough President James J. Lyons. "He'd say, 'Well, I don't much like public housing, but it's better than what's there,'" said Moscow. "There was no grand design in the Bronx, no special planning, no evil thought, but one thing and another we wound up with a solid phalanx of public housing. . . . It was a mistake, because we ghettoized too many poor people together. You had a feeling you were building the wrong thing, but everything was in the pipeline." Soon the Bronx rivaled Brooklyn's East New York for the densest assemblage of low-income projects in the country.

"It was like it happened overnight," says Carol Zakaluk, who grew up on 136th Street in Mott Haven, just across from the southern tip of a two-block-wide swath of public housing that runs north intermittently for twenty blocks. "One night the [old] buildings were there, and the next . . . suddenly everything was gone, and then over the course of a year or so you could watch the buildings rise floor by floor until they were finished. After that they took their sweet time putting in trees and grass—just dirt and those ugly, monotonous buildings."

The blight the new projects were supposed to cure simply spread to surrounding neighborhoods, and crime and petty vandalism within the projects themselves was worse than in the neighborhoods they replaced. Clara Rodriguez watched the construction from her home just a few blocks away on Brook Avenue and 138th Street. The buildings, she said, "were huge; they were ugly; and they were, most importantly, unsafe. Few of the old tenants became new tenants. People in the projects were afraid. It was an unfriendly place. Playing space was at a premium, and kids were a surplus commodity. Tensions were high. We felt sorry for the people in the projects. Sure, they didn't have roaches, but what about the quality of their life?"

Housing projects' dreary architecture, anonymity, and poor maintenance certainly contributed to tenant disillusionment, but a story about an East Harlem project with "a conspicuous rectangular lawn which became an object of hatred to the project tenants," related by Jane Jacobs, shows the larger issues at work. "A social worker frequently at the project was astonished by how often the subject of the lawn came up, usually gratuitously, as far as she could see, and how much the tenants despised it and urged that it be done away with. When she asked why, the usual answer was, 'What good is it?' or 'Who wants it?' Finally one day a tenant more articulate than the others made this pronouncement: 'Nobody cared what we wanted when they built this place. They threw our houses down and pushed us here and pushed our friends somewhere else. We don't have a place around here to get a cup of coffee or a newspaper even, or borrow fifty cents. Nobody cared what we need. But the big men come and look at the grass and say, 'Isn't it wonderful! Now the poor have everything.'"

More disruptive than housing projects were the highways of Robert Moses. The most notorious was the Cross Bronx Expressway, a 225-foot-wide, seven-mile-long trench of a highway that cut through the very heart of a dozen different neighborhoods, each of them solidly middle and working class, and evicted at least sixty thousand mainly Jewish and Italian Bronxites, along with a significant number of Irish, blacks, and Puerto Ricans. At first the expressway seemed like a political impossibility, but Moses' allies shrewdly pitched it as just one more example of the kind of grand, ambitious planning that had pulled the country out of the Depression and won World War II. "When the postwar program is finally executed," Borough President Lyons said of the Cross Bronx and a slew of other highways and housing projects Moses had planned for the borough, "the Bronx will be utopia itself." As for Moses, he treated the highway as a foregone conclusion, daring to oppose it like fighting the tides or the march of history itself. "There are people who like things as they are," he said. "I can't hold out any hope to them. They have to keep moving further away. This is a great big state and also there are other states. Let them go to the Rockies."

The Cross Bronx came, and writer Marshall Berman and hundreds of thousands of Bronx denizens like him lived with what it wrought. "For ten years," from 1950 to 1960, Berman wrote, "the center of the Bronx was pounded and blasted and smashed. My friends and I would stand on the parapet of the Grand Concourse, where 174th Street had been, and survey the work's progress—the immense steam shovels and bulldozers and timber and steel beams, the hundreds of workers in their variously colored hard hats, the giant cranes reaching far above the Bronx's tallest roofs, the dynamite blasts and tremors, the wild jagged crags of rock newly torn, the vistas of devastation stretching for miles to the east and west as far as the eye could see—and marvel to see our ordinary nice neighborhood transformed into sublime, spectacular ruins."

The process repeated itself with the six-mile Bruckner Expressway, which knocked down countless shops and factories on Bruckner Boulevard, once the commercial spine of the East Bronx; there was the eight-mile-long Major Deegan Expressway, which runs along the former ports of the Harlem River; the half-built and seldom used Sheridan Expressway, and the crisscrossing spiderweb of the Throgs Neck Expressway, New England Thruway, and Bronx River, Saw Mill, Mosholu, and Hutchinson River parkways.

Moses used the word "slum" to describe the areas he was knocking down, but they hardly fit the bill, most of them vital, working-class neighborhoods and many of them integrated by blacks and Puerto Ricans who had moved up and out of the slums. Torn asunder, the neighborhoods scattered middle- and working-class whites to the suburbs. Without that option, blacks and Puerto Ricans were packed into the severed limbs of what had so recently been whole communities.

And so the South Bronx spread. It began in Port Morris and Mott Haven, home to the seventeenth-century farm of Jonas Bronck, who gave the borough its name, and the site of Jordan Mott's ironworks, which cast the five-thousand-ton dome of the U.S. Capitol Building and thousands of manhole covers and sewer grates that still dot the city. Then on to Morrisania, settled in the late 1600s by Richard Morris, whose great-grandchildren included Lewis Morris—a signer of the Declaration of Independence—and Gouverneur Morris, aptly described by the subtitle of a 2003 biography "The Rake Who Wrote the Constitution." From there, the decay crept east, to a blunted peninsula jutting into Long Island Sound named Hunts Point, once a mansioned playground for the family and friends of jewelry purveyor Charles Tiffany (who first introduced America to the retail catalogue and a 92.5 percent–pure alloy of silver known as "sterling") and the descendants of George Fox, the founder of Quakerism. The South Bronx soon doubled in size when it was met by another stretch of blight spreading outward from the ravages of the Cross Bronx, through neighborhoods like Soundview, Bronx River, Tremont, Crotona Park, and Kingsbridge.

THE ECONOMIC AND SOCIAL BLIGHT QUICKLY COMBINED with another housing trend called redlining, which provided the key link to the fire epidemic of the War Years. During the Depression, the federal Home Owners' Loan Corporation (HOLC) decided that banks needed better mortgage lending guidelines, creating "Residential Security Maps" for every city in the United States with more than forty thousand people and grading each neighborhood's fitness for loans from A to D. The HOLC relied on hard data—mostly housing statistics and local economic indicators—to determine the grades (in the same tradition that FDR's uncle Frederic Delano, who was now the president's chief planner, had used when he was chairman of the Regional Plan Association). But the maps proved to be an early warning about the weaknesses of the kind of centralized, statistical decision-making that would come to dominate

American government and business in the ensuing decades, as complex issues were reduced to a handful of the most easily obtainable, and often misleading, statistics.

In one of the more humorous passages from *The Death and Life of Great American Cities*, Jane Jacobs discusses Boston's North End, a poorly graded neighborhood where for decades, Jacobs is told by a leading banker, hardly any mortgages or renovation loans were granted. But Jacobs finds this neighborhood, which all the planning textbooks and lending guides say is an abysmal slum, to be a vibrant, friendly, economically stable community. Calling a Boston planner she knows, Jacobs is told that the North End "has among the lowest delinquency, disease, and infant mortality rates in the city," and that the planner himself loves visiting the neighborhood "just to walk around the streets and feel that wonderful, cheerful street life . . . But of course we have to rebuild it eventually," he remarks oddly. "Why, that's the worst slum in the city. It has two hundred and seventy-five dwelling units to the net acre!"

"Here was a curious thing," wrote Jacobs. "My friend's instincts told him the North End was a good place, and his social statistics confirmed it. But everything he had learned as a physical planner about what is good for people and good for city neighborhoods, everything that made him an expert, told him the North End had to be a bad place."

The HOLC maps proved just as shortsighted in New York as they did Boston, and added a more pernicious element to the usual litany of unforgivable planning sins (like high density, old buildings, and a mix of residential, commercial, and industrial use): race. Race and religion have always been used to value real estate, with whichever group is being abused at the moment barred from buying and renting in whatever real estate markets are strong enough to turn away their money. But prejudice was a scattered thing, inconsistently applied and regularly—though not easily—overcome. A landlord who needed cash quickly might begrudgingly accept black or Jewish tenants who could pay. Real estate agents could be bribed by those with the financial wherewithal to do so. By creating detailed demographic maps that singled out blacks (and later

Hispanics) as detrimental to a neighborhood, the rigid classifications of the HOLC maps permitted no such flexibility, creating a handy federal reference guide that, in effect, forbade integration in every major city in the country.

Over the years, the HOLC maps, along with similar practices from the Federal Housing Administration and private lenders, threw real estate markets into disarray. People living in well-thought-of neighborhoods with even a small black population saw their property values drop overnight. Smelling blood in the water, scurrilous real estate brokers—who made commissions on sales of any kind, even panic sales—began the process of "block busting." Some spread self-fulfilling rumors of impending property value crashes ("Don't let this get around, but from what I've heard . . ."). In mixed neighborhoods, savvy brokers intentionally sold and rented only to black families in the hopes of sparking white flight—sometimes the mere sight of a black man (usually paid off by a broker) walking down the street or ringing doorbells to inquire about home prices was enough to incite a panicky exodus. In highly rated neighborhoods, loans became easier to come by—but only for the right kind of whites (the first round of HOLC maps singled out Italians and Jews as detrimental influences); otherwise the neighborhood's makeup would change, the rating would drop, and property values would follow. Redlining wasn't the only factor driving white flight and racial segregation in New York. Southern blacks, as economically distressed and unaccustomed to urban life as any immigrant group New York had ever known, were coming by the hundreds of thousands. Racism alone did push many middle-class whites out of the inner city.* But people have a

---

*Some have also read segregation through the lens of the "tipping point," a term coined by sociologist Morton Grodzins in the 1950s to explain how white families, perfectly happy to live in a racially mixed neighborhood, would suddenly move once blacks became predominant. The idea was popularized by RAND economist Thomas Schelling, who derived an formula that showed mathematically how even the slightest preference to live near neighbors of the same race can lead to total segregation. His 1971 paper on the topic, "Dynamic Models of Segregation," has since become one of the most cited papers in economics and, along with his work on game theory, the primary contribution that led to his 2005 Nobel Prize in

curious habit of dealing with their own prejudice when it's in their economic interest to do so. Redlining, on the other hand, incentivized and exacerbated racism and segregation, and the market quickly complied: in Brooklyn, blacks went from being the most integrated ethnic or racial group in the borough before the maps were released, to the most segregated by the end of World War II.

Underlying the neighborhood rating systems was a new theory that saw urban communities as biological organisms that progressed through a natural and unavoidable "life cycle," moving from birth to maturity, decline, and death. Some neighborhoods were fated to decline, or so the theory went, and making loans there would only be a costly delay of the inevitable. Advocated by influential academics and planners—including the Federal Housing Administration's chief economist, Homer Hoyt—the theory pushed redlining and racism deeper into official government policy and private-sector practice. In reality, there was nothing so inexorable about neighborhood decline (loans and a stable populace are a more effective fountain of youth than anything Ponce de León could have hoped for), but as wrong as the theory may have been, it was a self-fulfilling prophecy: without loans, the neighborhoods did, in fact, decline, giving the impression that the life-cycle predictions were correct all along.

The supposedly inevitable decline of inner-city neighborhoods also created the link between redlining and fires. Up to that point, New York real estate, even in marginal neighborhoods, was a good long-term investment. The operating profits weren't fabulous, but with some basic maintenance and repairs the value of the land and buildings rose steadily. It was the kind of investment that attracted local businesspeople, particularly budding immigrant entrepreneurs, who usually lived nearby, were accountable to renters, and maintained properties and neighborhoods for the long haul. Redlining made it almost impossible for these

---

Economics. It's a compelling idea, but both Grodzin's observation and Schelling's abstract theorizing ignore the very real economic incentives for segregation that redlining created, and as with the federally subsidized suburbs, it was those incentives that induced people to move.

landlords to get even small loans to install a new water heater, repoint the brick, or fix the roof. In poor neighborhoods, such loans serve the same function as rubber patches on a leaky raft: not the ideal solution, but a good way to keep your head above water.

With keeping buildings and neighborhoods afloat no longer an option, the only logical question for a businessman was how to salvage as many valuables as possible before abandoning ship. In most cases, this meant selling the building, and not to another traditional landlord interested in long-term investment but to a slumlord content to simply ride the sinking ship until it capsized. Known sometimes as "milkers," the slumlords would chop up apartments into smaller and smaller units, cut maintenance, repairs, even heat and hot water, to an absolute minimum, and charge whatever the market would bear. It took a few decades, but without proper maintenance the quality of the housing stock declined and the aging, overcrowded buildings became magnets for fires.

IT WAS A PERFECT STORM OF BLIGHT FOR THE BRONX. Redlining and clearance for highways and housing projects chased whites to the suburbs and further segregated the rising black and Puerto Rican populations. Rapid deindustrialization not only caused widespread unemployment and poverty, it changed the very character of (now non-) working-class New York. Men who had worked difficult, low-paying jobs to support their families suddenly found that they couldn't even do that. Children who watched their fathers go to work—saw the money and respect they earned, internalized the value of work, learned the discipline themselves by selling papers, running errands, or stacking boxes in a nearby store—suddenly saw and experienced very little of that. Social services dealing with the symptoms of joblessness—like unemployment, welfare, and food stamps—surged. Local politicians, who in past decades had secured the support of the newest immigrants by supplying jobs, now turned to those social services as the only rewards they could bestow upon loyal voters. Speaking about Spanish Harlem congressman Vito Marcantonio (a former law partner of La Guardia's, jokingly referred to by many as the "congressman from Puerto Rico"), one welfare official said that "the pressure he puts on our welfare centers in his section is terrific and continuous. He urges our workers to step up relief for the Puerto Ricans, as he does for the others, too, and it pays off." Add rising violence and drug and alcohol addiction, and an economically dysfunctional "culture of dependence" was becoming entrenched.

"It was a gradual thing, but I would say probably in the early or mid-sixties was when I discovered the increase in drugs and violence," says Genevieve Brooks Brown, who moved to New York in the 1950s as part of the Great Migration from the South, and lived just off Charlotte Street in the South Bronx. "On Jennings Street, there was like a market with vendors, and they would have goods and services out on the sidewalks and all. After one of the storekeepers was found murdered, that was really when you saw that the merchants fled, in about 1963. There were burglars, murderers, and all that. When they started preying on folks and they became victims, that was when a lot of them moved, up to Co-op City, Espinard Gardens in Harlem, anywhere where there was some kind of housing for the middle and lower classes. I mean, if somebody in my family gets mugged or attacked, you start thinking about safety. You know: 'It's time for us to go.'"

Once a destination of choice for upwardly mobile immigrants, the Bronx was becoming a place to escape from. Seeing the signs, landlords, who'd been subdividing apartments and skimping on repairs for years, turned to out-and-out neglect, particularly in apartments under rent control. The penalty for late payment of real estate taxes was so low that one deadbeat landlord told reporters it was "the cheapest loan in town." Since the city waited at least three years to seize a delinquent property, some landlords never bothered to pay back taxes at all, milking it for as much rent as possible until tenants stopped paying or the city took over the building. The half-abandoned properties—still home to average people just trying to get by—drew junkies, winos, gangs, and the other dangerous outcasts of an increasingly broken borough.

After years of inadequate maintenance and renovation, by the mid-1960s more and more of those dilapidated apartment buildings were going up in flames. Aging electrical wiring and outlets, as well as leaky oil- and gas-burning furnaces and water heaters, sparked thousands of blazes. When furnaces broke or a landlord didn't pay the oil bill, people used dangerous space heaters and gas ovens for heat and hot water. As substance abuse rose, more and more fires were started by junkies using lighters to dissolve heroin in water-filled spoons, nodded-out smokers dropping lit cigarettes, and neglected children playing with matches. Overcrowding was the worst. When a significant portion of the apartments in a neighborhood reached the point of "extreme overcrowding" (1.5 people/room), fire rates skyrocketed.

Even arson became an economically rational act in the Bronx's shattered housing market. As more and more of the poorly maintained and overcrowded buildings were lost to fire, some landlords realized that torching a building for the insurance money, then hiring a "finisher" to strip whatever valuables (copper wiring, lead pipes) could be salvaged, was even more profitable than milking it.

"About 1968, I was a rookie in the Four-Eight [Forty-eighth Precinct]," says Bronx native and retired Bronx police officer Howard Farkas. "And in this precinct there used to be a motorcycle cop. . . . He was dropped from the motorcycle unit and put back on the street. So he was lazy, a little bitter, just waiting for his pension and retirement. He didn't do collars anymore. So he responds to a fire on the south side of Bathgate [Avenue], near Claremont [Parkway]. Outside, people are saying, 'That guy did it!' and pointing out a Puerto Rican guy who was the super or something for some buildings in the area. The guy had been paid $100 or $150—a lot of money at the time—by the landlord to torch it. Like I said, [the former motorcycle cop] was not making collars at the time, so he called me and said, 'You looking?' and I was always looking. . . . It was a strange thing, I thought, torching a place for the insurance money. I'd grown up in the neighborhood and I'd never heard of anything like it."

Still, arson remained a small fraction of the total blazes in the city,

less than 1 percent according to fire marshal reports, through the early
1970s. The real problem was accidental fires caused by neglect and
overcrowding. The fires actually fostered the very conditions they fed on.
The rash of blazes convinced more Bronx landlords that the borough was
fated to ruin and buildings weren't worth maintaining. Displaced victims
were forced to pack into already decaying, overcrowded tenements in
nearby neighborhoods. An increase in fire rates was, in fact, almost
always preceded by an uptick in the number of public school students
transferring from fire-ravaged neighborhoods, paradoxically chased by
fire and re-creating the conditions that caused it. Mapped chronologically,
the fires spread outward like an infectious disease, consuming block
after block of the South Bronx and, increasingly, other victims of slum
clearance and redlining, like Brooklyn's Bedford-Stuyvesant, East New
York, and Brownsville neighborhoods, and Harlem and the Lower East
Side of Manhattan.

The Bronx collapses.

(Photo © 1982 Lisa Kahane, NYC)

NINE

Of Riots and Airmail

We can deal with rockets and dreams,
but reality . . . what does it mean? Ain't nothing said.
'Cause Freddie's dead.

—Curtis Mayfield, "Freddie's Dead"

East New York had been hardscrabble for as long as anyone could remember, home of Brooklyn's Jewish mafia, stomping grounds of Louis "Lepke" Buchalter—the only Cosa Nostra boss ever executed by the federal government—and his hit-man-for-hire syndicate, Murder Inc. In the 1950s, the area was saddled with the densest assemblage of public housing in the country, and as Jews and Italians streamed out of nearby tenements and row houses, it quickly became the neighborhood of last resort for black and Puerto Rican slum-clearance refugees, packed by the tens of thousands into the crumbling neighborhood. The area was, according to Mayor Lindsay's aide Barry Gottehrer, "an abandoned neighborhood, with one of the highest rates of infant mortality, drug abuse, abandoned buildings and welfare, and the lowest employment in the city. Many poor people . . . were finally dumped here, as were the 'problem families' who had been evicted from public housing."

According to Lindsay aide Robert Blum, the white section of the neighborhood was "just as much a wasteland as the almost completely Negro and Puerto Rican" parts. In 1966, there were seven crimes reported for every hundred residents of East New York. In a single year,

15 percent of the seven-to-twenty-year-old males in the neighborhood were arrested. Whites talked of blacks bringing crime, heroin, and violence to the neighborhood. Blacks talked about whites driving through black areas shouting, "Go back to Africa, niggers!" In the racial turf wars, the most heavily contested area was the last stop on the number 3 subway line, a triangular traffic island formed by the intersection of New Lots Avenue, Livonia Avenue, and Ashford Street, with blacks living to the north, Puerto Ricans to the west, and whites to the south. Tensions built throughout the summer of 1966, and on July 21, Mayor Lindsay came to the neighborhood for a meeting with white community leaders. Two hours after he left, an unidentified sniper shot and killed an eleven-year-old black boy on the street. A few hours after that, a group of white youths calling themselves SPONGE—the Society for the Prevention of Niggers Getting Everything—set up a picket line at the traffic triangle, chanting "Two, four, six, eight, we don't want to integrate." Rival black groups passed out leaflets: "Whitey has done it again—innocent Eric Dean shot down by white racist cops or gangs—whitey wanted for murder, justice now." Later in the evening, a three-year-old black child was shot and critically wounded. When black residents took to the streets to protest, a thousand policemen were dispatched to the neighborhood and spent the night dodging bricks, bottles, and Molotov cocktails. Under strict instructions not to provoke the crowd, the police kept their guns and billy clubs on their hips, and the violence passed. The next day, a mayoral walking tour of the Italian section of the neighborhood was met with a chorus of Bronx cheers and calls to "Go back to Africa, Lindsay, and take your niggers with you!"

The next summer, it was Spanish Harlem. The police shot a knife-wielding suspect, rumors spread, a crowd formed, an officer told people, "Go home. You didn't lose anything. You just lost another spic," and the crowd fought back. Following a riot plan worked up in part by Chief O'Hagan, who later wrote a book on responding to civil disorders, the next night the police once again took a bend-don't-break approach, not exacerbating the situation but not doing anything to stop rioters from smashing windows and looting stores, either. The third night was the worst. Police and snipers exchanged gunfire. One mayoral aide, taking cover from gunshots behind a police cruiser, asked the black police inspector crouching next to him what they should do. Echoing Tonto's line to the Lone Ranger, the inspector joked back, "What do you mean *we*, white man?" The police fought pitched battles with rioters as the violence spread across the river to Mott Haven in the Bronx, where seven cops were injured, one taking a fifty-stitch stab wound in the arm. A week later, there was rioting in Bed-Stuy. Firemen were so angry after a series of attacks that they refused to answer calls until they were promised a police escort for each rig.

Fortunately for New York, Lindsay proved remarkably adept at handling the riots. Unlike the mayors of Newark, Los Angeles, Washington, Detroit, and so many other American cities—content to walk amid a phalanx of police and National Guardsmen along ash-quiet streets the next morning—when riots erupted, Lindsay went where the action was. Recognizing Lindsay in Flatbush, protesters hoisted him onto their shoulders, and the sight of the relaxed, smiling mayor calmed the crowd around him. After Martin Luther King was murdered, Lindsay rushed to 125th Street in Harlem, speaking off the cuff with crowds, listening to cries of despair shouted from rooftops and windows. "The most courageous man I've ever seen," said one aide. "He looked straight at the people on the streets and he told them he was sick and he was sorry about Martin Luther King," wrote columnist Jimmy Breslin. "And there was no riot in New York."

"It was an incredibly fractious, combustible period," says Lindsay's former chief of staff, Jay Kriegel. "The normal tolerance society has today, where we let tempers cool, that didn't really exist in that period. It was always a tinderbox, ready to explode, and we were always on twenty-four-hour alert for a period of years."

Lindsay's reach went beyond New York. In 1967, President Johnson formed the National Advisory Commission on Civil Disorders to look into race riots; it is generally called the Kerner Commission, after its chairman, Illinois governor Otto Kerner. Vice chairman Lindsay was the group's driving force, running commission meetings, leading fact-finding missions into slums around the country, and penning (or, rather, having his assistants Peter Goldmark and Kriegel pen) the famous lines from the report's introduction, that the United States was "moving toward two societies, one black, one white—separate and unequal."

The results of the report proved less notable than the wording: a few Whiz Kid–administered War on Poverty programs long on technical aims and lofty intent but short on dollars or longevity. The programs proved particularly disappointing in New York, a city with a long history of riots and reasoned responses to them. The most notorious were the three-day Irish Draft Riots during the Civil War, the fighting so fierce that Union troops were sent from Gettysburg to put down the insurrection. Unlike the race riots of a century later, there were no august fact-finding commissions, or official, expert-approved response plans from the government. Instead, Tammany Hall handled the riots with an age-old counterinsurgency tactic: If you can't beat 'em, buy 'em—pouring jobs and informal relief funds into Irish neighborhoods in return for stability and the loyal vote of the new immigrants. The response wasn't scientifically reasoned; it was arguably inefficient and undoubtedly corrupt. But it was also successful, helping the Irish start the long, slow climb to the working and middle classes.

With New York's blue-collar economy hemorrhaging jobs, and most private-sector job creation in the 1960s and 1970s favoring educated white women over uneducated minority males, that task of bringing jobs to the ghetto fell to the government, a task made almost impossible by the politicking of former mayor Robert Wagner. During the 1961 mayoral election, Wagner broke with what was left of Tammany Hall and turned the city's civil-service unions into his own de facto machine. In return for their support, Wagner gave in to union demands that city workers be allowed to live outside city limits. Largely ignored outside civil-service circles, the concession proved to be one of the final nails in the coffin of working-class New York, all but encouraging white flight and the exodus of hundreds of millions of dollars in salaries and city tax revenues to the subsidized suburbs. Just as important, it meant that even a major expansion of the bureaucracy would result in few jobs for actual city residents, namely, poor blacks and Puerto Ricans. They were free to take civil-service exams just like everyone else, but the resolutely Italian and Irish police and fire departments, Italian sanitation department, and Jewish teachers and clerks unions were hardly inviting to most blacks and Puerto Ricans, and the white contenders for the jobs—from more affluent backgrounds and better schools, some prepared for civil-service exams almost from birth by their civil-servant parents—made for stiff competition.

WHILE THE RIOTS THEMSELVES LARGELY PETERED OUT after King's assassination and the "long, hot summer" of 1968, tensions between the ghettos and white authority figures continued to simmer, particularly for the whitest of all city departments: the fire service. In 1963, there were 21,961 false alarms in New York, about 17 percent of the total calls. In 1968, that number had almost tripled, to 60,945—27 percent of the total. False alarms have always been a guilty pleasure of bored children in poor neighborhoods. Like a clanging, mechanical genie-in-a-bottle, just pull a lever and in five minutes you'd summoned your very own roaring parade scene. For kids without much to do in neighborhoods no one seemed to care about, it was an enormous exercise of power—but one that was taking a terrible toll on busy companies. And the increase was even larger than the statistics showed. A company like Engine 82 in the South Bronx could easily catch thirty calls in a single night, going from call to call without stopping at their house for a break. With little time for officers to fill out alarm forms between calls, busy lieutenants routinely ignored the paperwork for false alarms and small fires. How often calls were disappeared varied from company to company. "Some guys wanted to say their house ran the most, those types kept track of everything," says one South Bronx fireman, but he estimates that as much as 10 to 20 percent of the alarms were thrown out in some busy houses.

Along with the false alarms came a rash of attacks on firefighters, particularly in the South Bronx and East New York. Bricks, rocks, and bottles were "airmailed" from rooftops, shots fired at speeding rigs (one South Bronx ladder truck had four bullet holes in it). As racial tensions flared, the union counted 114 attacks on firemen in just two weeks in July of 1968.

"We used to just have guys ride in the hose bed," says one South Bronx engine man. "Then one night someone tossed a dog—I'm telling you, a dog—off a roof and it landed right in the middle of the hose bed. We stopped having guys ride there after that."

Some firemen built protective roofs and strung chicken-wire netting over vulnerable spots on the rig; others started carrying blackjacks, pistols, and sawed-off shotguns for protection. ("Fire a couple rounds off into the air and you'd clear the airmailers off the roof for a little bit, enough time to get into or out of the building.") Vietnam vets on the job compared the incidents to Vietcong ambushes. On the Lower East Side, East 5th Street comes to an abrupt halt at Avenue D, where it runs into the sprawling Lillian Wald housing project. Neighborhood teens would open up a fire hydrant on 5th Street, flood a low section of the road near the dead end, and pour enough gasoline or lighter fluid into the moat to leave a thin film across the top of the water. Then they would pull a fire alarm, wait for a rig to cross the water, and toss a match, leaving firemen caught between the projects (where the airmail would be coming hot and heavy) on one side and a jury-rigged lake of fire on the other.

Most viewed the tensions through the larger political issues of the time. When UFA president Michael Maye was a boy, his mother would say a prayer each time she heard a fire engine pass by. "It made them seem kind of holy," he told a reporter. "Today they throw bottles and snipe at us. . . . We're the same men. Trying to do the same job. Well, we won't stand for it." As for City Hall, Maye said they were holding the cops back from investigating attacks and making arrests—the city so afraid of race riots it was ignoring basic police work in poor neighborhoods.

The supply-side of the problem was even more complicated. In some cases, the violence and false alarms were an expression of legitimate gripes with the fire department. Firemen had a reputation (often deserved, especially in poor neighborhoods) for helping themselves to some of the items they saved from flames.* Then there was the issue of damage—it's a lot easier to fight flames with a broad sword than a scalpel, and fire companies running from fire to fire all day and night were often a bit more liberal with the size of the holes they punched through walls to check for fire extension, or the amount of furniture they tossed out the window to keep it from catching on fire. "The most bigoted, racist guy in the company would give up his life to save a black child," says Captain Vincent Julius. "*Any* white firefighter would risk his life to save a black child, but sometimes he would do more damage to an apartment."

But the largest motivator for the attacks seems to have been the racial politics of the period; firemen were virtually the only white authority figures left in neighborhoods with little love for white authority figures. Most ghetto residents weren't pulling alarms or attacking firemen, but they weren't exactly rushing out to turn in their neighbor's kid to a corrupt police department or firehouse full of suburbanite Irishmen with a reputation for thievery.

And for all the problems with false alarms and attacks, the issue drew the attention of the media and department brass away from the real fire problem in ghetto neighborhoods: plain old fires, as even small blazes were transforming into a death sentence for apartment buildings,

---

*When he was a child, pioneering Bronx hip-hop DJ Kool Herc (born Clive Campbell) and his family were burned out of their West Bronx apartment. "When the fire department came in there they were looking for money," recounted Cindy Campbell, his older sister. "The fire was really in one room, but in the bedroom the drawers were pulled out. My father had a tin pan of quarters that he was saving, and that tin pan had at least three or four hundred dollars in quarters at the time. That was just missing."

sometimes even whole blocks in the redlined, slumlord-owned ghettoes. "Even in poor neighborhoods, in the fifties and sixties, there would be somebody boarding up broken windows and sweeping out the water and ash before we were even done rolling up the hoses," says Chief Vincent Dunn. "And then something changed. You'd drive past the same building a week later, and the windowsill would still be all charred, the window not even boarded up."

Fires in partially abandoned buildings rose 800 percent in five years, as the fires and abandonment fed on one another: fires turned inhabited apartments into vacant rooms, which, in turn, attracted junkies and kids who carelessly burned trash for heat, started blazes with errant cigarettes, or lit fires for kicks. By the second, third, or fourth wave of flame, most buildings had gone completely abandoned, attracting even more vagrants and fires. By the late 1960s, vacant buildings accounted for only about 0.5 percent of the buildings in the city, but 11 percent of the structural fires and almost 30 percent of multiple-alarm fires.

Confronted with the abandoned building problem, the real-estate-centric city government developed a kind of cognitive dissonance. In rich neighborhoods, apartment buildings were the most expensive in the world, and in poor neighborhoods, they were overcrowded. New York had been fighting a housing *shortage* for decades, and Lindsay was facing harsh criticism because the pace of new housing construction had dropped during his administration—the idea that there was housing nobody wanted just didn't compute. For the time being, the problem was small enough that city agencies could ignore the complicated issue, content to bulldoze the worst eyesores and let the others burn until they fell down of their own accord. The numbers were rising, though, from an estimated 2,900 vacant buildings in 1965 to 4,344 in 1969, a 67 percent increase despite the thousands of vacants the city had knocked down. Whole sections of the city were turning into ghost towns, and hardly anyone seemed to notice.

O'Hagan leads the FDNY contingent during the Saint Patrick's Day Parade.
(Photo courtesy FDNY Photo Unit)

TEN

O'Hagan's Choice

One of the functions of intelligence is to take account of the dangers that come from trusting solely to the intelligence.

—Lewis Mumford

On a late afternoon in January of 1969, RAND fire project head Edward Blum received an urgent phone call from fire headquarters. The department had suffered a serious defeat at the hands of the fire unions in labor arbitration. O'Hagan was meeting with the city's lead labor negotiators and needed RAND to come up with a precise way to measure the fire department's "workload," and significantly decrease it without hiring new firemen or opening new companies. And he needed it all by eight a.m. the next day.

Accustomed as they were to spending months carefully analyzing issues, it was a daunting task for RAND's researchers, but it was their best chance to live up to the lofty goals on which the institute had been founded. Since opening its doors a year earlier, NYC-RAND had struggled to get a foothold in city government. In city hospitals, where RAND analysts worked with professionals as well educated as themselves, interactions often devolved into petty intellectual one-upmanship, because RAND, as one bureaucrat put it, "has tensions with any other intellectually sophisticated group with which they deal." In the police department, RAND had the opposite problem, distrusted as arrogant

intellectuals.* For its work with the housing department, the city council
actually sued RAND for access to a confidential report on rent control
(RAND argued for ending popular rent-control regulations, advice
Lindsay quickly distanced himself from).

Things didn't start much better for the RAND fire project. "When
RAND came into their first meeting with us, they had this guy who had
these huge glasses, he looked like Dr. Strangelove," says Steve Isenberg.
"It wasn't the guy's fault that he couldn't see, but that's how that group
seemed, out of place. You'd talk to some of them and think, 'These guys
can barely communicate with me, how are they going to deal with the
guys in uniform?' "

Firemen wondered the same things. "Out-of-touch nerds," says one.
"You couldn't talk to guys like that."

"Oh, they thought they were going to straighten us out alright," says
one of O'Hagan's aides. "They had a real attitude about things."

But Chief O'Hagan's penchant for numbers and new management
techniques meant that the fire project enjoyed considerably more support
from the top. "The police, they thought we were going to make them look
bad," says RAND researcher Peter Kolesar, a young Columbia professor
when he joined the institute. "O'Hagan, though, was a young guy, a very
smart guy. Not educated, but smart. He saw this RAND initiative as a
way to advance his own agenda." For the project's first year, O'Hagan's
assignments were relatively small matters, but this gave analysts the free

---

*What influence RAND and other consultants did have on the police department resulted in a
short-lived experiment of splitting up partners to cover more ground, until one half of a lately
split-up pair was shot on patrol. Another consultant-approved initiative took police off foot
patrols and put them in cruisers, so they could be more mobile and respond to more calls.
This policy lasted for years, but arguably not to the department's benefit, as it left patrolmen
isolated—listening to the radio in their patrol cars—and increasingly disconnected from the
life and crimes of the neighborhoods they were supposed to be keeping an eye on. More recently,
police departments have trended in the opposite direction, back to the "community policing"
of yesteryear, when cops spent more time on the street, and had greater leeway to establish relationships within the community and monitor areas as they saw fit; that policy has been given
partial credit for the precipitous decrease in violent crime in American cities over the last two
decades.

time to research whatever they felt like and wait until they were called on for something more ambitious—such as providing the chief with new ways to cut workload.

The concept of workload was actually a fairly new entry into the FDNY's lexicon, introduced a few months earlier in preliminary contract talks with the unions. It can be a tricky thing to measure—different kinds of alarms and different-sized fires require different amounts of time and effort—but in terms of the total number of alarms and working fires, the FDNY's workload increased about 60 percent from 1964 to 1968. The unions wanted more fire companies and more men (i.e., more union members) to handle the increase, and cited the workload rise and a doubling of civilian fire deaths in the last six years to argue that that manpower should be on the table during the next round of contract talks.

Labor arbitrators eventually agreed, a shock to O'Hagan and department brass. Issues like the number of firemen and fire companies had always been left up to management—giving the unions say over them was like letting the inmates run (or at least have a seat on the executive board of) the asylum. O'Hagan had survived attacks on his authority from above by the commissioner and the old staff chiefs; now he would have to take back control from the unions and the rank-and-file below.

"Before O'Hagan, and even in his first couple of years as chief, people were feeling like no one was really in charge," says Chief Vincent Dunn. "When [the union] used to go to meetings with the city, there was never anyone from headquarters there. All of a sudden, John O'Hagan is showing up to these meetings with the city council, with the mayor, and he's interjecting, he's stopping us from getting what we want from the city. He had this attitude of 'I'm the boss, I'm going to run it.' . . . After the union won [the workload case], O'Hagan took control of that department like no chief ever had control. After that we had a saying: 'Lowery ran an office, but O'Hagan ran the job.'"

Labor arbitrators appointed a union-dominated group nicknamed the "FLAME committee" to come up with ways to stem the rising workload. Their recommendations were predictable: hire thousands of new firemen and open dozens of new "second sections"—companies added to busy firehouses that served as a backup when the first company was out on a call. To reassert his control over the unions, O'Hagan needed a counterproposal, and he thought RAND could provide it. His last-minute call over to NYC-RAND headquarters didn't leave much time, but it was the fire project's first chance to employ the "RAND approach." They started by analyzing a recent experiment with second sections that the department had tried after Engine Co. 82 went on more than six thousand runs in 1966. A RAND report sums up what happened next: "To relieve its workload, the department created a new company (E85) in July 1967, and put it in the same firehouse as Eng. 82. It was expected that Eng. 82's workload would be cut in half. But in 1968, Eng. 85's first full year of operation, Eng. 82 was still the busiest company in the city and Eng. 85 was the second busiest. Instead of helping the busy units, there were now two busy units," at an additional "annual cost of $600,000."

The problem with second sections, RAND decided, was false alarms. Companies in busy neighborhoods were out on calls so often that dispatchers were forced to send out less than the standard response of three engines and two ladders to each alarm. With Engine 85 able to fill in whenever 82 was out of the house, dispatchers could send a full response more often, but 85 was just an extra engine going on useless false-alarm runs.

For O'Hagan, this was the kind of innovative approach to firefighting he'd been dreaming of for years. Not only had RAND found a creative explanation for a vexing problem, that explanation was exactly what the chief wanted to hear: that the old way of doing business, of throwing more money and men and machines at a problem, wasn't going to solve anything; that the FLAME committee's second sections were a waste of resources. What the department needed was in-depth research, novel deployment and dispatch patterns, a creative, "more with less" mentality. It was like something out of the magazine articles about McNamara and the Whiz Kids turning Ford from a place where stacks of bills were measured with a ruler to one of the most statistically advanced companies in the world.

RAND's findings weren't enough to convince the city's labor relations board to nix the FLAME committee's second sections completely, but they let O'Hagan and RAND replace some of the proposed second sections with a new kind of part-time company. RAND's statistics showed that alarms peaked from the late afternoon to around midnight, particularly in fire-prone neighborhoods. If there needed to be more men and machines on the street, the chief argued, why not build a little flexibility into the system and create a few tactical control units (TCUs) that only operated during those peak hours? The companies would be housed in prefabricated Quonset huts that could be assembled for a fraction of the cost of a new firehouse, and quickly disassembled and moved as fire patterns changed. Building on RAND's criticism of second sections, O'Hagan also pushed a new plan for dealing with false alarms, called "adaptive response." RAND's analysis had shown that for the vast majority of legitimate alarms, never mind false alarms, the standard response of three engines and two ladders was more than adequate. With adaptive response, only two engines and one ladder would respond to fire alarms pulled in neighborhoods with high false-alarm rates.

Both of O'Hagan's measures ran counter to union philosophy. Adaptive response made sense for most alarms, but the fire service wasn't built around what *usually* happened, it was there to deal with worst-case scenarios, and anything that weakened preparedness for those scenarios didn't fly with the union. As for the tactical control units, they were just that—tactical, a purely pragmatic entity to be dispatched when and where they were needed, disassembled and reconstituted according to the whims of the brass at headquarters. As far as the union was concerned, devotion to "the job" and to the higher calling of saving lives was important in training firemen, but it was a little too abstract for the day-to-day. No one from headquarters was dragging your ass out from underneath a collapsed wall, or letting you sleep on a couch in the

Municipal Building if your wife kicked you to the curb for that trace of
Chanel No. 5 wafting from the hamper. Guys needed something more
immediate, more tangible, to devote themselves to, and the company
and the men who staffed it filled that role. Having a full-time, brick-
and-mortar firehouse went a long way toward building the culture that
trained men to risk their lives and subordinate themselves to the best
interests of the company—it was hard to build up a proper esprit de
corps when the corps wasn't even around most of the day. Make *some*
companies part-time, cut back responses to *some* fire alarms, the union
claimed, and there was no telling where it would end.

But adaptive response and the TCUs were a masterstroke from
O'Hagan and RAND. The union had built their manpower case on
numbers and rationality—like a 60 percent increase in alarms and more
than 100 percent increase in civilian deaths over the last few years—not
tradition or firehouse-culture intangibles, and unless they wanted to
undermine their credibility with the labor board, they had to play ball.
A deal was struck: eighteen new companies would be opened, a mix of
full-time second sections and TCUs that would operate from three p.m.
to one a.m. In deference to a state labor law requiring that fire companies
operate at full strength at all times of day (one of RAND and O'Hagan's
biggest obstacles to building a more flexible, efficient department), the
TCUs also had to be staffed by volunteers, not mandatory transfers.

RAND's second-section studies also made O'Hagan's decision on what
to do about the rising ghetto-fire numbers easier. Not a ghetto firefighter
by inclination or experience, the chief had stayed relatively aloof from
the issue, focusing on high-rise fire codes and the kind of quantitative
reforms he and Isenberg had been working on. O'Hagan knew he needed
to hand off responsibility for the issue to someone, and RAND's second-
section studies and contract proposals proved a successful audition.

Unfortunately, RAND's second-sections studies were also wrong. On
its face, it did seem that Engine 85 had done nothing to relieve Engine
82's workload, but in their haste to help Chief O'Hagan fight the FLAME
proposals, RAND missed a more important set of statistics than the

number of alarms a company was called out on. The number of runs a company goes on is a decent measure of how much work it does. But showing up to a fire that the first-due company already has under control only takes a few minutes. A false alarm is even quicker, just cruise by the box, make sure there's no smoke in the area, and head home—what O'Hagan's protégé and primary liaison with RAND, Chief Homer Bishop, used to call "the slide and glide." A much more accurate measure of real workload is the number of "workers": how many fires the company actually has to fight. When Engine 85 opened, Engine 82 dropped from the top spot on the workers' list to fourth. Engine 85 wasn't simply going on useless false-alarm calls; it was fighting thousands of fires (the fifth most in the department, right behind Engine 82). The rising number of fires and alarms in the South Bronx meant that Engine 85 hadn't turned 82 into a seldom used company, but it had done something much more important: averted certain disaster if Engine 82 had been responsible for not only the 3,803 workers it went on in 1968, but the 3,759 workers Engine 85 handled, too.

A quick glance at the department's workers' rankings after the FLAME second sections were opened would have shown RAND and O'Hagan how effective the new companies were. When a second section was added to the South Bronx's Engine 88 (Engine 88-2), 88-1's number of working fires dropped more than 30 percent.* A few blocks away, Ladder 27's workers fell 30 percent after 27-2 was opened, dropping it from eleventh on the workers' list to twenty-ninth. Engines 50, 41, and Ladder 17 in the Bronx saw similar drops when their second sections opened. In East New York, Ladder 103 fell from the third-busiest ladder company to the ninth after 103-2 was opened, experiencing a slight decrease in workers even as the number of fires in the neighborhood skyrocketed. "It was a big help to have two trucks and additional manpower on the

---

*Unfortunately, to open 88-2, O'Hagan closed another Bronx second section, Engine 46-2. The number of workers at 46-1 jumped 40 percent that year and 90 percent over the next five years; 46-1 remained one of the busiest engines throughout the 1970s.

scene," says retired fireman Joe Dirks, who worked in Ladder 103. "The neighborhood was going downhill, but not like it was a few years later. There was still a lot to be saved."

RAND and O'Hagan's tactical control units proved similarly effective, most of them among the busiest 10 to 20 percent of fire engines and ladders in the city despite their being open only nine hours a day, and helping significantly decrease the number of fires surrounding companies had to fight. Citywide, civilian deaths and the number of structural, nonstructural, and serious fires were all held in check for the first time in years after the openings started going into effect in 1969. By responding to fires more quickly and containing them, and by helping free firemen for inspections that prevented flames from breaking out in the first place, the tactical control units and FLAME openings helped *decrease*—not just spread out—citywide workload by nearly 10 percent. With a little breathing room, busy firehouses started community outreach and fire-awareness programs that cooled some of the racial tensions and brought false alarms and attacks on firemen down significantly (despite increased media attention that gave the opposite impression).

But like Dartmouth and Princeton football fans watching a penalty-filled game, Chief O'Hagan was in the thrall of an idea, and that idea blinded him not only to the impact of the FLAME companies but to the right way to approach the ghetto-fire problem as a whole. RAND wasn't the only contender for taking greater responsibility for ghetto fires. Alarmed at the rapid rise in fire numbers in his division, South Bronx Deputy Chief Charles T. Kirby wrote O'Hagan a six-page report with breakdowns of local fire trends and predictions for the near future. With just 13 percent of the city's total area and 18 percent of its population, Kirby wrote, the Bronx accounted for more than 26 percent of all the city's fires, and that ratio was increasing rapidly. Fires in places like Morrisania and Hunts Point near Engine 82 were spreading to other neighborhoods, including parts of the West Bronx with extremely high population densities that promised to "present fire and social problems exceeding any previously encountered in the city," unless something was done quickly. "In no instance during this period can we find a clear indication of [fire rate] leveling in any area of the Borough," Kirby wrote, with one exception: the area south of 149th Street was deteriorating so rapidly that in five years there might not be anything left to burn.

Kirby realized that combating the fire problem consisted of more than simply putting water on flames, writing that fires were ultimately a social and economic problem, both a cause and result of poverty: "The actual fires and the constant threat of fire must surely be a devastating horror to people required to live in houses in a deteriorating neighborhood," he wrote. "We also know that fire is a large component of the decay cycle and we can suspect that it adds to the uneasiness and insecurity of the poor. After years of fire experience, fire prevention—and fire investigation, I feel that it can be said that rather than being accidental, fire is largely a social problem and the Bronx has and will have its share of such problems."

Such a broad-based problem required a coordinated solution from the city, and to that end, Kirby recommended "that a very high-ranking member of the Department be a full-fleged [sic] member of all New York City Agencies dealing with housing, Redevelopment, and similar functional groups. . . . There are many more physical and social changes which must be planned to reverse the fire trend," he wrote. "If these are beyond the fiscal capabilities of the City or inequitable with our economic structure it does not relieve us completely of our obligation to point up problems as we see and forecast them."

Rejecting Kirby's recommendation that the department open up more South Bronx companies and coordinate with other agencies in the borough in favor of RAND's take on second sections wasn't a hard choice for O'Hagan. RAND was pushing O'Hagan's favored root approach for tackling problems: compartmentalize an issue, analyze it with comprehensive statistics, and charge ahead with a bold new solution. Kirby advocated the kind of traditional approach O'Hagan had made a career of eschewing—bringing together the concerned parties and hashing out a flexible solution. And if that wasn't enough, Kirby actually praised the effect that the newly opened FLAME second sections had on work-load, and suggested locations for opening up more. It is impossible to determine the exact mix of motives behind O'Hagan's decision to side with RAND over Kirby, but by all indications the chief's belief that the FLAME second sections were a personal affront to him played a role in the decision. O'Hagan was a true believer in the RAND approach, yet the fact that RAND told him exactly what he wanted to hear (that second sections were useless; that spending more money on poor, politically weak neighborhoods would do little good) blinded the chief to the very real success that second sections had in cutting the number of workers for their first sections and surrounding companies, and bringing workload under control.

In the "old days" of Tammany-style governance, O'Hagan and RAND's big ideas and ambitious reform agenda wouldn't have mattered much. Local ward bosses, irate at watching their constituents being burned out of their homes, would have drawn together the relevant authorities and cobbled together a plan. In all likelihood, fire patrols and building inspections would have been increased, negligent landlords brought into line, redlining dogmas put aside to make loans available, renovation and poverty programs put in place, fire-awareness campaigns begun—in other words, exactly the kinds of things Chief Kirby was recommending. Such plans would have been classic Tammany pluralism—true branch-approach problem-solving. The programs would be hastily assembled and muddled through by trial and error. Some would succeed, others fail, and most would be rife with backdoor politicking and corruption. It wouldn't have been particularly analytic, scientific, transparent, or progressive, but *something* would have been done, and done quickly. There were too many buildings, votes, and dollars being lost.

But New York City was no longer run on the Tammany model. The vast sums lavished on the Democratic clubhouses during the Moses years had left them largely unaccountable to their constituencies at the very moment when white flight and the Puerto Rican and black migrations struck the city. Instead of bribing the new arrivals with enough jobs and influence to secure their votes—as Tammany had done with previous waves of Irish, Italian, and Jewish immigrants—the county organizations had lined their own pockets by evicting and displacing the newcomers. By the time the party bosses woke up, the demographic shift in the Bronx was so massive, and the clubhouse so unpopular with minorities, it was clear that the old white working-class borough was on its way out, and the white-dominated machine would go with it.

"I remember when my mother and I went to see our congressman," said one Bronx native. "We wanted to talk to him about what was going on and see if we couldn't get the neighborhood working to fight [the growing crime, fires, and white flight], to stem the tide. He said 'Move to Co-op City,'" a massive middle-class housing project on the suburban northeast fringes of the borough.

Like slumlords in a redlined neighborhood, outgoing Dems could only grab what power and money were left and hold on for as long as possible, a plan that didn't include expending political capital fighting for new firehouses and home loans. In the meantime, the fires were actually displacing so many people that it was hard to build up any opposition to the established order. If anything, the machine was indirectly benefiting from the fires and dysfunction, so why fight them? The machine's competition, black and Puerto Rican political leaders, didn't show much more concern for the fires than did their clubhouse counterparts. Some of them actually benefited from the fires too, as the remaining white voters were chased from their districts, and money to deal with the housing, health, and economic devastation of the burnout poured into the social-service organizations they controlled. Ramon Velez, a Democratic party boss, head of the city's Puerto Rican Day Parade, and "the baron of a sweeping array of poverty programs in the South Bronx," as *The New York Times* put it in his 2008 obituary (Ed Koch called him "a poverty pimp"), told historian Jill Jonnes that "physical destruction is inconsequential. I care about my children being able to walk the streets and not be ashamed of their culture and their roots. I'm saying, don't steal my identity. Don't implant your values. I'd rather have no housing than sell my soul." A very rich man, thanks to the $300 million his organizations garnered in antipoverty funds over the years, Velez himself never had to make that choice. Even Bronx Congressman Herman Badillo had all but given up on the borough, telling Battalion Chief Alfred Benway not to worry about fire company closings and the epidemic of fires, he'd get federal funds to build new housing after the old buildings burned down.

No one with any power, it seemed, had any interest in saving the Bronx, and many were doing just fine letting it burn. Even city agencies were finding silver linings in the clouds of smoke. In 1968, Lindsay's planning commission recommended taking advantage of the burnout: "The South Bronx will be designated for urban renewal, permitting the City to acquire small vacant parcels and empty buildings. . . . This would prevent the reoccupation of worn-out industrial buildings and lot-by-lot fixing up or replacement of burned-out tenements." The report made similar designations for East Harlem and the Brooklyn neighborhoods of Brownsville and East New York, where fire and abandonment were doing the kind of slum clearance that the city no longer had the money or political will to do itself.

The housing department was actually judged by how much housing it *built*, not how much it preserved—if anything, more destruction meant more funds for rebuilding. The police department had mostly given up on the Bronx as a lost cause, finding it easier to ship their most violent, corrupt, and incompetent officers there than go through the hassle of trying to fire the civil service–protected cops. The advantages fires brought to politicians and bureaucrats may have been small, but they removed any incentive for the relevant power-brokers to go mucking about in the fire department's business, particularly with a competent, powerful chief like O'Hagan in charge.

O'Hagan's decision to side with RAND over Chief Kirby came at a time when New York's ghettoes were reeling from the effects of poverty, drugs, violence, and a dysfunctional real estate market. But they were also still standing. The Board of Education was still planning on building a new junior high and elementary school on Charlotte Street to house the recent influx of school-age children, surveyors noting that "this entire area has high-density housing that is in fair condition." In census tract 2 in the South Bronx, there were still 836 buildings providing shelter and employment. Ten years later, all but nine of those buildings were burned out and abandoned, their fate sealed by O'Hagan and an ambitious fire-modeling project RAND embarked on after their successful contract recommendations.

For the chief, though, the decision contained no such momentousness. In fact, for all the personal, political, and philosophical issues that motivated his fateful choice, as far as O'Hagan was concerned, it was just one aspect of a larger political battle he was waging for the good of the city and the department. This other battle, and the time, energy, and political capital it required, was the reason why O'Hagan's third option for handling ghetto fires—digging in and studying the problem himself, unleashing the keenest firefighting mind in the business on what was fast shaping up to be the most disastrous wave of fires any modern city had ever known—was never really an option at all. The chief had bigger fish to fry, and not in the slums of the Bronx, but in the high-rise canyons of Manhattan.

O'Hagan and Lindsay at the fatal One New York Plaza high-rise fire.

Support beams show faulty spray-on insulation.
(Both photos courtesy FDNY Photo Unit)

ELEVEN

Going Along to Get Along

August 5, 1970

Twenty-nine-year-old telephone repairman Charles Kuhn was working
on the thirty-ninth floor of the nearly completed One New York Plaza
building at the southern tip of Manhattan when he noticed a chemical
smell in the air. He walked over to a group of technicians to see if they
noticed it too, but was cut off by a man bursting out of the stairwell,
shouting, "There's a fire, there's a fire!" Everyone jumped in an elevator
and headed for the lobby, but the doors opened every few floors to take
on new passengers, the smoke thicker, blacker, and hotter with each stop.
On the thirty-third floor, the elevator doors opened again and a wave of
scalding smoke rushed in, but no people.

"It was pure black," said Kuhn. "It was just like night. It took all
the oxygen out of the air. There was nothing to breathe and I felt like
dying." The doors jammed open, and with heat piercing his skin, Kuhn
screamed, "Let me die!" Somebody else yelled "Fall to the floor!" over the
din of screaming passengers, and people dropped on top of one another,

trying to shield their faces and mouths. Eventually, someone managed to get the doors shut, and everyone rode to the lobby in smoky silence. "It must have been just a matter of minutes," said Kuhn, "but it seemed like hours. I never thought I'd live." Safely downstairs, people wondered who had rung the elevator on the thirty-third floor, and whether they'd made it out.

As Kuhn stumbled into the lobby, two building employees ferried Ladder 15 and Engine 10 up to the thirty-second floor. As the firemen left the elevator, the two men hit the button for the lobby, but the elevator lurched upward and stopped on the thirty-third floor, and the doors opened and jammed once again. One of the men took a belly full of smoke and was knocked out cold, but the other was able to close the doors and get them back downstairs. Firemen battling the flames on the thirty-third floor found a third stalled elevator. Inside, three men lay on the floor, shirts pulled up over their faces. One of them was still breathing and ultimately survived, the other two—including a security guard on his first day of work—didn't make it.

In charge of the 150 firemen who spent more than six hours putting down the flames, John O'Hagan raged at the fulfillment of the warnings he'd been making for years about the city's lax high-rise fire codes. "The thing that hinders us is the design and construction of the building," he told one reporter. The high-rise was "cheap, highly inflammable, and . . . of the common type used for economical purposes," he told another. "This type of building does not provide ventilation for firefighting. It doesn't even have a sprinkler system." The chief gave a similar report to Mayor Lindsay, who arrived in time to see some of the two-dozen firemen being carted to the hospital for smoke poisoning and burns.

Investigators later found that it was not a person but the fire itself that had called the three elevators to the thirty-third floor, the flames triggering elevator call buttons designed to detect heat from a person's finger. Chief O'Hagan had made warnings about the gimmicky buttons before, just one of a handful of design flaws he'd been pointing out to architects and developers for more than a decade. The New York Plaza building had all the standard faults in spades: thick-paned glass windows that took longer to break in a fire, trapping the heat and smoke like an oven. Spray-on insulation for load-bearing beams and columns, supposed to be fire-resistant for three to four hours, was, in fact, not tested at high enough temperatures and routinely fell off the beams during a fire, leaving them completely exposed. A gap between the interior walls and the external skin of the building, filled with flammable insulation, that allowed fire to travel between floors. A ventilation system that spread smoke throughout the building.

As O'Hagan had learned after the 23rd Street fire, tragedy creates an opening for reform, but that opportunity is fleeting. "Sprinklers, compartmentation, these real estate industry guys didn't want any of it," says retired chief Vincent Dunn, who worked on high-rise fire problems with O'Hagan. "When you saw that play, *Man of La Mancha*, you'd think, 'That's O'Hagan!' He was fighting windmills." But this time, the chief was prepared for quick action. Over the years, O'Hagan had cultivated relationships with forward-thinking architects and engineers who had the power to push for common-sense reforms (or, at least, not fight them). He became friendly with powerful real estate developers and businessmen like Jack and Lew Rudin, and John A. Coleman—the son of a policeman who worked his way up from a job as a Wall Street errand boy to a seat on the New York Stock Exchange—who schooled O'Hagan in the ways of New York power.

But in the years leading up to the One New York plaza fire, all of O'Hagan's influence hadn't been enough to stop the construction of a pair of 200-by-200-foot steel boxes that soared 1,350 feet into the air just a few blocks from New York Plaza, the top entry in a growing list of steel-and-glass high-rise "fireman killers" in Lower Manhattan: the World Trade Center towers. The largest buildings in the world, they were designed with a revolutionary new engineering style that made them incredibly light, allowed for the enormous open-floor-space plans that renters coveted, and left them remarkably susceptible to fire and collapse—design flaws that O'Hagan fought against, but was powerless to stop. "It was the one big battle [O'Hagan] lost," says a retired aide. "From then on, that was *his* issue."

After losing the WTC battle, O'Hagan realized that for the first time in his career, power—more than test-taking prowess, managerial skill, or technological competence—was what he needed to achieve his goals. He began seeking out that political capital more formally, by becoming active in the Brooklyn and Queens Democratic organizations and in the Catholic Church, which still had considerable political sway in the city. But for all his juice with the Democratic Party, the most important politician in the city was still O'Hagan's boss, John V. Lindsay. An independent Republican, Lindsay didn't know much Democratic inside-baseball, and actually thought of O'Hagan as an apolitical civil servant, an image O'Hagan had cultivated with his tough-minded approach to management and budget-making. "Lindsay liked O'Hagan because the fire service is a tough service to run," says one retired fire chief, "and O'Hagan *ran* the fire service."

Lindsay also believed in RAND, and saw O'Hagan as the only municipal department head giving the institute enough authority to fulfill its initial promise. It had been a difficult couple of years for both Lindsay and RAND. Lindsay had found himself in a fight for his political life in the 1969 mayor's race, losing the Republican primary and barely winning the general election as the Liberal Party candidate. As for RAND, the new city comptroller, former mayoral candidate Abe Beame, attacked Lindsay's $70 million consultant habit (up from $8 million under Wagner) and suspended payments to the institute for more than a year, forcing it to scrape by on money sent from RAND's Santa Monica headquarters and a $900,000 grant from the Ford Foundation.

But the mayor still had faith in RAND's ability to rationalize government and turn City Hall from a reactive muddler into a forward-thinking operation, one that would use computer models to predict and head off social and economic problems before they grew. Like President Johnson, so impressed with "that fellow from Ford with the Stacomb in his hair," Lindsay loved the numerically precise reports and recommendations that O'Hagan, courtesy of RAND, produced for him. "Lindsay really believed they were *supermen*," one budget aide said of RAND. "Their use of statistics and charts just dazzled him. The statistics made him feel the city was controllable with expertise." And while the mayor may not have understood exactly how such systems actually worked, he had faith that the wizards at RAND did. "I remember that I once wrote a speech for Lindsay and he made me use the phrase 'new budget science' three times in it," said one aide, "and I'm convinced he didn't know what the words actually meant." By giving RAND more responsibility and authority, O'Hagan was also securing his alliance with Lindsay just when he needed it most.

As with the 23rd Street collapse, the New York Plaza fire caught the attention of the press, and O'Hagan used every angle at his disposal to shine a light through the holes in the city's fire codes. Lindsay appointed a blue-ribbon committee to investigate the problem, and the panel came back with a report that read like it had been all but ghostwritten by the chief (some say it had). At the close of 1972, the city council passed Local Law 5, a first-of-its-kind fire code for high-rise buildings. It was a compromise bill, falling short of O'Hagan's ultimate goals, but it was a remarkable victory for a civil servant forced to battle the most influential political lobby in the city. The law became the crowning achievement of O'Hagan's career. One of the most important pieces of legislation in modern firefighting history, it has since become a template for building and fire codes in cities the world over.

Unfortunately, the most potentially dangerous high-rises in the city, the World Trade Center towers, were nearly completed. In fact, because the Port Authority was a bistate governmental body, the buildings weren't subject to *any* city fire codes or fire inspections. Norman Steisel, a Lindsay budget aide who years later, as Mayor David Dinkins' first deputy mayor, was responsible for overseeing the evacuation efforts after the 1993 World Trade Center bombings, says that O'Hagan's warning's were prophetic. "The evacuation efforts took hours," observes Steisel. "They were slowed significantly because of the lack of ventilation and

communication; the sprinkler system was totally lacking; stairwells
didn't have emergency lighting and were filled with smoke . . . all of which
would have been significantly better if they had [had] to follow Local
Law 5." After the 1993 bombings, the buildings were forced to comply
with many of O'Hagan's regulations, a decisive factor, according to
Steisel, in the mostly successful evacuations after the September 11
attacks. On 9/11, "those buildings were evacuated very quickly," says
Steisel. "Building management experts and emergency responders have
observed that tens of thousands of lives were saved, and in 1993 I don't
know if that would have been possible."

But while O'Hagan was busy accumulating and spending political
capital to pass Local Law 5, the situation in the city's ghettoes was
rapidly deteriorating. "I used to cry like a baby sometimes," says Artie
Wohlgemuth, who worked in a TCU company in Brooklyn. "They
burned like matchboxes, those houses. I remember hearing tapes of
some of the calls when they came into the dispatchers' . . . just awful."
Harlem chief Joseph Galvin broke down in tears while testifying before
Congress about the destruction of neighborhoods and the toll that the
lack of money was having on the fire department—overworked men,
broken rigs, antiquated equipment.

But riding high on his recent successes, O'Hagan continued to
cultivate his image as a hard-nosed manager intent on cutting waste.
He began threatening the unions and boasting to City Hall that he
could run the department on 7,500 men instead of its current 14,000
uniformed personnel. He made steep cuts in "nonessential" operations
like preventative fire inspections, upkeep, and repairs, and, despite
a slight uptick in arson for profit, fire marshals. Intent on running a
smaller, more flexible department, the chief was proud of his ability to
cut budgets; it was an opportunity to show his management prowess
and fiscal responsibility. "O'Hagan was all about efficiency," says Chief
Vincent Dunn. "He was like a Donald Rumsfeld in that department . . .
or like those [Whiz Kids] at Ford."

Despite the success of putting more firemen on the streets with the

FLAME second sections, in April of 1971, Lindsay imposed a hiring freeze on all uniformed services, which cut the number of firemen and officers from more than fourteen thousand to twelve thousand in less than two years. Brand-new firehouses sat empty because there weren't enough men to staff them. O'Hagan was even able to cancel some of the FLAME second sections he'd agreed to open, because of the lack of manpower. Overworked, understaffed, and furious with O'Hagan and the city for reneging on the contract agreement to open more second sections, the fire union president told the volunteers who staffed O'Hagan's TCUs to request transfers, and the program had to be shut down.

Wherever the blame lies for closing the TCUs (and though it was arguably backed into a corner, it was the union who ultimately pulled the plug on them), the cuts were a serious blow to the neighborhoods they operated in. Open for just nine hours a day, three TCUs in the Bronx fought 10,000 fires in 1970, making them by far the most cost-effective companies in the city. Now those fires would have to be fought by the already overworked nearby companies (some had to work 50 percent more fires the next year), and others called in from farther away to spread out the burden. Making matters even worse for the Bronx, O'Hagan closed Engine 85—the original second section that he and RAND were convinced served little purpose but that was, in fact, one of the busiest companies in the city. (As an apparent act of retaliation, Engine 85 was perhaps not so coincidentally headquartered in the same house where UFA president Michael Maye was a fireman.) But to outside observers unfamiliar with the complicated politicking of the fire department, the closings looked like just another example of O'Hagan's management prowess, his uncanny ability to use numbers and careful research to "do more with less."

Impressed with O'Hagan's ability to handle the hiring freeze, in 1971 Lindsay asked him for more cuts. At the time, the mayor was preparing for his long-awaited run for the presidency. Despite the Goldwater disaster of 1964, the Republican Party had grown increasingly conservative over the years and put Richard Nixon in the White House in 1968. In August

1971, Lindsay switched to the Democratic party in the hopes of securing the 1972 nomination to take on Nixon in the general.* With Lindsay gearing up for a presidential run, O'Hagan knew the mayor was willing to cede authority to anyone able to cut budgets and keep their department under control while he was preoccupied with national politics. It was the perfect opportunity to show off his managerial skills, and he turned to RAND for help with the cuts.

While O'Hagan was fighting for Local Law 5, RAND had expanded their second-section study to work on the questions O'Hagan and Isenberg had puzzled over years before: how to predict fire patterns and where and when to open fire companies to more efficiently fight those fires. From the fire reports O'Hagan and IBM had computerized over the years, they were able to create computer models that replicated when, where, and how often fires broke out in the city, and how quickly fire companies were able to respond to them. The models estimated which areas received faster and slower responses, and from there RAND could determine which companies could be closed with the least impact on response times. When Lindsay asked for budget cuts in 1971, RAND and O'Hagan devised budget-cutting options, such as turning some companies into TCUs instead of full-time companies, that wouldn't require widespread closings, but the unions rejected the ideas, and negotiations generally devolved into petty bickering and macho bluster. (One union man actually showed off by walking along the thin ledge of a balcony, hundreds of feet above the ground, outside the negotiating room.) RAND ran its models and recommended closing six companies and moving seven others (or closing thirteen companies and opening seven new ones, depending on how you looked at it). About half of the companies closed or moved were genuinely redundant—houses in Lower Manhattan that were built when most of the city's population was

---

*Lindsay eventually suffered an embarrassing defeat in the Florida primary (prompting Brooklyn Democratic boss Meade Esposito to say, "I think the handwriting is on the wall; Little Sheba better come home") and dropped out of the race.

crowded into tenements south of 14th Street—and some of the openings were well placed. But the models also suggested closing some of the busiest ghetto fire companies in the city, including four FLAME second sections. Some of the new locations were equally puzzling, coming in places like sleepy Staten Island and the suburban Bronx neighborhood of Throgs Neck.

How had models designed to make the least painful cuts and the most useful openings suggested closing some of the busiest fire companies in the city and opening companies in neighborhoods with few fires? How had systems analysis—designed specifically to favor scientific rationality over political and personal bias—given such dangerously irrational and politically expedient advice, allowing O'Hagan to close the second sections he saw as a personal affront and cut budgets in neighborhoods too weak to fight back?

In the more than sixty years since their inception, systems analysis and computer modeling have become *the* central decision-making tools for complex problem-solving of all stripes, from Wall Street stock-picking and making economic projections to health-care reform initiatives and global-warming studies. RAND's fire modeling project was something of a turning point in this rise, the most statistically advanced and politically influential initiative of its kind, an early leap in the automation of governance and decision-making. But the project also became a template for the dangers of using the root approach and systems analysis for tackling complicated problems with real-world implications.

A MODEL FOR PREDICTING AVERAGE FIRE COMPANY TRAVEL TIMES

PETER KOLESAR

R-1624-NYC
JUNE 1975

is Report we propose and test a simple model for predict
ire company travel times (the elapsed time between when
s its house and when it arrives at the scene of a fire)
es that, in a given region of a city, the expected trave
sest responding fire company, ET, is given by

$$ET = \alpha + \beta \left[\frac{A}{n - \lambda ES} \right]^{\gamma}, \qquad (1)$$

the physical area of the region (square miles), n is th
mpanies stationed there, λ is the expected number of ala
and ES is the expected total service time (in hours) of
nies that respond to and work at an alarm. α, β and λ
ng values that depend on the physical characteristics o
ield measurements and simulation experiments have valida
New York City and have shown that, in most regions of th
is approximately

$$ET = 2.2 \left[\frac{A}{n - 0.5\lambda} \right]^{0.3} \qquad (2)$$

as been used as a rule of thumb in estimating how
nge with increases or reductions in fire company s

It has been employed in studies that have led to
nt changes in New York City and, consequently, to

-5-

III. COMBINING THE TRAVEL TIME AND RESPONSE DISTANCE MODELS

Now we combine the travel time model with the response distance model
and, by so doing, we relate expected travel time in a region to a few easily
measured parameters. To motivate the approximation and the supporting data
analysis that follows, we begin with s

Consider a particular region of th
ditional expected travel time when the
denote the cumulative probability dist
ET, the unconditional expected travel
away), is

$$ET =$$

Assuming the validity of the travel ti

$$ET = \int_{0}^{2d_c} c_2 \sqrt{\frac{\overline{x}}{a}} \, dF_D(x) + \int_{2d_c}^{\infty} \left(\frac{v_c}{a} \right.$$

Recognizing that both segments of the
inequality we have:

$$ET \leq \begin{cases} 2\sqrt{\dfrac{ED}{a}}, \\[2mm] \dfrac{v_c}{a} + \dfrac{ED}{v_c}, \end{cases}$$

However, by ignoring the inequali
addition, we replace ED by (3), obtain

$$ET \approx \begin{cases} c_1 \left[\dfrac{A}{n - \lambda ES} \right]^{1/4}, & \text{if ED is "small} \\[4mm] c_2 + c_3 \left[\dfrac{A}{n - \lambda ES} \right]^{1/2}, & \text{if ED is "large."} \qquad (7b) \end{cases}$$

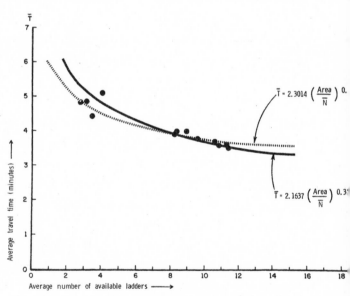

Figure 2.   Average ladder travel time vs. average number of ladders
available--North Bronx Region, Data Set 2.

How do you argue with that?

TWELVE

Quantifying the Unquantifiable

If you only have a hammer, you tend to see every problem as a nail.

—ABRAHAM MASLOW

Before RAND's studies, the FDNY had measured fire coverage the same way since the days when straining firemen pulled coal-powered steam engines along cobblestone streets ("since the days of the white mice," Steve Isenberg might have said): by looking at "external" measures of success, like the number of fatalities and injuries, or the value of damaged property. When the numbers seemed low, firemen patted themselves on the back. When the numbers seemed high, they asked the city for money to hire more men, buy better rigs, and build new houses. Minimizing deaths and damage are a fire department's reason for being, but are difficult to translate into systems analysis because they are subject to so many random variables. By external measures, the jump in firefighter deaths from eight in 1965 to eighteen in 1966 makes it look like the department's safety procedures were going rapidly downhill. In fact, safety had improved markedly under new Chief O'Hagan, but, by chance, an unpredictable variable—the basement extended beneath the Wonder Drug store on 23rd Street—killed as many firemen in an instant as had died in the line of duty in the previous two years. Remove a single day from 1966, and the department's fatality rate would have dropped by 25 percent instead of rising 125 percent.

In some ways, gauging fire coverage is a bit like judging a pitcher. A pitcher's basic job is to limit the other team's offense enough that his own team can score more runs and win the game—so it would seem that an external measurement like a pitcher's win-loss record is the best indicator of how he performed in a given season. But a pitcher's win-loss record is so dependent upon factors that are completely out of his control (namely, how many runs his own team scores) that more internal measurements are needed. One of the first developed was earned run average (ERA), the average number of earned (i.e., not caused by a fielder's error) runs a pitcher gives up for every nine innings he pitches. Ultimately, the external result—how many games a pitcher wins and loses—is the most important thing to a team, but by gauging a key internal statistic, ERA gives a fairly accurate indication of which pitchers are the most likely to give the best external results.

The internal statistic RAND chose to measure was response time, the lag between when an alarm is called in and when a fire company arrives at the alarm box. RAND's job was to determine the best location for fire units, so response time was a natural choice: it could be easily quantified—just hand out stopwatches to the lieutenants—and the variances would show which areas were the best protected and which the least. From there the researchers could use the same playbook RAND's Albert Wohlstetter had laid out years earlier with his SAC basing study: build a model of when and where fire alarms occur and how quickly they are responded to, run it under various conditions (open a company here, close a company there), and determine the most efficient way to allocate companies.

Internal measures of success, though, are useful only when they have a strong correlation with the more important external measures. Earned run average is a far-from-perfect statistic, but the fewer runs a pitcher gives up, the more games he's likely to win. The problem with response time is that a fire company's job goes far beyond getting from the

firehouse to the alarm box. Firemen need to find which building the fire
is in, coordinate with other companies, gain access to the fire, rescue
anyone stuck inside, stretch and hook up hoses, prevent the fire from
spreading, and put it out, and how quickly they do this varies from
neighborhood to neighborhood and building to building. In poor
neighborhoods in particular—where aging buildings spread the flames
faster, overcrowding meant more potential victims, and heavy doors
and bars installed on the windows to prevent break-ins made access
difficult—driving was often just a fraction of the time spent before a
company could actually fight the fire.

RAND realized the problems with relying solely on response time, and
researcher Ed Ignall later wrote a memo to seventeen fellow researchers
and FDNY officials, laying out the difficulties: "We do not have good
measures of the extent of fire when fire companies arrive . . . delays in
discovering fires are sometimes long, sometimes short . . . Some fires
grow quickly, others grow slowly," and he warned that "effects like these
can cripple a naive approach to estimating the value of response time."

Here RAND faced a crucial decision. Their studies were predicated on
the assumption that they could build models that accurately represented
how the fire department worked in reality. Response time was easy to
measure and model, but it fell far short of representing all the factors
that go into fighting a fire. Another statistic, "firefighting flex time," was
much more useful, measuring the time between when an alarm comes in
and when firefighters actually began fighting the fire, but was harder to
gather: expecting a fireman to check a stopwatch as his rig pulled up to
an alarm box was one thing, asking him to check it as the water started
gurgling from the hose under his arm was another. The other reason
flex time was a better measure of firefighting—because it was as variable
and inconsistent as real life—also made it much harder to convert into
a model. So RAND made a fateful choice: gather the response-time
data, model it to the best of their abilities, and put their concerns about
response time's shortcomings to the side.

Within the broader field of systems analysis, this weakness—having to ignore certain realities because they are too complex to quantify—is so common that it even has a philosophical justification. Simple models, the conventional wisdom of the field holds, are better than complex models, because it's harder to keep track of all the moving parts in a complex model. This is true enough, but it raises the question: If modeling can't handle complexity, why bother with it in the first place?

"With RAND, they would start off with these very ambitious plans for simulation and then end up with something you could do on the back of an envelope," says Matthew Crenson, a professor of political science at Johns Hopkins, who studied NYC-RAND for his Ph.D. dissertation on the use of analytic models in public policy. "That's all they had time for. They wanted answers right away and they wanted to help Chief O'Hagan."

For all the data-gathering and complicated modeling that was to come, RAND was building its elaborate castle on a foundation of sand—the deeply flawed assumption that modeling response time was the same as modeling firefighting operations as a whole. It's a common mistake made by modelers. In fact, just a few years earlier, McNamara's Whiz Kids entered the Vietnam War working under a similarly flawed assumption. To model the Vietnam conflict, they viewed the war in Vietnam as a "war of attrition," with each side exacting "blood and treasure" from the other until the weaker side sued for peace. To measure the success of a war of attrition, all they had to do was calculate how much damage the United States was inflicting, how much they were receiving in turn, model the two outputs to determine more efficient inputs (battle plans, troop movements), and adjust strategy accordingly. Except that Vietnam wasn't a war of attrition—Vietnamese Communists were willing to fight to the last man standing. Communist leader Ho Chi Minh said as much to the French colonial forces he fought before fighting the United States: "You can kill ten of our men for every one we kill of yours. But even at those odds, you will lose and we will win." Yet a war of attrition was the only conflict the Whiz Kids could model, so they ignored the realities on the ground and charged ahead.

Basing their work on flawed assumptions turns out to be the greatest weakness of systems analysts, and—along with faulty data, the information gap and culture divide between modelers and the systems they are trying to model, and political influence—one of the four most common weaknesses of analysts when trying to model complicated systems. It's almost a function of psychology—among the first things a new schoolteacher learns on the job is that right-brained, creatively oriented students are more likely to ask all sorts of annoying questions when they're given a task: Why are we doing this? Shouldn't we be studying X instead of Y? But left-brained, analytically inclined students are more likely to take an assignment at face value and go to work on it—it's the process that fascinates them, not the broader issues surrounding it.*

While RAND's researchers were ultimately responsible for their flawed assumptions, it's a bit like expecting a cement-truck driver to ponder whether building new roads is the best way to alleviate the nation's transportation problems—thinking about that isn't his job, and thinking it out loud might actually get him fired. Ultimately, RAND's analysts were modelers, number-crunchers. Response time could be modeled, and so they modeled it. Veterans like O'Hagan or RAND's liaison with the department, Chief Homer Bishop, were in a much better position to judge the usefulness of response time than firefighting neophytes like the RAND analysts, but they signed off on the project and it moved forward.

NYC-RAND's next step was to hand out stopwatches to a small number of companies and use those times to predict how quickly fire companies as a whole responded to fires. Sampling is nothing unusual in social science research—the kind of thing pollsters do before an election—and with a large and representative sample, the results can be

---

*The same process has occurred on Wall Street, where the recent financial crisis has revealed that a number of previously successful financial models rested on a handful of shaky assumptions (like perpetually rising real estate values, or credit markets that never seize up), which caused massive losses when the economic conditions changed.

extremely accurate. But RAND distributed watches to only fifteen of the FDNY's nearly four hundred units, ten of them in Manhattan, one in the Bronx, and two each in Brooklyn and Queens. Of the fifteen units, two were chiefs' cars and thirteen were ladder trucks. So RAND's sample didn't take into account the fire engines that were the bulk of the FDNY's companies and vastly underrepresented the boroughs with the largest population (Brooklyn), landmass (Queens), and highest fire rates (the Bronx). Even the ten Manhattan companies were skewed, all of them located downtown.

A bigger problem with the response-time studies was the second major weakness of analytic modeling systems: faulty data. Bad information is, of course, a problem with studies of every stripe, but there's no soft-pedaling or room for gray areas in model-building: either you use the numbers you have, or you don't. And because most models are multilayered, even a tiny discrepancy can create exponentially larger inaccuracies when the model is completed and run. RAND researchers were proud of the time they spent "in the field," and the rapport they developed with headquarters brass like O'Hagan and Chief Homer Bishop. "It was in our nature," says RAND's Peter Kolesar. "We were academics with a very real-world orientation. We slept overnight in the fire stations, went on calls. There was a lot of work out in the field to help get a sense for the problems."

That there would be some ball-breaking and even genuine suspicion as soon as firemen "took one look at this dimpled kid about twenty-three years old, with glasses that looked like milk-bottle bottoms and hair down to his shoulders," is natural. (One fire chief tacked up a poster of a bikini-clad woman under the heading "The RAND Model" in his office.) But firemen were so suspicious of RAND that some of them sabotaged the response-time data. "We never trusted them," says one fireman. "These were efficiency-expert types. We figured they were there to close houses, why would we give guys like that information?" Some officers reported faster response times to look good. Others reported slower times to make the company look overworked. A few left the stopwatches behind the wheels of their rigs and let gravity do the rest, ignoring or making up times after the fact.

With a little more historical knowledge of their own field, RAND might have avoided the faulty-data problem. During World War II, the Navy operations-research team charged with improving attacks on U-boats used a series of post-mission questionnaires filled out by flight crews to study their search patterns. Sending a team of researchers out into the field, they realized the bomber crews tended to fill out the forms haphazardly when they returned to base. "Hell, I didn't think anyone ever read those damned reports," one pilot told them. Able to convince flight crews that the forms were important, the researchers used the new, accurate data to revamp search patterns and drastically improve mission success rates.

Along with flawed assumptions and faulty data, this brings up the third major problem with modeling systems, the information gap and sometimes cultural divide between modelers and who or what they are trying to model. The Navy's operations researchers—men who had devoted their lives to numbers—assumed that weary flight crews would show the same devotion when they filled out their questionnaires. They were able to overcome this obstacle by going out in the field, realizing their mistake, and convincing airmen it was to their benefit to fill out the forms accurately. But RAND never learned from their predecessors' mistakes. RAND did have some inkling that there were problems with the data. They knew the union was against the stopwatches and went to great pains to subvert the studies—RAND's Peter Kolesar later wrote in a paper on the fire studies that "some stopwatches were thrown against firehouse walls or dropped mysteriously off the fire trucks." In an e-mail message, he writes that "the participating companies certainly did not meet our own criteria for an optimal experimental design. . . . We had to take what we could get, and we had to live with deliberate malicious actions to undercut the experiment. . . . Alas, so it is in the real world." After eliminating some times that they thought were incorrect, RAND moved on to their real field of expertise, turning data into models.

RAND's next step was to use the years' worth of fire reports O'Hagan had been keeping to build a "simulation model" of when and where fires broke out, and how quickly units could respond to those fires. The model was essentially an early version of the computer game SimCity, with RAND, as the game's player, coming up with new firehouse configurations to try to minimize response times.* Predicting fire rates was a problem in and of itself. As any investor will tell you, past performance is no guarantee of future results, particularly when it comes to predicting something like the rapidly changing fire rates in the Bronx. The shortcomings of using response times and the faulty response-time data were put on the back burner when RAND's simulation model turned out to be too complex for contemporary computers to handle (this was a time when the computer game Pong was still years away from development), making it impractically slow and expensive to run.

To cope with the setback, RAND hoped to re-create the behavior of the simulation model with a pair of "analytic models," equations that could be calculated much more easily than the simulations could be run. RAND broke Manhattan, Queens, Brooklyn, and the Bronx (suburban Staten Island was modeled separately) into twenty-one different regions. The first model calculated how quickly fire companies would respond to fires, and showed response-time discrepancies from region to region. Once it was determined which regions should gain or lose a company, the second model would show where within those regions companies should be opened and closed to most efficiently respond to fires. Politically, this would be difficult to do; no one wants the local firehouse closed or moved, but RAND was concerned only with efficiency, not politics. Until, that is, they weren't.

The best way to cut response time is to put as many fire companies as close to as many fires as possible. Let's say two fire companies are moved from neighborhood A, which has three thousand fires per year,

---

*SimCity was actually inspired by the work of MIT professor Jay Forrester, one of the first systems analysts to use computers to simulate complex systems like urban economies and real estate markets. Forrester, it turned out, produced similarly naive studies. His model of urban real estate markets, for example, failed to include the suburbs—the predominant influence on mid-twentieth-century urban growth—as a factor in any of its calculations.

to neighborhood B, which has fifteen thousand blazes. Even if this raises response times in neighborhood A by thirty seconds and drops them by only twenty seconds in B, the greater number of fires in B means that the *average* response time will drop, exactly the kind of efficient reallocation of resources one would expect RAND to want. But this kind of fire-company clustering means moving units from low-demand, often wealthy neighborhoods, into high-demand, almost invariably poor neighborhoods. "The residents of the low-demand region probably would not stand for such a poor level of service," wrote RAND's Warren Walker. "They pay their taxes (in fact, they probably pay more taxes than the people in the high-demand area) and they are entitled to a reasonable level of service. It would seem that they are being penalized for being careful and having few fires." There's some validity to the point, but it's interesting that researchers, who never voiced similar concerns at the myriad factors in their models that put poor, high-demand regions at a disadvantage, were so sensitive to the single disadvantage faced by the middle- and upper-class residents of low-demand regions, who "would not stand" for it (and, being middle and upper class, had the power to fight back).

This concern led RAND to put each of the twenty-one regions into one of seven "hazard categories" ("valuable commercial," "high-density high fire-hazard residential," etc.) and compare only regions from the same category. This meant that RAND was no longer trying to balance fire coverage throughout the city, only between neighborhoods it deemed similar, and this became the primary reason for the irrational recommendations the models eventually came up with: ghetto neighborhoods lost companies not because their regions were necessarily better served than the city as a whole, but because they were better served than other regions in the same hazard category (in most cases, were other underserved ghetto neighborhoods). Sleepy suburban neighborhoods in places like Staten Island and commercial districts gained companies because they were underserved not compared with the rest of the city, but compared with other (often overserved, at least in comparison with places like the South Bronx) suburban and commercial districts.

The problems didn't end there. In RAND's reports a variety of graphs show an almost perfect correlation between the actual response times they collected and the equation that predicted response times. But, writes William Corrigan, whose Ph.D. dissertation examined and re-created the RAND studies, "this excellent fit is illusory." The problem was that RAND didn't show actual response times, just *averaged* response times, thus eliminating all the outliers and other wrinkles in the data. As Corrigan puts it, "Using only the means [i.e., average] can lead to misleading interpretations of the . . . model, specifically, that it fits the data much more closely than, in fact, it does."

One of RAND's analytic models assumed that in the most congested city in America, traffic played no role in response time, rigs able to cruise through Midtown Manhattan at rush hour at the same speed as through Queens at midnight.* It also assumed that fire units were always available to respond to an alarm directly from their firehouse, a rarity in places like the Bronx, where every company in a neighborhood, sometimes in the entire borough, could be out fighting fires at the same time. The assumption that all companies were always available explains why the FLAME committee second sections were singled out for closure. According to the model, second sections, which were called into service only when the first section was out on a call, appeared to be useless—a reflection of RAND and O'Hagan's previous assumptions but a reversal of reality. The models also downplayed the importance of companies on the edges of the regions RAND broke the city into. These units responded to alarms in neighboring areas as well, but RAND treated each region as an island unto itself, underestimating border companies' usefulness.

Strangely enough, RAND's faith in these analytic models may be

---

*The source of this assumption was the faulty response-time data. Because the data was taken mostly from Manhattan neighborhoods, RAND found only "small variations . . . in different regions of the city," small enough, in their minds, to justify assuming that "the average velocity for a given distance is almost constant throughout the city." And although "average response velocities vary somewhat by time of day," RAND found, the variances within their undersized, unrepresentative sample were small enough to "be ignored for many planning purposes."

rooted in the failure of their original simulation model. There's an old modeler's dictum that's the rough equivalent of "missing the forest for the trees": solving the equation doesn't necessarily solve the problem. It's a warning about the tendency of modelers to become so wrapped up in the complicated process of building a model that they can forget that the model isn't necessarily a perfect stand-in for reality. It's a saying RAND would have done well to remember. According to RAND reports, when analysts ran the slow, expensive simulation model to compare the results with the analytic models, the two matched almost perfectly, perhaps confirming the accuracy of the analytic models in the researchers' minds, despite the fact that the original simulation model was itself based on questionable data and faulty assumptions.

Had the analysts taken a step back from the models, perhaps they would have thought there was something fishy about closing companies in the most fire-prone neighborhoods in the country and opening them in Staten Island. But lost in a modeler's world that was increasingly divorced from reality, the fire project had "stepped through the looking glass," as RAND physicist Sam Cohen once said of his colleagues who worked on systems analysis, "where people did the weirdest things and [used] the most perverse kind of logic imaginable and yet claimed to have the most precise understanding of everything . . . because it all sounded so damn rational and so damn reasonable as to be unassailable."

There was certainly reason to be proud of the studies. No one had ever attempted to even quantify government services in such a large-scale manner, and RAND had then gone two steps further, using those quantifications to predict future trends and recommend policy steps. To O'Hagan, it was the culmination of his dream of rationalizing the bureaucracy and turning it from a reactive to a proactive entity. For RAND researchers, years of political battles, budget shortfalls, frustrating setbacks, and, most important, painstaking work, had finally come to fruition.

Their colleagues agreed, with RAND publishing a score of well-received papers, winning the prestigious Lanchester Prize in Mathematics "for the best contribution to operations research and the management sciences," second place in the Franz Edelman competition (known in the field as "the Super Bowl of operations research"), and a NATO Systems Science Prize. In the burgeoning academic field of emergency-response service, the models became foundational studies. HUD paid RAND to translate their models for other cities around the country.* Insurance adjusters used them to determine the level of fire coverage (and thus set fire-insurance rates) around the country, which, in turn, led cities to conform their fire-service patterns to the models to bring those rates down.

But the accolades and influence had less to do with the actual value of the models than with an intellectual vacuum. Because no one had ever performed such studies before, there was no way for the RAND models to be comprehensively checked by fellow experts. Fire experts didn't have the requisite quantitative training, and the only systems analysts and modelers who'd ever studied fire departments were on the RAND fire project. Like Albert Wohlstetter's SAC basing study, RAND's sterling reputation and the researchers' confident tone and clever equations were enough to convince people that the models were accurate.†

When they heard serious technical criticism, the RAND team didn't take it seriously. In the late 1970s, husband-and-wife research scientists Deborah and Rodrick Wallace, who received copies of RAND's reports from the fire officers' union, published numerous critiques of the studies in academic journals. Instead of refuting the Wallaces' technical criticisms, RAND wrote them off as leftist ideologues with an axe to grind. This was in many ways true—the Wallaces accused RAND and the Lindsay

---

*Through HUD, the RAND models were sold to cities throughout the country, including St. Louis, Washington, Tampa, Denver, Wilmington, Hartford, Jersey City, Hoboken, and Tacoma. None of those cities used the models to cut fire service as deeply as New York, but cuts were made and a number of the cities experienced serious fire problems. In particular, Jersey City, which received an influx of fire refugees from New York in the late 1970s, watched as even its city hall burned in 1979.

†As William Corrigan wrote in his Ph.D. dissertation critiquing the models: "The glaring omission concerning the . . . model is the lack of critical analysis of the model itself. Seemingly, the intuitive appeal is so great that many do not question its effectiveness."

administration of being part of a malicious attempt to burn down poor neighborhoods. In reality RAND researchers had noble intentions and thought their work was doing some real good for the fire department.

"We thought we were going to save the city," says NYC-RAND's Arthur Swersey, who also worked on what turned out to be a very successful revamping of the department's dispatching process. "Many of us would have never worked on a military project for RAND . . . we were liberals who really wanted to help."

But while the Wallace's political claims may have been baseless, their technical criticisms of the models, which RAND largely ignored, were largely correct. The same thing happened when the chief researcher at HUD (which had helped fund the fire project and purchased the studies from RAND) responded to a RAND report with some serious suggestions for improving it. A copy of the critique was passed around the RAND office and the margins quickly filled with dismissive comments, including a note next to the HUD researcher's name: "This is a female!"

IF RAND DID HAVE ANY DEEP-SEATED DOUBTS ABOUT THE accuracy of their work, they could rest assured that the decision about where to open and close companies rested with Chief O'Hagan, and RAND trusted the chief completely, even looked up to their boss. "He was a bigger-than-life guy," says RAND's Rae Archibald. "Big ego, big temper, very smart, and he let the other chiefs know it. But open to learning as well . . . I remember a class he was taking at Columbia University to get his MBA, and he would start talking about things, like, 'Rae, I learned a lot doing some stupid exercise on growing the hosiery business, do you know how the pantyhose industry started . . .' And charismatic in an old-fashioned way. He would lose his temper and yell, and then put his arm around you and say, 'Let's go have a drink!' "

As far as Archibald and his fellow researchers were concerned, if RAND's models suggested the wrong companies, O'Hagan and Chief Homer Bishop, who was more intimately involved with the studies, would know better and overrule them. "Ultimately, the decision was O'Hagan's," says one researcher. "Sometimes he took our advice and sometimes he didn't." O'Hagan was the preeminent firefighting expert in the city, maybe the whole country, and RAND trusted him to make decisions on the merits alone. "He was a great civil servant," says Archibald. "When John O'Hagan was chief, virtually no politics were involved in decision-making."

But O'Hagan was far from the impartial civil servant that RAND and Mayor Lindsay thought he was. Political and personal biases weighed on the chief as heavily as anyone, and as his luck would have it, the flaws in the RAND model matched those biases perfectly. On the personal side, the FLAME committee and its second-section recommendations had been the biggest challenge to O'Hagan's authority since staff chiefs had kept him in the dark about the 23rd Street collapse. Thanks to RAND's studies, he did genuinely believe second sections were an inefficient use of resources, but this belief and his grudge against the FLAME committee blinded him to the second sections' very real value. When the RAND models came back saying they could be cut with little loss in fire coverage, he had every reason *not* to dig deeper and find out whether this was actually true.

"O'Hagan went after those [second] sections," says Chief Vincent Dunn, who worked under O'Hagan at FDNY headquarters at the time. "He was a good manager but *of course* personality gets in there. O'Hagan was tough and he wanted to go into the lion's den. If he made cuts in those busy neighborhoods, the union would know he was for real."

On the political side, O'Hagan was staking out a reputation as one of the most intelligent, progressive bureaucrats in the business. He'd been the youngest fire chief in department history and now, seven years into the job and still just forty-six years old, he was primed for something bigger: fire commissioner, maybe even electoral politics. The key to any promotion, though, would be helping the mayor and maintaining his own reputation as a hard-nosed, efficient manager. To do that, O'Hagan needed to make cuts and—to avoid stepping on any politically influential toes—needed to make them in politically weak neighborhoods. The RAND models recommended doing just that, and gave him the political cover of being able to blame the closings on scientific studies that were out of his hands—after all, who could argue with numbers?

And O'Hagan believed in RAND himself. They were bringing to the fire department exactly the kind of proactive, statistically driven, professional management style he had long dreamed of. Part of RAND's very appeal was that they often turned up counterintuitive recommendations—if that meant closing companies in busy neighborhoods, so be it. While RAND's recommendations generally aligned with O'Hagan's political interests, even when they didn't, he chose political concerns over statistical accuracy. O'Hagan was too smart to ever tell the researchers which houses he wanted closed and which left open. "But," admits RAND's Rae Archibald, who was later hired as an assistant fire commissioner, "there was no question that where the commissioner kept his car was not a house that was going to be closed. . . . If the models came back saying one thing and [O'Hagan] didn't like it, he would make you run it again and check, run it again and check."

When the results still didn't come back to his liking, O'Hagan's men handled the problem. "Mostly we used [the RAND models] for the cuts, but if they came back saying to close a house in a certain neighborhood, well . . . if you try to close a firehouse down the block from where a judge lived, you couldn't get away with it," says retired chief Elmer Chapman, who ran the department's Bureau of Planning and Operations Research, which worked with RAND and, in later years, ran the models after NYC-RAND was shuttered. In those cases, continues Chapman, you could simply skip down the list of closings to a company in a poor neighborhood. The models said there were less painful cuts to be made, "but the people in those [poorer] neighborhoods didn't have a very big voice."

As Chapman pointed out, though, O'Hagan rarely needed to ignore RAND's recommendations, because for the most part, RAND suggested closing exactly the kinds of companies the chief wanted to cut: FLAME second sections and militantly pro-union companies in the South Bronx, where there weren't any politicians or businessmen powerful enough to make a stink about the closings.

As for Mayor Lindsay, if he'd ever looked closely at the cuts, he might have questioned them. But he was busy dealing with the broader issues of the city and preparing for his own run for the presidency. He didn't know much about the Bronx, and knew less about systems analysis and fire. O'Hagan and RAND's assurances that he could trot out the first round of scientifically determined policies he'd dreamed of for so long, cut budgets, and not hurt fire coverage in the process was more than enough for him. Beyond the initial request for budget cuts, the mayor's office had almost nothing to do with how those savings were achieved, leaving it up to O'Hagan and RAND.

"I decided that neither I nor my [budget] engineers knew [as much about the fire department budget as Chief O'Hagan]," says David Grossman, former assistant to Fred Hayes, who was budget director at the time of the cuts. "Most commissioners I would not make that statement about, but with the kind of collaborative relationship that we had [with O'Hagan] there was really no problem."

"It was a reflection of the enormous regard everybody held John O'Hagan in at City Hall and throughout city government," says Anthony Smith, who was the mayor's office liaison to the fire department. "O'Hagan ran that department so completely and was so knowledgeable. . . . [Issues like which houses to close] were left to him."

Political influences on how the models were used—along with faulty assumptions, bad data, and information and cultural gaps between modelers and who or what's being modeled—rounds out the four most common flaws in purely quantitative attempts to understand and model complex situations. "There's the big irony of research," says Professor Matthew Crenson. "Anytime an issue is important enough to justify research, there are enough interests out there that will influence things." Sometimes that influence comes in the form of out-and-out fraud, as happened with firefighters who lied about response times, O'Hagan's willingness to close companies not recommended by RAND when the political situation called for it, and in Vietnam, where military brass faked the "body count" of enemy soldiers to give McNamara and his Whiz Kids a rosier view of the supposed war of attrition than was accurate.

More often, that influence doesn't come in the form of malfeasance but rather ignorance-inducing wishful thinking. Like football fans watching a penalty-filled football game, people have an extraordinary ability to see what they want to see. RAND and Lindsay wanted to believe O'Hagan was an apolitical civil servant. O'Hagan wanted to believe that RAND's studies were accurate and that he really could cut budgets, close houses he held a grudge against, and not significantly hurt fire coverage. Lindsay wanted to believe that the kind of whiz-bang, scientific management of the bureaucracy that he'd long hoped for was finally coming to fruition. And in all three cases, they weren't just *fans* of these ideas, their jobs *depended* on them. And so, everyone involved was willing to look the other way as plans to close busy fire stations went into effect while the neighborhoods around them burned to the ground.

The closings go into effect.
(Photo courtesy New York *Daily News*)

THIRTEEN

A Disproportionate Share
of the Economies

To err is human—and to blame it on a computer is even more so.

—ROBERT ORBEN

When the company closings were announced in the fall of 1972, they were met with pro forma outcries from the fire unions. In a column for the civil-service newspaper *The Chief*, UFA President Michael Maye told the old fable of the farmer who saves money by giving his mule one less handful of hay each day, until the mule keels over dead, the surprised farmer exclaiming, "Just when we had him down to a full days' [*sic*] work without eating!" O'Hagan's predecessor as chief, Edward McAniff, stepped back into the spotlight to join a union lawsuit to stop the closings. "To the blacks and Hispanics living in poor, ghetto communities," he said, fire protection "is considerably inferior to that provided in the more affluent communities in the city, and is substantially below what I would consider to be the minimal level of necessary and essential protection of life, safety of a person, and property."

To O'Hagan's surprise, the uproar spread to the press and public. Part of the problem lay in City Hall's mixed message on the exact purpose of the cuts. The officials called the cuts a chance to increase productivity, but were forced to admit that saving money was part of the motivation. But if that was the case, why weren't other departments making similar cuts? And why were they targeted at the very neighborhoods that were burning?

Columnist Pete Hamill, one of the city's most influential journalists and certainly no knee-jerk union advocate, wrote that "the solution is more men, at whatever cost that might be," pointing out that the city was spending $3 million a year on graffiti removal and $15 million to add orange signals to traffic lights, but was only going to save $600,000 on each closing. One of the companies to be closed, Squad 6, he wrote, had suffered eighty-two fire fatalities in its Upper West Side and Harlem coverage area over the last seven years. Another story revealed that the department had spent $15,000 renovating a firehouse two months before announcing it was going to be closed, and installed a safety gate on the fire pole the day *after* the announcement. Even politicians were getting in on the act, with recently elected Queens Borough President Donald Manes calling the closings a dangerous gamble. But press speculation and public outrage were of little consequence. The independence of politicians like Lindsay is generally viewed as an asset, because they aren't bound to any of the corrupting influences of a major party. The flip side is that they are not accountable to the voices of reason within those parties either; Lindsay was able to ignore the protests of Democrats and Republicans alike as he eagerly awaited a few million dollars' breathing room in his budget.

All that could hold up the closings were the two lawsuits filed by the unions against the city, which claimed the cuts were racially motivated. That was where RAND's models came in. There is a classic economics experiment in which two volunteers are paired up and given $10. The "Proposer" gets to decide how the money will be split, and the "Responder" can either accept the offer or reject it, which will leave both of them penniless. Usually the Proposer goes the benevolent-dictator route and decides on an only somewhat skewed split, say $6 or $7 for himself, and the Responder agrees. When the Proposer gets greedy, giving himself $8 or more, the Responder generally rejects the deal, and neither gets anything. But when told that the split has been decided by a computer, the Responder tends to assume the divvying up to be the unbiased findings of a machine and takes what's given, no matter how uneven the split. Therein lay the strength of the city's case for the fire closings. The unions claimed the city was unfairly targeting black and Puerto Rican neighborhoods, but RAND could provide reams of jargony technical reasoning and complicated equations that gave the whole process the air of impartiality. The judge concluded that the cuts were based on "exhaustive analysis," not race, and threw the lawsuit out. Five thousand people showed up to a union protest on the steps of City Hall, but the decision had been made and the cuts went through.

When the South Bronx's Engine 88-2 was closed in the winter of 1972, its first section, 88-1, nearly doubled its number of working fires, jumping from the thirty-ninth busiest engine in the city to sixteenth. When nearby Ladder 27-2 was closed, 27-1 went from twenty-ninth to twelfth. The Brooklyn neighborhood of Bushwick was filled with blocks of row houses built with "common cocklofts"—shared attic space that ran the entire length of the block.* With no fire-stop between buildings, a few seconds delay in response time could mean the difference between a fire that was contained to the second story of a building, and one that got up into the cockloft and burned out a whole block. Having already lost a TCU the year before, Bushwick lost Engine 217-2 in the 1972 cuts, and Engine 217-1's number of workers rose 128 percent, moving it from the 126th to thirty-first busiest engine. In nearby East New York, Engine 233's number of workers rose by 70 percent after 233-2 was closed.

WHILE THE SOUTH BRONX AND CENTRAL BROOKLYN BURNED in 1973, Lindsay was wrapping up his mayoral career. He had swept into office with such great expectations in 1965—New York's answer to JFK, intent on cleaning up government, revolutionizing the bureaucracy,

---

*Theories on the etymology of "cockloft" vary, from "cock" as a term for bales of hay stored in the space, to the practice of keeping a rooster there at night as a fire alarm.

and bringing the verve and vigor back to the Rotting Apple. In the eight years since, the city had been rocked by race riots, spiraling rates of crime, drug abuse, unemployment, welfare, and, of course, fires. Lindsay himself looked like a beaten man, his face lined and hair grayed by his two tumultuous terms. While Lindsay is generally blamed for these troubles, many were far beyond his control, the result of decades of bad economic and urban planning locally; national economic, racial, and violence problems; and major cuts in federal funding for city programs after Nixon was elected and the War on Poverty disassembled. Even worse, he was sure to be replaced by the same Democratic wheelhorse he'd beaten eight years before, Abe Beame—who was running largely unopposed in the general election after a close Democratic primary victory—and already promising to undo most of Lindsay's bureaucratic reforms. But Lindsay made sure to bequeath his most important administrative reformer to the new administration, elevating John T. O'Hagan to commissioner on September 11, 1973, after Robert Lowery, Lindsay's longest-serving appointee, stepped down. O'Hagan also retained his role as chief of department, only the second man to wear both hats since the department was turned from a volunteer outfit to a professional force in the 1860s.

While there'd been increasing rancor between O'Hagan and the unions over the closings, his reputation for professionalism led some to hope for a thaw in labor relations.* Many still thought of him as the same no-nonsense professional who'd only become chief because the threat of a union lawsuit prevented the city from passing him over for the job. But O'Hagan had changed over the last nine years. He missed all but one of the first five funerals given for firemen after his promotion to commissioner. Once he had pursued power in order to enact reforms and save lives, but increasingly he sought power for its own sake. The transformation was

---

*O'Hagan went to great lengths to keep his fingerprints off the 1972 closings, with Lindsay and Lowery taking nearly all the heat. Even union higher-ups like Chief Alfred Benway, who had publicly blamed everyone but O'Hagan for the closings, didn't realize his central role in them.

slight at first, but noticeable to those who worked with him closely. "The way he spoke, the words he used, started to change," says one retired chief who worked with O'Hagan at headquarters. "Before, he talked like a manager, 'efficiency,' 'modernization,' things like that. But more and more he talked about power, politics, things like that. His vocabulary was different." There was a change in the way he carried himself as well, donning the suit and tie of a civilian commissioner over the uniform of a chief. "He always used to tell me, 'They look down on you in the uniform,'" says Captain Sandy Sansevero, whom O'Hagan hired as his executive assistant when he became commissioner. "The politicians didn't see uniformed guys as professionals, so he didn't wear the uniform."

Still smarting from the TCU closings, eager to assert his own "more with less" philosophy, and fill the power void left by lame-duck Lindsay, O'Hagan made a stand on contract negotiations just weeks after his promotion. Using inside information from O'Hagan and his source in the union hierarchy, city negotiators reneged on a last-minute deal they'd struck with the unions, prompting a department-wide strike that lasted a few hours, both sides fortunate no serious blazes broke out in the interim. Despite some serious miscalculations by O'Hagan, which instigated the strike, the union suffered nearly all of the negative PR, and after the mayoral election, Beame kept his fellow Brooklyn Democrat O'Hagan on as commissioner. And once again, RAND's models proved vulnerable to the fourth major weakness of modeling systems: political influence. In a perhaps less-than-subtle retaliatory move for the strike, O'Hagan closed two more second sections, including Engine 41-2, the home of union president Dick Vizzini, just as he'd closed the second section in former union president Michael Maye's old house after Maye killed the TCU program.

To that point, the RAND cuts had been a remarkably effective tool for O'Hagan. Within the department, they showed the unions that he was willing "to go into the lion's den," and close busy units, as Chief Vincent Dunn put it. More broadly, they helped O'Hagan cut budgets, curry enough favor with Mayor Lindsay to pass Local Law 5 and become commissioner, and helped further cultivate his rock-solid reputation as an efficient manager who could be counted on for loyalty.

With the union on its heels and his job as commissioner secure, O'Hagan was ready to stop the fire company closings. Because their recommendations were so neatly aligned with his own interests, O'Hagan had shown more faith in the RAND models than he perhaps should have, but he was too savvy a fireman to think he could continue closing ghetto fire companies indefinitely while the neighborhoods around them burned. The day after O'Hagan announced he was closing Engine 41-2 in Vizzini's old house, a fire in Bushwick killed a young mother, her son, and her six-month-old daughter. The deaths, said Vizzini, were the result of a slow response after the recent closing of nearby Engine 217-2. Ten days later, another fire broke out just a few blocks away. Two police officers spotted the blaze and evacuated all the residents, but firemen couldn't contain the flames before they reached the common cockloft and spread in both directions down the block, burning ten buildings and leaving fifty people homeless on one of the coldest nights of the year.

Along with cutting more than a dozen companies and a 20 percent reduction in manpower thanks to the hiring freeze that had been in effect since 1971, the toll for years of shoddy upkeep on rigs, fire hydrants, and other equipment was finally coming due. Each of the department's sixteen thousand street-side alarm boxes was supposed to be inspected every sixty days, but cuts left them uninspected for upward of seven years. More than five hundred were rendered inoperable by a single snowstorm. In March 1974, after a malfunctioning alarm delayed firemen more than twenty minutes, five-year-old Christa Solo was pulled from her burning home alive but died en route to the hospital. A sixty-five-year-old Queens man had died under similar circumstances a month earlier, but because he held on in the hospital for a few days, the death wasn't technically considered a fire fatality. "Almost every day, a citizen claims he pulls a box and gets no response," dispatcher Richard Hanrahan complained. "Believe it or not, we've even had people pull a false alarm and complain that nobody came."

"It's possible that with fourteen thousand boxes, we have some that are out," O'Hagan told a reporter. "But I wouldn't suspect any large number." In reality, there were sixteen thousand boxes and thousands of them were malfunctioning, but when budget cuts and faulty equipment were the undeniable cause of death for an elderly man and five-year-old girl, the commissioner had little choice but to downplay and dissemble.

Some of RAND's innovations that were supposed to make up for closing companies and cutting manpower were falling flat. RAND's most publicized advance was "slippery water," a process of adding a polymer to the water in a fire engine, which reduced friction enough to pump the same amount of water through thinner, lighter hoses, requiring fewer men on each company to carry the heavy hoses. Unfortunately, the water turned out to be a bit too slippery, causing firemen to slip and fall at fire scenes, and the program was discontinued after a few trial runs (the manpower cuts, however, continued).

The next technical development involved fire alarm boxes. With traditional mechanical fire boxes, when the alarm was pulled, it transmitted a signal to dispatchers, who then sent out fire crews. As part of the adaptive response plan, RAND recommended installing call-box alarms that let callers tell dispatchers about the size of the fire. To justify the expensive new boxes, RAND pointed out that very few people called in false alarms on the phone, the vast majority coming from alarm boxes. But they were confusing causation with correlation: people didn't call in false alarms because telephones are in people's homes and could be traced (although they never were).

Veteran dispatchers and firemen thought the boxes were a terrible idea. "It's a toy," fire marshal Tony Keisel said of the voice alarms. "And now the toy on the street talks back to you." Early testing of the boxes confirmed their suspicions, but the new call boxes were part of a broader efficiency plan to cut back responses further. RAND and O'Hagan's comprehensively-plan-and-charge-ahead root approach didn't leave much room for the kind of rethinking the faulty boxes required, so RAND hid the problem by calling the false alarms "diverted alarms," and recommended the boxes be installed throughout the city. False alarms rose sevenfold where the new boxes were installed, and to deal with the explosive rise in prank calls, dispatchers began ignoring "no-voice contact" alarms altogether. But this led to many legitimate fires' being missed or ignored, including one fatal fire when a deaf and mute child in East Harlem was unable to communicate through the voice box and no fire crews were sent.

The new technology was also prone to mechanical failure. After the FDNY spent $8 million (more than the annual operating cost of all the closed companies) installing a thousand new boxes, they had to replace every one of them because of a wiring glitch. Lightning storms made the boxes send in false alarms, sometimes dozens coming in simultaneously, leaving dispatchers to guess which were real and which were false. Operating on an electrical system akin to Christmas lights, when one voice box was activated, every other box on that circuit—usually twenty to thirty boxes, but often running closer to a hundred—went inoperable, and fires were left to burn without dispatchers realizing it.

In New York's poorer quarters, fires were morphing from a serious problem to a defining element of life. Entire blocks went from crowded to uninhabited in a matter of months. On the Lower East Side of Manhattan, the constant din of sirens was so loud in the evening that people scheduled their phone calls for the afternoon and late at night.

"You'd go up on the roof of a building after a fire and look out around you and see another fire here, another fire there, they were just everywhere," says South Bronx fire captain Tom Henderson. "The Bronx was fucking anarchy at the time, like the Wild West, and nobody gave a shit."

Something needed to be done, and, given the adequate time, incentives, and money, there was no one more qualified to handle the problem than John O'Hagan. But that was not to be the fate of the commissioner, or the poor neighborhoods of New York.

To Beame and the county Democratic organizations, O'Hagan was an ideal commissioner: a respected, competent administrator who had paid his political dues, could be counted on for a favor, and knew how to play the game of municipal politics. What's more, he was ambitious. That was usually the trouble with fire chiefs: they'd advanced as far as they'd ever imagined; with little to gain or lose, they were willing to fight City Hall for what they thought was best for the department. As a chief, O'Hagan had wanted to be commissioner and had proven himself amenable to political influence, and as commissioner he was still short of his goals. He wanted to see his reforms enacted across the bureaucracy, and to attain the kind of power necessary to do that, he needed to move on from the fire service. O'Hagan would have to start relatively low on the totem pole (deputy mayor in charge of civil service, city council), but, to make even that first step, Beame and the machine knew he needed their support and thus could be counted on to remain loyal, to go along to get along. Facing a growing budget gap in his first year in office in 1974, Beame called on his fire commissioner for help.

Traditionally, in a bureaucracy, mayors and politically appointed commissioners try to cut budgets, and civil-service chiefs try to increase them. *Chief* O'Hagan had tried to change the rules of the game by bringing efficiency to his department like a commissioner or mayor, but it had upset the balance of power—by 1974, he knew how dangerous further closings would be, but he had shown off his budget-cutting, controversy-killing models, and now Beame expected *Commissioner* O'Hagan to use them.

"When you study the history of the bureaucracy," says Chief Vincent Dunn, "it's a little like the tides. When there's a rising tide and the government has money and the unions have clout, the government starts getting bloated and inefficient. It's just the nature of things. But O'Hagan was cutting when nobody else in city government was cutting, and the fire service doesn't get any consideration for the earlier cuts. Had he not interfered with the ebb and flow of bureaucracy, and let fire service become bloated when the rest of the bureaucracy was, things wouldn't have been as bad."

O'Hagan was now forced into the role he'd always disdained, a political commissioner trying to prevent cuts and still maintain his power within the machine. Beame's initial request for $26.9 million in savings, almost 10 percent of the department's entire budget, came as a shock to O'Hagan, and would have necessitated closing more than seventy companies and laying off more than 2,500 firemen (20 percent of uniformed personnel). Arguing for no cuts was out of the question; the best O'Hagan could hope for was to scale them back enough to stave off a disaster. Eventually, O'Hagan was able to persuade Beame to accept an $8.3 million cut that closed eight companies, two fire boats, a specialty division, and a "seventh man" program that assigned firemen from slow engine companies to work as extra bodies on overworked companies.

Once again, O'Hagan turned to RAND for help, but with the knowledge that this was his last opportunity to do so. Never a fan of Lindsay's pet project, Beame had renewed RAND's contract for another year to let them wrap up their studies and help O'Hagan with his cuts, but with the city's budget future looking bleak, it was clear the institute's days were numbered. RAND ran the models one last time, and came up with cuts that affected second sections and busy ghetto companies almost exclusively. Ladder 17-2, which worked along a stretch of the South Bronx's Mott Haven neighborhood known as "Gasoline Alley," was shuttered. In nearby East Harlem, Engine 91-2 was closed and 91-1 more than quadrupled its number of workers, going from the 107th to the fourth busiest engine company in the entire city. A few blocks away, Ladder 26-2 was closed and 26-1 went from the top fifty to the top ten over the next four years. Engine 50-1 in the South Bronx went from 1,934 workers in 1973 to 4,175 in 1975 after 50-2 was closed. In East New York, the sixth-busiest ladder company in the entire city, 103-2, was closed. "The closing of the second section made a big difference," says fireman Joe Dirks, who worked in Ladder 103. "It was a big help to have two trucks and additional manpower on the scene . . . but the department needed to make cuts. It was just terrible to see, though, the whole neighborhood just deteriorated so quickly." Other neighborhoods were hurt when fire companies were moved to cover the holes left by the closings. Ladder 43 in East Harlem was moved a half-mile south, still on the periphery of the neighborhood, but much closer to the tony Upper East Side. Ladder 58 in the South Bronx was moved more than a mile east, to the other side of Crotona Park, where neighborhoods gutted by Robert Moses' Cross Bronx Expressway were burning at a furious clip.

As they had with the 1972 cuts, the unions sued, saying they were racially targeted. And just as with the 1972 suit, testimony and reports from O'Hagan and RAND won the day. "The specific decision as to which fire companies would be eliminated," wrote U.S. District Court Judge John M. Cannella, "was premised solely upon the neutral, nonracial, scientific, and empirical data available. . . . That the ordered closings will take place in the areas in which they will, was, in the opinion of the Court, a fortuitous circumstance." RAND's technical jargon and reams of data seemed able to quell almost any dissent, leaving the firemen and community activists who questioned RAND's recommendations sounding like backyard mechanics questioning NASA rocket scientists. With tens of thousands of apartments burning to the ground each year, the *New York Times* editorial page came out heavily in favor of the closings, saying there was "no justification" for union complaints and citing one RAND analyst who said the cuts would have no serious impact on coverage.

But John O'Hagan no longer seemed so convinced. In an unexpected moment of candor with reporters, the commissioner gave a rare glimpse into his struggle with the scientifically determined budget cuts he had created and lost control of. The FDNY was "being asked to carry a disproportionate share of the economies," he told reporters. "We're cutting back because the city is in a desperate fiscal plight, and I don't think we had any alternative. If the mayor feels this is necessary to be done, then we're going to support the mayor. . . . We're very hopeful that this won't result in a loss of life. But I can't give a guarantee."

Sign of the times.
(Photo courtesy Allan Tannenbaum)

FOURTEEN

New Math

Because the city's structures are bony—city people live in buildings, not tents—the city itself resists these changes demanded of it. The very massiveness of its structures promises lack of adaptability. The solid buildings are so fireproof that city officials must plan conscious destruction as a preliminary to rebuilding. Catastrophic conflagrations can no longer be depended on to remove obsolescences even though these accidents served New York, Chicago, and San Francisco so effectively in the past. The European cities have been similarly served by wars, as well.

—ROGER STARR

Only the thoughtful ask, "What is happening to us?" The popular cry is, "Who is doing this to us?" and its satisfying sequel—"Just let me get my hands on him!"

—FRED SCHWED, JR.

By 1974, budget deficits were nothing new for New York City, and no one knew this better than Abe Beame. While the mayor of New York spends the money, the task of collecting it (and telling the mayor how much he can spend) lies largely with the city's comptroller. Theoretically, New York is obligated to have a balanced budget each year—unlike the federal government, it can't simply print more money—but it is also allowed to borrow money to meet budget shortfalls by issuing municipal bonds, which are tax-free for the lenders and have a fairly low interest rate. In 1965, the city was unable to balance its budget, prompting then mayor Wagner to issue bonds with his assurance that "a bad loan is better than a good tax."

During the 1965 campaign for mayor, both Beame and Lindsay denounced the bond sale as irresponsible, and in Lindsay's first year in office, he passed a series of new taxes that balanced the budget and let him pay off Wagner's bonds. But the 1965 budget deficit was similar to the misunderstanding surrounding the "City in Crisis" narrative. City Hall wasn't just having a temporary budget problem after a few years of bad fiscal management; it was on the verge of a much deeper decline in revenue thanks to years of backward economic planning. For two decades, New York City had been spending billions of dollars to bulldoze and zone its industrial and economic base into oblivion. It had cleared taxpaying neighborhoods for highways and subsidized high-rises that paid few or no taxes at all. Middle-class taxpayers were chased to the suburbs, many of them city employees suddenly free to live and pay taxes outside the city, thanks to Wagner's cave-in to union demands. Even during the economic boom years of the mid-1960s, the F.I.R.E. industries that were supposed to be a more profitable replacement for working-class New York couldn't hold up their end of the bargain, and those bubbles were about to burst.

The decline was slow at first, but by 1970, Lindsay and Comptroller Beame (who'd taken his old job back from Lindsay's 1969 rival for mayor, Mario Procaccino) were forced into increasingly complicated financial maneuverings to keep the city afloat. Their routine was almost choreographed, with Lindsay warning of a looming "budget shortfall" that would force "payless paydays," and tens of thousands of layoffs, and Beame swooping in to save the day with a new source of cash (except, of course, for John O'Hagan and the compliant fire department, which largely acceded to Lindsay's budget cut requests). It turned out that Beame and his staff's revolutionary budgeting skills mostly involved hiding billions of dollars of debt where no one could find it. "The tradition in New York," said the dean of New York University's School of Public Administration, Dick Netzer, "is that the budget is a fake piece of paper from the start of the fiscal year. There's confusion, lack of knowledge, obscurity, and use of stealth. The people who make up the budget feel defenseless, somehow, if anybody can figure out what's going on."

Each success convinced Beame and Lindsay to embark on further budgeting gimmickry, rolling over this year's debt to next, claiming next year's revenue for this year, and using ever more elaborate financial instruments to hide the mounting arrears.* In many ways, the comptroller's office was decades ahead of the economic curve, presaging the financial scandals of the 1990s and 2000s, when businesses like Enron and accounting companies like Arthur Andersen used similar "modern budgeting techniques" to hide debt, inflate earnings, and con investors.

Beame and Lindsay were, of course, driven by nobler goals than inflated stock prices and personal riches. New York City, the city they loved and were charged with watching over, was losing money and on the verge of social collapse. The mayor was risking his hide on an almost fortnightly basis to prevent rioting in the streets; if the magicians in the comptroller's office could help save the city with a few financial gimmicks, so be it. Business, they figured, is cyclical. Like the cartoon character Wile E. Coyote, who repeatedly ran off cliffs but didn't start falling until he looked down, as long as the borrowing held until the city's financial picture turned around, things would be fine.

But New York's budget shortfalls were not just the result of fairly predictable three-to-five-year business cycles; they were part of a much deeper economic decline. Making matters worse, New York had wed its economy to the most notoriously fickle of industries, finance, and the financial world was about to go through its biggest downturn in decades.

---

*The city's fiscal year officially ended on June 30, so Beame suggested that Lindsay "save" $25 million in teacher salaries by sending out checks in early July instead of late June and counting them against the next year's budget. Lindsay called the idea "stopgap financial juggling," but Beame sent the checks out late anyway and was praised by the press for his financial acumen. (Lindsay went along with the gimmick the following year.) Lindsay later agreed to perform the same operation in reverse with educational aid from state and federal governments. The money came in the autumn, but the city counted it on the June balance sheet, once again pushing this year's shortfall into next year, and borrowing to cover the difference.

The Middle East oil embargo, stagflation, and a host of other national and international economic factors conspired to erase nearly 50 percent of the stock market's value from 1973 to 1975. Then on May 1, 1975, the SEC abolished the fixed fees that stockbrokers charged investors for buying and selling stocks. The discount brokerage industry was born, fees collapsed, and Wall Street lost $600 million dollars in fees over the next three years.

Even the city government's own exuberance to help its suddenly essential white-collar industries proved counterproductive. The reason the government needed to give tax abatements to convince real estate developers to build more high-rises, and the Rockefellers needed a governmental body like the Port Authority to front the billion-plus dollars needed to build the World Trade Center and keep it off city tax rolls, was that the free market wasn't strong enough to support their construction, even during the boom years. With white-collar businesses retracting just as all that new office space opened up—66.7 million square feet from 1967 to 1973, twice as much as during the run-up to the Crash of 1929—the laws of supply and demand kicked in and the commercial real estate market collapsed. Rents dropped by a third, and vacancy rates skyrocketed, particularly downtown, where the Rockefellers had bet so much public money on the WTC. Along with a construction standstill, losses on Wall Street rippled out to lawyers, accountants, architects, engineers, and other white-collar fields that depended on Wall Street largesse, and from there to the service economy they supported (retail stores, bars and restaurants, taxi drivers, dry cleaners, maids, doormen). Fortune 500 companies found they had trouble recruiting new employees to work in crime-ridden, fire-plagued Gotham, and many relocated their headquarters to cheaper, more hospitable climes. All told, 500,000 jobs disappeared from 1969 to 1975, on top of the hundreds of thousands of industrial jobs the city had lost over the previous ten years.

By early 1975, the big commercial banks that underwrote the city's bonds—keeping some for themselves and selling most of them to pension funds and other investors—were growing nervous about the city's nearly

$10 billion debt (it would eclipse $12 billion by the end of the year) and
the increasingly opaque budgets coming from Mayor Beame. The banks
continued underwriting and selling the bonds, assuring investors they
were a rock-solid investment, but quietly sold off billions of dollars'
worth of city bonds they held in their own accounts. Then, in the spring
of 1975, the Urban Development Corporation—a public authority that
former governor Nelson Rockefeller (who had just left Albany to become
Gerald Ford's vice president) had created to handle the residential end
of his massive building projects*—went belly-up with $2 billion in tax-
free bonds still on its books. The UDC had nothing to do with New York
City bonds, but to the average investor they looked similar enough to
stay away. Between the UDC collapse and the flood of New York City
paper being dumped by the underwriting banks, the market for New
York City bonds dried up almost overnight. The lending window was
shut, the city unable to borrow any more money.

Beame should have understood the city's financial problems as well as
anyone, but the years of consequence-free borrowing seems to have lulled
him into a false sense of security. The idea that the city would be shut out
of the bond market, that the banks the city housed and which had made
so much money from underwriting city bonds would no longer lend it
money, that New York—NEW YORK!—would be left teetering on the
verge of bankruptcy was simply unthinkable. But it was the reality.†

In the midst of an unprecedented financial meltdown that few had
seen coming, the media and politicians made a frantic rush to assign
blame. The budgeting tricks hailed just a few months before were exposed fairly quickly. New York State Senate Majority Leader Warren M.
Anderson said that Beame's top budget aide had "the three shells out
there and the pea in his pocket. Most of the occupations for which

---

*Rockefeller, the joke went, suffered from a serious "Edifice Complex."
†Journalist Jack Newfield said Beame's reaction was like that of the watchman on the *Titanic*,
promoted to captain after hitting the iceberg he failed to spot, then feigning shock when the
boat sank.

he's suited have been declared illegal." Despite engineering most of the borrowing when Lindsay was mayor, and nearly doubling city debt in his first year in office, Beame received less of the blame for the crisis than Lindsay, whose reputation was so damaged that by 1978 *The New York Times Magazine* was calling the fifty-six-year-old former mayor "an exile in his own city." In 1980 he ran for Senate but finished a distant third in the Democratic primaries, with just 16 percent of the vote, and less than 15 percent in the heart of his home Silk Stocking District. He stayed out of city politics until 1996, when, as he was struggling to pay for treatment for his Parkinson's disease, Mayor Rudolph Giuliani appointed him to a pair of unpaid jobs on city committees to make him eligible for health coverage and a city pension that helped support the former mayor until his death in 2000.

"In a way, he's a rather sad figure," said one friend of the former mayor's. "He can't accept the fact that life is just unfair sometimes, and that he's had to take the fall for what happened to the city. He's obsessed by that, plagued by the feeling that he's been scapegoated."

But the scapegoating wasn't aimed at Lindsay so much as at the tax-and-spend liberalism he had come to represent. His and Beame's financial gimmicks had only been necessary because the city was taking in less money than it was spending—who was responsible for that? The decades of slum and industrial clearance that cost billions, decimated the city's tax base, and yoked it to Wall Street's fortunes was too long and involved a story to make for good headlines. The issue of handouts was much better fare.

New York's budget was weighed down by two kinds of subsidies: those the city gave to the poor, and those it gave to the upper and middle classes and the business community. The point of origin for most of the country's labor and housing regulations, the New Deal, and many of the War on Poverty's marquee programs, New York was famous for its liberal social welfare policies. Sometimes that liberalism was taken advantage of. As the city hemorrhaged jobs, the 1970s became, as journalist Pete Hamill put it, "the years of 1,200,000 people on welfare, an entire city sitting on the stoop." Nine percent of those welfare recipients were ineligible. Engine 41 in the South Bronx was right next to a city welfare office. "Every month it was the same thing," says one fireman. "The street would be lined with out-of-state cars—Georgia, New Jersey, wherever. I remember this one guy, used to double-park his Cadillac, get out wearing a slick suit, collect his check, and head right back out of town. It was crazy."

But reputation aside, New York was fairly restrained in its social-service spending. Despite laying claim to the second-highest unemployment rate in the nation, New York actually had the second-lowest welfare rate of the country's ten largest cities. New York did spend a good deal of money on other social welfare programs in the inner city, but they ate up a much smaller portion of the city's budget than most assumed.

Just as expensive, but less well known, were handouts the city gave to Wall Street, real estate developers, and other politically influential interest groups (and the "retainer regiments" that trailed them). The government-subsidized office building boom of the 1960s made the cost of building anything but luxury housing all but prohibitive. So the city decided it needed to swallow a spider to catch the fly, and further interfered with the market to undo the unintended consequences of the original interference by borrowing on the bond market and lending the money to middle-class-housing developers. By 1975, New York was $3 billion in hock for the program, almost a third of its total debt. The city's expense sheet was littered with a host of other, smaller but costly corporate welfare projects, like the $100 million it spent to renovate Yankee Stadium while the neighborhood around it burned.

Even less well known were real estate tax exemptions. The World Trade Center alone cost the city $700 million in lost real estate taxes by 1979, and under Wagner and Lindsay the city granted tax abatements almost willy-nilly to spur development. All told, the portion of New York City real estate off the tax rolls rose from 28 percent in the mid-1950s, to 40 percent by 1976. But those abatements generally went only to new construction. When property managers complained about the imbalance, the city swallowed a bird to catch the spider, extending exemptions and abatements to older buildings as well. And unlike the straightforward handouts of programs like welfare, these handouts were usually well hidden: instead of simply cutting the rate at which buildings were taxed, the city dropped assessments on the value of the buildings being taxed, from an average of 82.2 percent of market value in 1960 to 48 percent by 1975. Sometimes the assessment drop was in conjunction with a slight rise in the tax rate, allowing real estate companies to claim hardship (look, higher tax rates!) while actually paying less.

But 1975 was not a year in which American politicians, reporters, and ordinary citizens were prepared to give equal scrutiny to social welfare programs and business subsidies. For a decade, Americans had been *hearing* about how much their government was doing for minorities and the poor, with programs like urban renewal, slum clearance, and the War on Poverty. In return for that investment, they got inner-city race riots, spiraling rates of drugs, crime, family dysfunction, and welfare, and staggering budget deficits. Of course, many of the social programs that were supposedly helping the poor more closely resembled the lawn in the Harlem housing project that Jane Jacobs described: "The big men come and look at the grass and say, 'Isn't it wonderful! Now the poor have everything.'" Even War on Poverty programs were, as Daniel Patrick Moynihan put it, "oversold and underfinanced to the point that their seeming failure was almost a matter of design." But a backlash against social-welfare spending was brewing, and Gotham—bankrupt, burning down, and begging for loans—was about to become a whipping boy in the ensuing morality play.

WITH THE BOND MARKET DRIED UP, THE STATE STEPPED IN and created the Municipal Assistance Corporation, aka "Big MAC," a governmental authority that would take over the city's debt and issue new, state-backed bonds to prevent bankruptcy. Dominated by lending banks, corporate board members, and Democratic wheelhorses, MAC's take on who was to blame for the city's insolvency was fairly predictable.

As one MAC spokesman had told reporter Robert Fitch, "It's the fucking blacks and Puerto Ricans. They use too many city services and they don't pay any taxes." Most politicians and reporters were a bit more tactful in their wording, but the general message was the same. The city had became a "fiscal junkie," in the words of *New York Times* reporter Steven Weisman, feeding its liberal spending habit with a steady dose of loans until it was too strung out to get anymore. Reporter Ken Auletta wrote a book about the fiscal crisis, called *The Streets Were Paved with Gold,* and blamed the city's financial predicament on a failed experiment in "local socialism." The most thoroughly wonkish account of the fiscal crisis came from former budget bureau staffer Charles Morris. Though Morris paid little attention to the enormous cost of the tax abatements and subsidies the city handed out to developers, readers who made it through the assembled charts and statistics found an otherwise even-handed account of what drove the city to bankruptcy. But for those who simply read the oddly discordant title, *The Cost of Good Intentions: New York and the Liberal Experiment* was more of the same.

The city's fortunes were supposed to take a turn for the better on July 1, 1975. Mayor Beame was in Albany, meeting with Governor Hugh Carey and state assembly and senate leaders to hash out a deal to bring more aid money to the city. Big MAC was going to start selling $3 billion in bonds that would put the city back on its feet. And in return for the money, New York was going to pay for its sins, laying off forty thousand overpaid, nonessential workers and cutting back on liberal spending programs. It didn't quite work out that way. First, it started to look as if some of the people being laid off weren't quite so nonessential. A week earlier, firemen Thomas Newbert and Richard Weiser had pulled a man from the flaming wreckage of Eastern Airlines Flight 66, one of only a dozen of the 124 people onboard to survive a crash landing at JFK airport in Queens. A few days later, they were given commendations for valor, and a couple of days after that, told they'd be laid off. Newbert's wife, a police officer, was also axed, but the government still had to pay both of them: they filed for unemployment until they could find new jobs.

Then came word that talks between Beame and state leaders to bring more state aid to the city had fallen apart, the diminutive mayor storming back to New York to hold the city together, he told the newspapers, as the layoffs went into effect. His presence didn't help much. After five thousand laid-off policemen turned in their badges and guns, about five hundred of them made their way to City Hall for a union rally, carrying signs that read "Burn City Burn" and "Beame Is a Deserter, a Rat." After the rally, a few hundred opened up the playbook of the antiwar activists they had jostled with for so many years, and took it to the streets. Blocking off nearby Brooklyn Bridge with wooden police barricades, the laid-off cops stormed the bridge, hurling beer cans and bottles at their former colleagues, harassing motorists, and rocking trapped cars to chants of "Turn it over!" One former policeman carrying an American flag used the spiked flagpole to slash tires. The bridge was blocked intermittently for five hours, with police officers on duty at the scene reluctant to intervene. "We could be on the other side tomorrow," said one. "They've been driven to this by the politicians."* One of the most common chants from the protesters was "We want DeLury!" in support of the president of the sanitation workers' union, who had just called what one reporter deemed "the most well-organized wildcat strike the city had ever seen, a 100 percent effective spontaneous walkout." The garbage strike lasted two days, leaving about 60 million pounds of trash rotting in the July heat.

Meanwhile, MAC salesmen were wondering if perhaps the party line on what caused the city's bankruptcy had worked a little too well, with almost no one interested in investing in the Kremlin-on-the-Hudson. "We called it Big MAC," said one MAC board member, "but everyone thought it was the same old hamburger meat. It was New York's, and it didn't smell very good to them."

---

*One of the trapped motorists was a professor on his way to New England to give a lecture on the city's fiscal crisis. The protests weren't the only bridge trouble the city had that day. After drawbridge operators were laid off, the bridges were left down to let cars cross, but this blocked water traffic, a violation of federal law—which led the Coast Guard to sue the city to open the bridges.

Unable to sell the bonds, a group including Beame, Governor Hugh Carey, and Carey's budget director, former Fred Hayes protégé Peter Goldmark, went to Washington, hats in hand.

With New York City increasingly reviled around the country, and Ford facing stiff competition from Ronald Reagan and the conservative wing of the Republican Party in the 1976 presidential election, the president refused to lend the city any money. "The people of this country will not be stampeded," Ford said in a speech in October of 1975. "They will not panic when a few desperate New York officials and bankers try to scare New York's mortgage payments out of them." Ford eventually compared the city's debt to an unwanted baby the city was trying to leave on the federal doorstep. Never afraid of invective, the front page of the *Daily News* put it a bit more succinctly: "Ford to City: Drop Dead."

What happened next was an odd precursor to the federal bank bailouts to come thirty years later. Ford's comparison of the debt to a child was more apt than he realized—abandoned by the city, perhaps, but desperately wanted by its real parents, the banks and other investors who were still owed more than $10 billion by the city. Afraid of losing their investment, they ratcheted up the rhetoric, warning that if New York defaulted, it would freeze up the entire tax-free bond market, causing a series of rolling defaults by dozens, perhaps hundreds, of cities and states across the country as investors refused to buy more bonds. Like AIG, they said New York City was too big to fail, could even take modern capitalism down with it, and Ford relented and lent the money to the city. (Unlike AIG, the New York City bailout came only in the form of a loan that New York paid back, with interest, years before it was due.)

With the money came more budget cuts to help pay the nearly $2 billion in debt service the city had to pay each year (by 1977, debt service made up a third of all city expenses), and those cuts were doled out in a fashion familiar to anyone who'd been paying attention to New York's root-approach bureaucratic reforms during the Lindsay years. Big MAC was renamed the Emergency Financial Control Board (EFCB) and given control of the city's purse strings, a kind of technocratic shadow government that oversaw the installation of new budgeting systems, conducted efficiency studies on the municipal workforce, and made more across-the-board budget cuts. The city government was in desperate need of a house-cleaning, but like so many centralized, top-down approaches to reforming the complicated bureaucracy, many seemingly logical cuts actually cost more than they saved. Across-the-board cuts made in the city's bloated clerical departments ended up including many of the auditors responsible for collecting the hundreds of millions of dollars that the city was owed in delinquent taxes and utility bills. Health clinics, which kept uninsured people from going to expensive emergency rooms, were shuttered. Day-care programs that helped single mothers work and stay off welfare were closed. The subway, already sagging under the weight of years of neglect, had police patrols, cleaning, and repairs cut back further, and this kick-started a cycle of fewer people wanting to ride the dirty, dangerous, unreliable trains, which meant less rider revenue and money for upkeep, and so on. Most layoffs were done by seniority—a particular problem in the police department, where the youngest, cheapest, and often most energetic and effective officers were let go, and better-paid old-timers were left to ratchet up the overtime hours because of the lack of manpower.

Amid years of economic and social decline, drugs, crime, and family dysfunction, there seemed to be an almost daily horror story coming out of New York. "On Fox Street," in the South Bronx, wrote journalists Jack Newfield and Paul Du Brul, "a nine-year-old girl is raped and thrown off a rooftop. In Harlem, two men freeze to death in a slum building owned by a landlord named Gold, who lives in Miami. In the Bronx, Hans Kabel, seventy-eight years old, and his wife Emma, seventy-six, commit suicide together after being robbed and terrorized in their own small apartment. They leave a suicide note behind that says, 'We don't want to live in fear anymore.'"

In Spanish Harlem, a fourteen-year-old boy died of a heroin overdose and it didn't even make the papers: a twelve-year-old had OD'd recently, and fourteen wasn't newsworthy. On garbage-strewn Delancey Street on the Lower East Side, homeless men sold used syringes they'd scrounged from burned-out buildings turned shooting galleries, the insides still caked with bloodrust. Open-air drug markets, street-corner prostitutes, collapsed tenements, garbage-strewn lots—New York was not only inspiring postapocalyptic thrillers like *Escape from New York* and *The Warriors* but beginning to resemble them. (The horror film *Wolfen* was shot on Charlotte Street). In the South Bronx, the city began painting street addresses on the roofs of buildings—fires had become so common that people stopped calling them in, figuring someone else would, and the fire department relied on passing helicopters to radio in the fires and addresses.

"The smell is one thing I remember," says Captain Tom Henderson. "That smell of burning—it was always there, through the whole borough almost."

In the South Bronx neighborhoods where Henderson fought fires, teachers noticed the smell, too, as their students' clothing took on the acidic tinge of the world of ash and smoke they lived in. "It's very difficult to generate enthusiasm," said one teacher, "when you feel everything is terminal." Youth gangs dominated Bronx street life, long-haired Puerto Rican and Afro'd black kids flying cut-sleeves and gang colors, wearing leather jackets emblazoned with swastikas, fiery skulls, and names like the Ghetto Brothers, Reapers, and Black Spades. Recruiting from the chaotic, drug-filled streets of the Bronx, the gangs brought a sense of structure, discipline, and family to kids who often had none. Inductions were simple enough—walk an "Apache Line" in a local playground, as fists, clubs, and whatever else was handy beat on you from both sides. Or crowd into a project elevator at the top floor, with the new man in the center—if he was still standing when it reached the lobby, he was in. For the hardest crews—top divisions of the Savage Skulls and Black Spades—it was Russian roulette in a burned-out vacant, a one-in-six chance you didn't walk out. Some dabbled in black and Puerto Rican nationalist politics. Others worked as pseudo-vigilante groups in lawless neighborhoods where cops rarely tread, harassing heroin pushers and staging brutal "junkie massacres" in vacant buildings.

The economic and social collapse that had sprung from bad planning theories hatched decades earlier came full circle when Abe Beame's housing commissioner, Roger Starr, pushed a new planning theory that justified and tried to extend the city's budget cuts. Like his friend Irving Kristol, Starr was a disillusioned Trotskyite-turned-neoconservative, who cast himself as a commonsense critic of the red-tape-entangled world of city politics, but he traded in the same tired fantasies of Le Corbusier and Moses—cities, economies, and people treated as little more than chess pieces moved about by all-knowing planners and politicians. Even the use of words like "community" were retrograde, he wrote, because they "suggest that, in the area described, people have thrown down their swords and spears; that they have created not only their own safety but a web of love and kindness, understanding and mutual support, which it is sacrilege to tamper with . . . a significance they never earned." Despite decades of urban-renewal evidence to the contrary, he wrote that "provided only that a certain homogeneity of social class and income can be maintained, American communities can be disassembled and reconstituted about as readily as freight trains." Calling his new theory "planned shrinkage," Starr suggested evicting the hundreds of thousands of residents living in places like the South Bronx and central Brooklyn en masse, and moving them elsewhere. "Stretches of empty blocks may then be knocked down, services can be stopped, subway stations closed, and the land left to lie fallow until a change in economic and demographic assumptions makes the land useful again."

Starr's idea wasn't entirely new, similar theories had been floating around academic circles for some time, beginning with the neighborhood life-cycle ideas that undergirded redlining. More recently, former RAND researcher Anthony Downs, one of the first thinkers to apply game theory to real estate markets, had called for the government to actively participate in the life cycle by pushing inner-city neighborhoods into the final abandonment stages. A "new means," he wrote, "of comprehensively 'managing' entire inner-city neighborhoods should be developed to provide a more effective means of withdrawing economic support from housing units that ought to be demolished. . . . Whole neighborhoods of high-school-district size would be demolished and replaced by newly constructed developments occupied by middle-class residents who would initially establish high standards and maintain them henceforth." The demolition would go hand in hand with his "dispersal strategy" to end the high concentrations of inner-city black poverty by pushing blacks out to the suburbs. As a member of the Kerner Commission, Downs wrote much of the report, including the concluding chapter on preventing further riots, "The Future of Cities."

As for Starr, his pitch for forced resettlement on a scale that would have made Robert Moses blush created an uproar in the city's poor neighborhoods, and Beame forced him to resign. Starr's real mistake, though, wasn't his ideas so much as his candor—the city already had a de facto planned shrinkage policy; Starr just wanted to admit as much and manage it more comprehensively. Big MAC head Felix Rohatyn floated a similar plan to bulldoze and "blacktop" most of the South Bronx. But unlike Starr, who answered to a mayor who had to run for office, Rohatyn answered only to MAC bondholders, and they agreed with him.

Brooklyn burnt.
(Photo courtesy FDNY Photo Unit)

FIFTEEN

The Fiscal Crisis Kool-Aid Test

In a marvelous, sad way, the South Bronx is an enormous success story. Over 750,000 people have left in the past twenty years for middle-class success in the suburbs.

—NEW YORK CITY PLANNER ED LOGUE

Despite years of boasting that he could run the department on 7,500 men and a fraction of the budget, O'Hagan knew the 1974 company closings had gone too far. With the city teetering on the brink of insolvency a year later, Beame was asking for the largest round of cuts yet. "When he got word of the [fiscal crisis] cuts they wanted him to make, he came to see me," says O'Hagan's former press aide, Frank Cull. "And he said, 'These cuts are gonna happen, what would you do if you were me?' And I told him, 'This is out-and-out unconscionable. Hold a press conference, tell them you can't make these cuts, and resign as fire commissioner.' He looked at me, said, 'You're not all wrong.' There was a part of him that liked that idea, riding off into the sunset as Don Quixote. But he just smiled, thanked me for telling him what I'd do, and that was that. . . . There was talk that he might be made deputy mayor, or maybe run for office, and he just couldn't quit like that, not after all those years. I still thought he could have had a political career, standing up like that against the cuts, people would have loved him—but it just wasn't something he could do."

"What could he do?" says O'Hagan's former assistant Sandy Sansevero. "If he didn't make the cuts, they would have found somebody else who would have. End of story."

But O'Hagan had options besides just going along quietly with the cuts, or resigning in protest to be replaced by a political flunky; he had the soft power of his own impeccable reputation and years of careful alliance-building within the bureaucracy and the city's Democratic clubs. Corruption, kickbacks, and payola were rife in Beame's clubhouse-dominated administration. Of the tens of thousands of city employees laid off, scores of clubhouse hacks were rehired under one guise or another. *Some* money could always be found when powerful people needed it, but O'Hagan never fully expended his political capital to claw back whatever funds he could for his department.

There were more indirect ways of staving off the cuts, as well. O'Hagan knew the authority the RAND models held in the minds of the uninitiated. He also knew that the models were easily manipulated, and had fudged the data himself to avoid cuts in politically powerful neighborhoods—a process that could be run in reverse just as easily. "When they were trying to close houses" in the 1980s, says Captain Tom Henderson, the vice president of the fire officers union at the time, "I'd tell the brass, 'They want to make cuts? Here, you give them this list, tell them these are the first houses to go,' and on that list I had Seventy Two Engine up in Throgs Neck, I had companies near assemblymen's houses, companies in rich neighborhoods, places where if they announced a closing you'd have the whole neighborhood out rallying the next day, politicians making speeches, all that. They couldn't close houses like that and they knew it, so you told them those were the only houses that could go and suddenly they didn't need to close houses so bad."

But O'Hagan stood pat, and on July 1, 1975, he oversaw nearly a thousand layoffs and thirteen company closings. As it turned out, Henderson's ploy to recommend closing companies in wealthier areas first might have worked. Initially, there were twenty-six companies closed, but thirteen of the more politically powerful ones were reopened within a week when some spare change was found under the municipal couch cushions, and more were reopened a few years later, after neighborhood protests and persistent hectoring from influential local politicians. But with the city's purse-strings held by MAC, and some of the most powerful people in government convinced that the ghettoes should be allowed, even encouraged, to die, closed companies in places like Bedford-Stuyvesant, the South Bronx, and Harlem weren't coming back.

Along with the company closings, equipment and repair budgets were cut to almost nothing. Where busy engines once had at least five, and as many as six or seven firemen per shift, now there were four. Many crews had found ways to adapt to the earlier cuts and the lack of available companies and manpower they caused, but the latest round made even their jury-rigged firefighting impossible.

"After the [first two rounds of] cuts, it took a lot longer for the truckies to show up," says Artie Wohlgemuth, who worked in an engine company in Brooklyn. "So my lieutenant pulls me aside one day and says, 'Artie, how about we do this. You take a hook and ladder and operate as a truckie.' I'd do it by knocking out windows, climb up the rear of the building and knock out a skylight, maybe rip a hole in the roof. It was against department rules, but we had no choice." Yet after the staffing cuts, Wohlgemuth's engine crew needed him back on the hose line, leaving no one to vent the flames. "When the fiscal crisis came along, you're talking four guys on most rigs, there weren't enough guys to do our regular job, never mind filling in for a ladder truck."

A few years earlier, John O'Hagan had been asking bold questions about bureaucratic structure and had a team of Whiz Kid Ph.D.'s at his beck and call. Now RAND was gone, shuttered a few months before the 1975 Summer of Insolvency, and he was reduced to the role of a triage medic, holding his once proud department together with duct tape and twine. Without his brain trust around, he was finding it increasingly difficult to save money or outsmart the unions that fought his every move tooth and nail. To save on overtime, O'Hagan had his chiefs deny sick leave. So the union told firemen who felt sick to show up to work and, as soon as they fought a tough fire, claim lightheadedness and get sent to the hospital. The carbon monoxide levels in a fireman's blood are usually so elevated after fighting a fire that most doctors will immediately pull him out of work for a week—so instead of paying time and a half for someone to cover a single shift, the department had to find firemen to cover for a full week's worth of shifts. (Other measures, like having dispatchers call in alarms moments after a shift change, as happened during the Waldbaum's fire, were more successful at cutting costs.)

As the cuts mounted, fire rates continued to rise. With fewer companies to respond to calls and fewer men in each company to fight the flames, fires that would have burned a single room or apartment spread to the entire building, and sometimes whole blocks. The number of fires that became "serious" (i.e., grew large enough that all responding units had to fight the flames or multiple alarms had to be called) rose by 40 percent from 1974 to 1977. By 1977 the busiest companies were going on more than eight thousand runs and seven thousand workers a year, 50 percent higher than when the cuts first started in 1972. Companies like Engine 82, which for years had been at the top of the list, were sinking further and further down, with hardly anything left to burn in their coverage area. Near Engine 82's house, the police department's 41st Precinct—once known as Fort Apache, because it was a government stronghold in hostile territory—was coming to be known as Little House on the Prairie, a solitary outpost surrounded by empty expanse.

Through it all, O'Hagan supported the mayor and stood firmly behind the cuts. "O'Hagan drank the Kool-Aid," as one fire chief puts it, even supporting astounding claims by City Hall that the cuts didn't significantly affect service, citing a slight decline in fire fatalities from 1975 to 1976. Subsequent investigations revealed that almost fifty deaths had been mysteriously missed—turning the slight decrease into a 20 percent increase—but it was years before that information came to light.

The one thing the ghettoes did receive was the renewed attention of the city's top firefighter, but his primary target was a bit off-base: arson.

Even at its peak, arson rates stayed south of 7 percent of total fires, and even those arson blazes were mostly in the abandoned shells left behind by the earlier wave of conventional fires. "What we found," says Dr. Rodrick Wallace, who conducted exhaustive studies into arson in parts of Bushwick and the South Bronx, "was that there was a pattern of [accidental] fires in a neighborhood, followed by arson in the abandoned buildings. Arson was only a problem after an area had already been burned out."

By 1977, though, the arson problem was attracting the kind of attention a decade of fires never had. First came the blackout riots, followed closely by President Carter's visit, the World Series blaze, and a CBS news feature that brought national interest to the arson issue. (The prevailing demographics of the Bronx—Jewish building owners, Puerto Rican landlords and torches—gave the process its most common nicknames, Jewish Lightning and Gasoline Gomez.)

For all the attention that intentionally set fires garnered, in reality arson was dwarfed by conventional, accidental fires. Chief O'Hagan knew this better than anyone, but he also knew that all the media hype would translate into city funding, and any money for fighting fires—even if it was aimed at a secondary problem—was a blessing. O'Hagan capitalized on the short-lived attention to start fire-marshal street patrols that responded immediately to fires, investigated suspicious blazes, and helped step up fire inspections that prevented conventional fires.

Even more important than O'Hagan's tardy attack on arson was the fact that he kept the department from falling apart completely during the worst of the War Years. His biggest fight came after a well-liked South Bronx fireman, family man, and union rep fell from his engine and died on the way to what turned out to be a false alarm. His death was a major news story, with some calling for the nine-year-old boy who'd pulled the alarm to be thrown in jail. But the press never picked up on the full story of the fall. "There was a promotion party at the firehouse," says a fellow South Bronx fireman. "He had a couple of pops in him before that call."

"He wasn't a drinker, but that night there was a party in the firehouse and he had a couple of drinks," says another fire officer. "The union made sure that never came out, but he was drunk."

Chief O'Hagan knew full well what had happened, and shortly thereafter issued Regulation 202, banning drinking on the job. "Some guys in the firehouse just hated O'Hagan," says former fire commissioner Tom Von Essen, who was a young South Bronx fireman and union rep when O'Hagan was chief. "Almost irrationally, and it was mostly because of 202. I remember being angry too, 'What, I can't have a glass of wine with my dinner?' But that wasn't what it was about, guys having a glass of wine, it was guys getting drunk, falling off rigs, getting hurt at fires, getting killed. I don't know what the percentages were, but you can bet, with a lot of accidents on the job, somebody had been drinking at some point."

Within the unions, O'Hagan had developed a reputation as a hypocrite, a man who'd forgotten where he'd come from in his long climb to power, but he kept an iron grip on the department during the toughest stretch in its history. On top of the incredible workload, frequent deaths and injuries, and the cuts and hiring freeze that exacerbated them, the department was roiled by the broader culture wars facing society at large. Women sued to take the firemen's exam, politicians pushed for affirmative action, the 1973 strike split the department almost down the middle; even seemingly trivial matters, like young firemen defying the ban on long hair, sideburns, and beards, turned into serious conflicts within the insular, conservative department. Through it all, O'Hagan maintained a level of constancy and discipline sorely lacking in other departments.

In the sanitation department, garbage trucks would ignore whole sections of the South Bronx, Harlem, and central Brooklyn, even dump trash in vacant lots. The police department, in particular, fell into disarray. The Knapp Commission, formed after allegations brought by Officer Frank Serpico, uncovered department corruption on a scale not seen since the days of Tammany mayor Jimmy Walker, and after that things only got worse. "After the Knapp Commission, cops felt like City Hall was against us," says one retired police officer. "Guys just didn't care, they were showing up until they could get a pension."

"We used to have [cops] come by the firehouse all the time, to relax or get some sleep. On duty, I'm talking here," says one retired South Bronx firefighter. "That, or they'd be in the pump room at the pool in St. Mary's park, playing cards. No one kept an eye on them, and no one cared."

But the fire department held together. "It was just bedlam," says former union president Jimmy Boyle. "[O'Hagan] was very antagonistic with the unions and there were bitter, bitter fights, but he held it together. He fought to get rid of the drinking and he won. He fought to make guys shave their beards and he won. And you know all the innovations—things like tower ladders and masks, all the information we have now on how to fight fires, all the things guys take for granted today—we forget, he had to fight for all of that, he had to go against all the old-school guys to get that. During the War Years, with all those fires and all that craziness, if it wasn't for O'Hagan, I don't know that the fire service would've made it through like it did."

Still, O'Hagan's relationship with the rank and file had reached a point of no return. "Things got really ugly," says Chief Vincent Dunn. "A lot of guys really hated O'Hagan, I mean picketing his house, saying things about his family, all that. I remember his wife used to come out and give coffee to the union guys when they picketed the house. . . . I was a young guy at this point, working in headquarters, real ambitious, and I remember one day the payroll came in and I got a quick look at it and saw that O'Hagan made seventy-five bucks a week more than the chief I worked for. I said, hey, seventy-five dollars? You become the head of General Motors or GE and you start slashing and saving, you're not making thousands more, you're making *millions* more. So I said to myself, 'Do I want people showing up at my house, picketing, bothering my family? For what? An extra seventy-five dollars?' All I can say is that he was a faithful guy, religious, and . . . he *ran* that department, no matter how bad things got, the toughest civil servant I've ever met. If he hadn't, who knows what would have happened to the fire service."

Despite the dissension in the ranks, after two years of fiscal austerity it started to look like O'Hagan had played his political cards right. According to department brass, Beame nearly made O'Hagan a deputy mayor during his first term, and things looked good going into the 1977 mayoral race. "The talk in the Bronx," says one Bronx clubhouse member, "was that if Beame won the primary, then O'Hagan might run on his ticket as city council president, or be named deputy mayor, and that Steve Murphy," a Bronx Dem who was O'Hagan's first deputy commissioner, "would take over as commissioner."

But Beame couldn't hold up his end of the bargain. After twelve years of the reformer–clubhouse dialectic, the city decided it wanted something new, and Beame finished a disappointing third in the Democratic primary behind Congressman Ed Koch, a one-time reformer from Greenwich Village with a keen ear for the increasingly conservative tenor of the times, and Mario Cuomo, the eloquent secretary of New York State from Queens. Koch won the general election a few months later. With O'Hagan politically vulnerable, the unions leaked a story about the commissioner making assistants drive his daughter back and forth to college in Massachusetts, and it was subsequently revealed that a fire charity O'Hagan helped run had paid for his MBA classes at Columbia University. Already looking to clean house, Koch fired O'Hagan as commissioner and replaced him with Augustus Beekman, a popular fire chief and the department's second black commissioner.

Because he had tenure, O'Hagan could have stayed on as chief, but his dismissal as commissioner was an embarrassing indication that his time had come and gone. After thirteen years as chief of department and four as commissioner, John T. O'Hagan retired to become a technical consultant like the RAND analysts who once worked for him, building on his experiences with RAND to conduct efficiency studies for departments around the country and abroad on issues like fire company locations, response times, and staffing sizes. While he stayed close with many of his former assistants at headquarters, within the department O'Hagan became a bit like his former boss, John Lindsay—a reminder of bad times better forgotten—known to most younger firemen only as the asshole commissioner who closed companies and sprang surprise sobriety tests.

Twelve years after his retirement, O'Hagan returned in 1989 to the fire training academy he'd helped build, to speak at the dedication of a plaque commemorating the twelve men who died in the 23rd Street collapse, the tragedy that had launched his quest to reform the department twenty-three years before. His body ravaged by cancer, the once boy-chief, still only in his early sixties, looked gaunt beneath his crisp blue suit and striped club tie. Before the ceremony, he chatted with his former headquarters hand, Chief Vincent Dunn, now running O'Hagan's old command, Manhattan's high-rise-filled Third Division. After a brief ceremony, O'Hagan stepped to the podium to deliver the dedication speech. October 18, 1966, he said, had been the worst day of his life. Through a bit of luck, good or bad, he'd had the pleasure of knowing every one of the twelve men who'd died, particularly Deputy Chief Thomas Reilly, who had replaced him as head of the Third Division.

The old chief didn't dwell on the past, though, looking, as always, for what could be learned going forward. "If one listened carefully to O'Hagan's message," wrote one of his former assistants, "it really was aimed at the present and future. He really was saying that, although inevitably firefighters will be lost in the line of duty, we cannot become complacent and let down our guard. For with proper safety equipment and state-of-the-art technology, coupled with progressive and repeated intense training, firefighters can reduce the dangerous hazards they face during their daily performances of duty." A year later, John T. O'Hagan died peacefully in the Bay Ridge home where he'd hung wallpaper upside down in the kitchen while waiting to find out if he would be the youngest fire chief in the department's history.

O'Hagan's influence has lasted well beyond his retirement or death. The oxygen masks, tower ladders, high-rise fire codes, and rigorous standard operating procedures O'Hagan fostered remain intact, both in the FDNY and departments around the country that followed his lead. The smoke detectors, fire-resistant building materials, furniture, and clothing he helped make a foregone conclusion in most homes have helped cut American fire fatalities by 75 percent over the last four decades. Under his watch, women began taking the firemen's (now fire*fighters'*) tests, and soon joined the department. O'Hagan's protégé and liaison to NYC-RAND, Homer Bishop, who many say was like a son to him, went on to become the chief of department himself in 1988 (though he was diagnosed with leukemia soon after, and died just a few months before O'Hagan did). Even younger union men grew to appreciate him for his professionalism, innovation, and ability to keep the department functioning under circumstances no one could have foreseen.

"I realized, when I became commissioner," says Tom Von Essen, a South Bronx fireman in O'Hagan's time, and later president of the firefighters union and the fire commissioner on September 11, 2001, "how hard his job really was. The decisions he had to make, the battles he had to fight. Guys like us in the Bronx, we didn't appreciate it at the time."

But O'Hagan's influence lived on in a very different way in the streets of the South Bronx, Brownsville, Bed-Stuy, Harlem, and the Lower East Side. In the thousands of lives lost, and homes destroyed by fire. In the once vibrant neighborhoods where upward of 70, 80, 90 percent of the buildings and residents vanished; the places where Jimmy Carter, Ronald Reagan, and Mother Teresa came to marvel at the spectacular ruins and wonder just how it was that the richest city in the world could burn down.

But while that influence would live on, the men who came to define the era when New York burned—John O'Hagan, John Lindsay, and the analysts of the New York City–RAND Institute—were not around for the last great fire of the War Years.

Waldbaum's supermarket, moments after the collapse.
(Photo courtesy FDNY Photo Unit)

SIXTEEN

Waldbaum's Revisited

Evening of August 2, 1978

Louise O'Connor had seen it happen right before her eyes, but she still couldn't believe it. Hours later, she sat with the kids, Billy Jr., Lisa Ann, and Jean Marie, watching television news reports of the supermarket collapse and the six men who died in it. "Is that Dad?" Billy Jr. asked as the screen showed a fireman being pulled from the rubble.

"Dad's dead, right?" said one of his sisters.

Louise thought about how two days ago she and Billy were having a cup of tea at a friend's house and he'd started teasing her.

"I hope you learn to save money when I'm dead," he'd said.

"I don't even know how to work the camera if you die," she shot back, laughing.

"If the undertaker fools around with me," said Billy, "I'm going to knock the clock in the kitchen off the wall."

"Okay," she had said. "And if I go first, I'll do that if he fools around with me."

Louise kept staring at the television. "He was on the roof, he waved to us and we waved back. Then the roof collapsed," she said. "I knew it was over right there." The phone rang as she talked and Billy's father answered. It was the department calling. Had Billy worn his uniform belt when he went to work?

"You mean they couldn't recognize him when they found him?" she asked. "You mean he looked so bad they couldn't identify him without his buckle? Our three babies . . . I can't believe it. He saw us, he was on the roof. Can you believe he's dead?"

Whatever a fireman might want to keep out of his home—love letters from a girlfriend, dirty magazines—he keeps in his locker. If he dies on the job, the men in his company go through it before his family. The men of Ladder Co. 156 never had the chance to do that with Billy O'Connor's locker. After the call from the department, Louise and Billy's uncle Phil, who'd searched for him in the Waldbaum's rubble earlier that morning, arrived at the firehouse to gather his things. "The lockers are on the third floor of this house," one of the firemen on duty said later. "She talked about how Billy had never let her come up to the third floor, and now she was finally going up there."

A few hours later, most of Ladder Co. 156 was asleep in the bunk room, but one probey lay on a cot in the TV room watching Jack Benny reruns. "He came here with Billy," the veteran on watch told reporter Pete Hamill, who spent the night in the house. "They were in school together. He's been walking around all night. He can't sleep. He can't get over what happened, I guess." Then he told Hamill about Charles Bouton, who'd died in the collapse with Billy. The night before the fire he'd shown up to the firehouse with a new crew cut and a smile on his face. That morning he'd borrowed one of his kids' bikes to ride down to the barbershop. It'd been a while since he'd been on two wheels but he pedaled hard and picked up speed down a hill. Approaching a stop sign, he grabbed for the brakes but found there were none, missing a car by inches as he barreled through the intersection. "The crew cut almost cost me my life," Bouton had said, laughing. "Maybe he'd have been better off if he got clipped by the car," the fireman told Hamill.

The next day, the search for answers began, with most people coming to conclusions that befitted their position. The department itself blamed arson, the fire supposedly set at the behest of local mobsters as part of a union extortion racket. Months later a homeless drug addict named Eric Jackson was convicted of arson and sentenced to twenty-five years to life. Still, that didn't explain the surprise collapse. Union president Dick Vizzini blamed the delayed second alarm and the lack of manpower for that. "Death was the grim paymaster," he told *The New York Times*.

Chief of Department Francis Cruthers found no fault with the response or the tactics at the scene. "It was almost classical," he said of the roof approach and the venting. "I thought the fire was fought well." Having more men at the scene, Cruthers said, wouldn't have prevented the collapse, may have even been a blessing in disguise. "There's just as much chance more people might have perished." Only eight months retired, John O'Hagan blamed the deaths on the kind of unprofessionalism he'd spent his career trying to stamp out of the department: slow houses in suburban neighborhoods that didn't run very much, a probey waving at his family from the roof of an active fire. Reading the newspaper accounts in his living room, he raged at the fulfillment of decades-old fears, now powerless to do anything about them.

But the blame for the Waldbaum's fire was more complicated than any of that. Of the firemen at the scene, not one, not even decorated officers with decades of experience, knew the first thing about fighting fires in buildings with a truss roof. The construction style was a serious hazard, and in areas where it was common, officers and fire crews took extraordinary precautions. But there was nothing about truss roofs in the department's safety literature, probey school, or training bulletins. "When I heard on the morning of August 2, 1978, that six firefighters had died in a timber truss roof collapse," wrote Chief Vincent Dunn, who investigated the fire, "I asked myself some very disturbing questions: did

I know about truss roofs? Not enough to have ordered the men off the roof before it collapsed. Would those six men have died if I were the chief-in-command of that fire? Yes, they would have. . . . Looking back, I find it hard to believe that, with the tremendous amount of bulletins, circulars, and directives issued to the department by the division of training, a subject as important as truss roofs was never covered. But it was not."

Such an oversight seemed strange in the wake of John O'Hagan's leadership. The 23rd Street collapse had happened under extremely similar circumstances—a hidden fire and the collapse of a building that had been altered without the buildings or fire department's knowing it. After 23rd Street, O'Hagan had worked tirelessly to prevent such a needless tragedy from ever happening again, creating a list of checkpoints and standard operating procedures for different types of buildings, constantly updating the department's safety and training bulletins to impart the latest techniques, stressing the importance of engineering to his chiefs, urging them to keep blueprints of local buildings in their cars, as he did. After thirteen years of trying to prevent exactly the kind of information gap that caused the collapse, how had it happened again? As it turned out, just as with the burning of New York's poorest neighborhoods under his watch, O'Hagan's lack of experience and interest in the ghettoes of the Bronx was behind this oversight as well.

"On the officers' union board," says Captain Tom Henderson, "we had Mike Vukovich, a very smart guy, he was the real sage on our board, and he was the captain of forty-eight truck [Ladder 48] in Hunts Point, and he was the one who told me about the truss roofs. I can remember him in the office, sitting back in his chair tapping a pencil, explaining that to us, saying, 'We had those things in Hunts Point.' Up in the warehouses up there, truss roofs were pretty common, all these old-timers from the Bronx knew all about them.

"Vukovich even knew about the 'rain roofs,' like at Waldbaum's. With the truss roofs, the water would stay on them, so they'd build a little dome where the water could come and roll right off 'em. He knew how weak they were, how they could fall. I had just taken the captain's test at the time, and I said to him, 'All that studying and I don't remember there being anything about truss roofs in there.' And he just said, 'Maybe because there *is* nothing in there.' It was an indictment on the job, I always thought, that guys up in the Bronx knew about these things but there was nothing in any of the training bulletins that said anything about truss roofs, so no one really knew about them."

The widows of the six victims later won a wrongful-death suit against the fiscal crisis–strapped buildings department and fire department, for not training firemen to deal with truss roofs or conducting the building and fire inspections that should have turned up the structural flaws and code violations in the supermarket years ago. After winning the case, the widows' lawyer, Robert Sullivan, obtained a new trial for Eric Jackson, the man convicted of the six arson murders, by showing that statements made by a fire marshal that Jackson wasn't guilty were kept from the defense and that the police and fire department investigators couldn't agree on whether the fire was even arson. (One fire investigator later admitted to Louise O'Connor that evidence was trumped-up in the search for blame.) Jackson was eventually acquitted on all counts and the fire deemed accidental, probably the result of faulty electrical wiring.

From a distance, it seems strange that the last great fire of the War Years would be a blaze in a bustling supermarket in a white, middle-class, largely suburban neighborhood. But on closer inspection, the Waldbaum's fire was emblematic of the period it brought to a close. Like the generation of planners and politicians led by Robert Moses, John O'Hagan had spent his career dealing with not just the city's fire problems as they were, but as he thought they would be, overlooking the blighted tenements and decaying warehouses of the Bronx to focus on the gleaming high-rises of Midtown Manhattan. And to fight fires in that city of the future, he'd devised the techniques of the future: cutting-edge technology, advanced communications systems, and, most important, a new method of quantifying and rationalizing the city itself, turning departments like the fire service from staid, reactive bureaucracies into efficient, proactive organizations run by numbers and computers, not tradition and intuition.

The old ways of doing business certainly had their irrationalities and shortcomings. But in the quest to rationalize and centralize from the top down, to focus on the big picture and the comprehensive plan, the realities of a bottom-up jury-rigged city had fallen through the cracks. Just as neighborhoods consumed by flame were pushed to the side by the city and the department responsible for protecting them, so too were the lessons to be learned in those neighborhoods. Like the War Years themselves, the Waldbaum's collapse was a presumed act of arson that turned out to be caused by big ideas, misaligned priorities, and the lost lessons of the Bronx.

Rising from the ashes.
(Photo courtesy Henry Chalfant)

Conclusion

Life is not an illogicality; yet it is a trap for logicians. It looks just a little more mathematical and regular than it is; its exactitude is obvious, but its inexactitude is hidden; its wildness lies in wait.

—G. K. CHESTERTON

The history books," writes Steven Johnson, "tend to orient themselves around nationalist story lines: overthrowing the king, electing the presidents, fighting the battles. But the history book of recent *Homo sapiens* as a species should begin and end with one narrative line: We became city dwellers." Along with that move to the city has come a fundamental shift in the way that we perceive, organize, and understand the world around us. Millions of years of evolution have hotwired our brains to turn the seemingly disconnected events of life (dark clouds, water falling from the sky, a violent flash flood) into coherent, cause-and-effect storylines with implicit messages (if you see rain clouds, head for the hills!). Animals, of course, have the same capabilities—just ask Pavlov's dogs—but it's the depth of our ability to gather and analyze information and pass that understanding on to others that makes us human.

For millennia, we have been able to organize our thoughts and experiences around narrative, using past experiences—our own, those of people we know, stories handed down from religion and myth—to make decisions about how to live. The gradual transition of nomadic bands of hunter-gatherers into settled communities, nations, and empires certainly tested the reach of human understanding and decision-making. But the last two hundred years or so—when we have grown from a planet of fewer than a billion people, with only 3 percent of them living in cities, into one of nearly 7 billion, with roughly half of us packed into crowded urban environments—have put the limitations of our Neolithic brains into stark relief against the backdrop of a postmodern world.

Society has had more than a few growing pains during this most recent transformation, and the nomenclature used to categorize the last two centuries gives us a hint as to why. We have gone from the so-called Industrial Age to the Information Age: first we built this utterly new, impossibly dense, unimaginably confusing modern world of ours; then we tried to make sense of it all. Our method for understanding this new world, though, is in fact the same one that Mesopotamian farmers developed tens of thousands of years ago to keep track of their increasingly large crop yields: numbers.

Through a combination of brain structure and sentimentality, narrative is still the dominant form of human communication and persuasion, from newspaper stories, novels, and television shows, to the canned anecdotes of political candidates, who, to rally support for health care reform, talk about how Edna K., of Ames, Iowa, can't pay for her cancer treatments. But increasingly, for those stories to have an impact, we the audience need them put into a broader context, extrapolated into a world of numbers where Edna K. is no longer just Edna K., she's a stand-in for tens of millions of uninsured and underinsured Americans struggling to pay the bills.

For all the seeming disparity of the primary issues behind the burning of New York—the isolated, root-approach governance of progressive reformers; slum and industrial clearance; the collapse of New York's ghettos; the RAND firehouse closings—it is this shift, from using narrative to using numbers to make complex decisions, that connects them all. In that sense, the War Years are more than just a dark period in the history of a single city. They're a chapter in the broader story of how statistics have implanted themselves so deeply into the way cities and governments are run that number-driven efficiency is no longer a reformer's crusade; it's conventional wisdom, simply the way business is done.

Using numbers to help govern is of course nothing new, but it was the information revolution kicked off by inventions like the adding machine and the modern slide rule, and the resultant rise of scientific management and progressivism, that truly transformed statistics and the way we use them. Muckrakers like Jacob Riis used statistics to overwhelm readers with the scale of society's problems. What Episcopalian relief society could possibly hope to feed, educate, and Americanize impoverished Ukrainian Jews "packed at the rate of 290,000 to the square mile"? What good were a few settlement houses or disease wards in neighborhoods "that turned out in the last eight years a round half million beggars," and produced cholera epidemics in which "tenants died at the rate of one hundred and ninety-five to the thousand of population"? The only group up to the task, in the estimation of concerned reformers, was a new kind of efficient, scientifically managed government.

Of course, this analysis ignored the very real aid that the government and Tammany Hall were already providing to the poor in return for votes. Political machines were the antithesis of scientific management, using an anecdotal approach to decision making based on experience and secondhand stories, not statistical trend lines. It was a far from perfect system. Anyone who didn't vote the right way couldn't get his story heard. Tammany's upper ranks were filled with powerful slumlords and sweatshop operators whose very survival depended on exploiting the immigrant poor, and they stymied labor and housing improvements at every turn. But there was a genius to the structure, a sort of organizational humility: Tammany chieftains and ward bosses didn't pretend to know what was best for individual precincts or neighborhoods on the basis of some statistical measurement. They were more ploddingly reactive, letting constituents come to them with new ideas for improving things and backing the ideas that seemed most credible or were the easiest to drum up support for. Intrinsically connected to the street, machine bosses had no time for abstract notions of how impoverished immigrants should be housed or fed or educated; they were forced to contend with the problems of the slums as they were. After all, stray too far from reality and someone with a better sense of what voters wanted would up and take your place.

Utopian reformers had little interest in the incremental changes of a muddling political machine,* and disasters like the Triangle Fire and the daily tragedies documented in *How the Other Half Lives* merely confirmed their belief that Tammany was incapable of addressing society's problems. For ambitious progressives like Robert Moses, only sweeping reforms and grand societal shifts would do, and to fight poverty they used the same scientific techniques that muckrakers like Riis had used to bring the problems to light in the first place. Through exhaustive census, health, and architectural surveys, reformers could map out entire city districts and "see" the impact that widening a street, building a park, or adding new tenement regulations would have. A few thousand slum apartments could be wiped out here, fifty thousand people would finally have indoor plumbing there—all of it orchestrated from afar just as a stock broker might roll over an investment portfolio, or an industrialist reconfigure his assembly lines.

The intellectual justification for urban renewal was built on numbers. It was only through statistics, Jane Jacobs points out, that there "arose the supposed feasibility of large-scale relocation of citizens. In the form of statistics, these citizens were no longer components of any unit except the family, and could be dealt with intellectually like grains of sand, or electrons. . . . The larger the number of uprooted, the more easily they could be planned for on the basis of mathematical averages."†

---

*Even the very real benefits the machine provided could be ignored by political adversaries. Jobs programs were often seen as nothing more than corrupt and wasteful vote-buying, and the slow march of upward mobility was often denigrated, as yesterday's huddled masses were turned into tomorrow's saloonkeepers, "slumlords," and "fat-paunched bundles of corruption," as F. Scott Fitzgerald's Amory Blaine put it.
†It's no wonder that Roger Starr was so shocked at the acrimonious reception of his calls for planned shrinkage and his assertions that "American communities can be disassembled and

New York was at the vanguard of this transition, but the same process has occurred all over the country and the world. From Boston's West End, Chicago's Cabrini Green projects, and San Francisco's bulldozed Fillmore District, to the high-rise "suburbs" of Paris and astringently formal cities like Brasilia (so rationally subdivided by its Le Corbusier–inspired designers that it came complete with Orwellian-sounding designations such as Hotel Sectors North and South—neighborhoods located, appropriately enough, near Lake Paranoa). Scientific policy-making in New York received a double boost from Robert Moses, who not only was the philosophy's greatest practitioner, but also killed its enemy with kindness, fattening up Tammany with so much "legal graft" during the slum-clearance era that the machine bulldozed and chased its own constituency to the suburbs.

After systems analysis churned out clunkers like the Vietnam War, the Whiz Kid dream of a world where the complicated task of governance was handled by model-wielding technocrats was put on hold. But this was less the result of a rethinking of the role that purely quantitative tools should have in complicated decision-making than the unintended side effect of a rejection of the political paradigm that had propped up scientific governance in the first place: the centralized, root approach to problem solving. The root approach depends almost entirely on statistical analysis. Just as John Lindsay could never be expected to find the right pothole filler as quickly as the clubhouse savants of Tammany, no central planner can gain the experiential understanding of conditions on the ground that a local expert does. What a central planner can lay claim to are statistical tools that compile and distill so much information that local knowledge seems unnecessary. Sometimes this is useful—a statistician looking at death rates is often better at spotting public health problems than a local physician who doesn't see the broader trends—but when root-approach planners are in charge they often give far too

---

reconstituted about as readily as freight trains." He was just giving voice to the conventional wisdom of his field.

much leeway to their like-minded number-crunching brethren, leaving the Dr. Strangeloves to run amok.

For America, the two decades following World War II proved tailor-made for the root approach. The World Wars had been fought and won; there was little chance of the country's going over to Communism (the McCarthy Red Scare aside); the economy boomed; the Democratic and Republican parties were at their most congenial. It was a unique Age of Consensus, and governing the country seemed to call only for cool, thoughtful rationality: lining up the numbers, weighing the costs and benefits—a job for nonpartisan experts who remained above the political fray. At the pinnacle of American power were "Wise Men" like Robert Lovett: boarding school and Ivy League compatriots who filled presidential cabinets, sat on one another's corporate boards, and made the behind-the-scenes deals that really mattered, regardless of their political affiliation. ("I don't care whether a man is a Democrat or an Igorot," JFK famously told the head of his transition team, Clark Clifford. "I want the best fellow I can get for the particular job.")

Just as important were the people who implemented those decisions, the college-educated "Organization Men" who staffed the government and private industry. For both the leaders and the middle managers, governance was not the experiment in hurly-burly adaptation and incrementalism that it was for the working-class decision makers in city and state politics. It was an exercise in grand ideas conceived by a few powerful men, debated by a few more, and administered to the masses from on high: programs like the Marshall Plan and the founding of NATO, the Housing Act of 1949 and the Highway Act of 1956, and revitalized New Deal institutions like Fannie Mae and the Federal Housing Administration.

But by the 1950s, cracks were beginning to show in the façade. Poets tend to be a bit ahead of the curve on such matters, and in 1956, Allen Ginsberg's poem *Howl* transformed the highways and skyscrapers of Moses-era New York into Moloch, the bull-headed god of Middle

Eastern antiquity who demanded mass child sacrifice. "Moloch whose buildings are judgment! Moloch the vast stone of war! Moloch the stunned governments! / Moloch whose mind is pure machinery! Moloch whose blood is running money!" (It's only fitting that another great sage of the Beats, William S. Burroughs, was the grandson of the inventor of the Burroughs adding machine.)

Along with the artists, intellectuals like Jane Jacobs and Nobel Prize–winning economists like Herbert Simon, Friedrich von Hayek, Milton Friedman, and James M. Buchanan convincingly attacked the notion that a privileged elite should or even could make decisions for the rest of us. Central planners spent too much time worrying about theoretical cities to understand real ones, Jacobs wrote—those matters were better left to the corner shopkeeper, the housewife on the stoop. Planned economies (like the Soviet Union's) were too slow to react to changing market conditions and consumer desires, said Hayek. According to Herbert Simon, the whole notion that central planning rested on—that there was such a thing as "perfect information" that could be found and applied to complex decisions—was a fiction.

As the ideas developed, so did their political application. Where the youthful left had staged a largely uncoordinated rebellion, by the late 1970s the reorganized right of Barry Goldwater and Ronald Reagan found that its most effective rallying cry was a rejection of root-approach elitism. The Whiz Kids had fought a war against poverty, the Gipper noted, and poverty had won. Bureaucrats and red tape were gumming up the machinery of capitalism by punishing profitability and stifling entrepreneurialism. In Great Britain, Margaret Thatcher and the Conservative Party rode the same wave into power. On both sides of the pond, the economic policy most associated with this movement has been tax cuts, but those cuts were originally pitched (before the rise of supply-side economics) not as a good in and of themselves, but as an indirect means of keeping government planners down: simply starve them of funds.

After the Reagan Revolution, the top-down root approach was

increasingly out of fashion in America governance, but in the private sector and quasi-governmental bodies that were sheltered from public scrutiny, the technocracy thrived. After his ouster from the Pentagon, Robert McNamara took over the World Bank, which along with the International Monetary Fund dispensed huge loans attached to a series of expert-approved economic reforms usually known as "conditionalities" or "structural adjustment programs." Number-crunchers have of course made their mark all over private industry, but particularly on Wall Street, where physics Ph.D.'s and MIT analysts began showing up in the 1970s and 1980s. Initially they faced skepticism, derisively dubbed "quants" by the trade-from-the-gut old-timers in charge (like the Whiz Kids, the quants quickly adopted the derisive term for themselves). Slowly, though, Wall Street came around, as the quants exploited tiny inefficiencies in the market to maximize profits, and developed risk models to help banks keep an eye on just how much money their traders were risking.

As the root-approach failures of the 1960s and 1970s faded from memory, and number whizzes enjoyed so much success in the quasi-public and private sectors, model-wielding technocrats and their root-approach enablers returned to government as well.* In Great Britain during the 1990s, Tony Blair and Gordon Brown's Labour Party developed an array of statistical tools to measure the job performance of everyone from sanitation workers to cabinet ministers. To cut costs and improve services, the British National Health Service was revamped along quantitative lines drawn up by Alain Enthoven, a onetime RAND analyst, Wohlstetter acolyte, and McNamara Whiz Kid turned health care academic.

At the federal level in America, the Bush administration's foreign policy used the centralized, root approach for overthrowing and

---

*One of the great ironies of the anti-root-approach rallying cries of Reagan- and Thatcher-era conservatism and its rejection of big government is that conservative politicians were forced to look to the private sector (where the high-handed root approach flourished) for new ways of running the government.

rebuilding a foreign government (Iraq) to a degree not seen since the days of McNamara's Vietnam policy, the result perhaps of having a foreign policy team composed of former RAND hands like Condoleezza Rice, Paul Wolfowitz, and Donald Rumsfeld, and Albert Wohlstetter acolytes like Richard Perle and Zalmay Khalilzad. (The invasion of Iraq was, in Perle's words, "the first war that's been fought in a way that would recognize Albert's vision of future wars. That it was won so quickly and decisively, with so few casualties and so little damage, was in fact an implementation of his strategy and his vision.")

At the municipal level, perhaps the most famous example of statistical decision-making is the NYPD's CompStat system, which has received the lion's share of the credit for New York's precipitous crime drop since the early 1990s. Introduced by Mayor Rudy Giuliani and Police Commissioner William Bratton, CompStat tracks crime trends block by block and demands accountability from police in high-crime areas. In 2000, Baltimore introduced a citywide version of CompStat called CitiStat. More recently, Michael Bloomberg has tried to quantitatively rationalize the business of governing to a greater degree than any New York mayor, perhaps any American mayor, since John Lindsay. A former Wall Street technocrat, and creator of the Bloomberg Terminal electronic stock ticker, Bloomberg, writes *The New Yorker*'s Ben McGrath, believes in "big-picture governance, of the sort that can be measured only through Scorecard Cleanliness Ratings, NYCStat Stimulus Trackers, and sustainability indicator dashboards."

Unfortunately, the same mistakes made by urban-renewal bureaucrats, NYC-RAND fire modelers, and McNamara's Whiz Kids have repeated themselves, even in the private-sector applications where they seemed to find their greatest success. The stock market, it turns out, doesn't always follow the laws of probability. According to the dominant risk models, the odds of 1987's "Black Monday," when the stock market lost 23 percent of its value for no apparent reason, were less than 1 in a sextillion (that's a 1 with twenty-one zeros after it). But Black Monday did happen, as did the series of "once in a million years" financial tumults that roiled the markets in 1997,* wiped out a bevy of quantitative hedge funds in the summer of 2007, and sparked the financial collapse of 2008. Naive models not only were unable to predict such cataclysms (few experts were, either), but also played central roles in creating them—from the herd mentality of computer-driven trading, to the risky gambling of bankers who were convinced they'd mastered the risks and irrationalities of the market with science.

In international economics, the original "structural adjustment program" was New York City during the Big MAC years, when a group of bankers and unelected bureaucrats imposed rigid financial restraints on the city in return for loans. A mixed success when the planners actually lived in the city they were structurally adjusting, the IMF's and the World Bank's approach has proved even more problematic when applied to far-flung countries that have little of the social, political, and economic history that American and European planners often take for granted.

In British attempts at rationalizing government, much of the quantification bordered on the absurd (measurements of "birdsong" were used in quality-of-life indices for British villages), but the real problems came in more substantive programs such as the National Health Service, where managers resorted to fraud to make their numbers look better. To cut down on waiting times, hospitals created what became known as "hello nurses," the medical equivalent of Wal-Mart greeters. The hello nurse's job was to welcome patients and mark them down as admitted (thus cutting wait time), even though they had received nothing in the way of medical treatment. To improve surgery numbers, simple procedures such as vasectomies and bunion removals were upped, and serious surgeries pushed back.

In New York City, CompStat certainly played a role in bringing down crime statistics, but that seems to have had more to do with pure power

---

*Famously bankrupting the ultimate quant hedge fund, Long-Term Capital Management, run by a pair of Nobel Prize–winning economists and former colleagues of Mayor Bloomberg's from the investment bank Salomon Brothers.

politics than with the illuminating power of numbers. Throughout the 1970s and 1980s, the NYPD had grown increasingly insular and hierarchical. New ideas were shunned, policies were made at One Police Plaza instead of on the streets, and there seemed little that anyone, even mayors, could do about it. In its original form, CompStat actually had a touch of Jane Jacobs, shaking up the power structure by decentralizing the decision-making process and giving greater authority to local precinct captains and cops on the beat to police their neighborhoods as they saw fit (provided they could show statistical evidence that it was working). Baltimore's version of CompStat has few of those branch-approach elements, and police brass and politicians there have been accused of faking crime statistics to make themselves and the system look good— an issue that formed one of the more fascinating subplots in the last few seasons of *The Wire*.

More recently, Mayor Bloomberg has brought back not only statistical governance, but root-approach planning as well. Most of his defining initiatives have been massive top-down development projects. Some, like the stadiums for the Yankees and the Mets, were bequeathed from his predecessor, Rudy Giuliani, but most have been Bloomberg's own. Banks including Goldman Sachs were handed hundreds of millions of dollars in government subsidies to build new headquarters. One project proposed building a football stadium over Manhattan's West Side railyards as part of a plan to host the 2012 Olympic Games.* (The stadium project was killed by community opposition and Albany lawmakers, and the area is now slated to become Hudson Yards, a mix of government-subsidized residential and office towers.) A similar plan to cover downtown Brooklyn's railyards with a basketball stadium and high-rises passed the necessary legislative hurdles (despite a $1 to $2

*The Olympic bid was spearheaded by investment banker Dan Doctoroff, who later became Bloomberg's deputy mayor and is now the president of Bloomberg's media company, and by Lindsay's former chief of staff Jay Kriegel, who helped fight off attempts by Congress to prevent the city from using eminent domain and giving the land to developers.

billion price tag for the government), yet while the basketball stadium is on track to be built, the rest of the project is on the back burner thanks to a lack of funding and the current glut of luxury housing and office space already on the market. The Bloomberg-backed rezoning of vast swaths of the city (the largest rezoning since 1961, when industry was barred from much of Manhattan) and most of the mayor's development agenda have fallen prey to the financial crisis as well, leaving the city pockmarked with subsidized office towers built for banks that wouldn't exist without federal bailouts, and high-rise luxury condos that no one seems to want anymore.

Although Tammany Hall and its anecdotal approach to governance are long gone, the elements that built it have been alive and well in New York over the last few decades. They provide an alternative history to the conventional wisdom that Gotham was saved from on high by technocratic budgets cuts and police reforms, and trickle-down cash from Wall Street's scientifically acquired billions, and a different model of how the city might recover from its current plight. It's a story of rebirth and renewal written by ordinary people hailing from the most famous victim of the root approach, the South Bronx.

STAND ON A SOUTH BRONX STREET CORNER IN THE LATE 1970s and you'd see him. Sticking his head through the shattered side window of a stripped car left on the street to rust. Standing in the middle of an empty lot, soft-eyeing the piles of trash dumped by some lazy city sanitation crew or mobbed-up private refuse company looking to save on dumping fees. Wispy-thin and loose-limbed in his Super PRO-Keds sneakers and a Kangol hat, Joseph Saddler was always tapping his fingers, keening his ears for some faraway rhythm, listening for the *beat*. He heard it in the shake and rattle of old steam pipes on cold nights, the clanking rumble of the elevated 5 train, like the world was giving him a private concert everywhere he went. Saddler had been too young and too Bronx-bound to ever know Radio Row's speaker shops and electronic equipment scrap bins, before the area was bulldozed to make way for the World Trade Center, but the destruction of the Bronx had taken care of that for him, the abandoned buildings, garbage heaps, and junked cars providing all the free speakers, wire, and stray bits of circuitry that a kid with a soldering iron and a little know-how could hope for.

The same week that the South Bronx's Engine 50-2 closed in April 1974, Saddler left his apartment a few blocks away, bound for his first all-night jam, a DJ spinning records till six in the morning at the Cedar Park Recreation Center near the Harlem River. Herc, they called the guy, Kool Herc, throwing dance parties in the rec room of the project his family had moved to after being burned out of their home in the central Bronx. When it was warm outside, Herc spun in city parks and concrete playgrounds, where someone would unscrew the base plate of a streetlight and boost juice straight from the city source. If anyone complained, the cops were usually too busy chasing murders and rapes or hiding from their supervisors to care. And few people complained, most of the neighbors just glad the kids were doing something besides dealing drugs and killing one another. That was one of Herc's rules—no gang colors, no beefs—and the man and his crew were big enough to enforce it. So the cut-sleeves stayed home and the girls and the gangs came to dance like supplicants at the feet of the man who controlled the music, all the aggression gone into shaking out their limbs and crowding into circles to watch whoever was in the center spinning and kicking and popping and locking. Break dancing, Herc had started calling it, because people danced best on the get-down part—the bridge, the break—when the vocals went silent and the high notes faded and there was nothing but bass, drums, *beat*.

After that night, Saddler knew it was time to take his private concert public, and started wheeling shopping carts full of DJ equipment down to the Mott Haven Projects Park on 142nd Street and Willis Avenue, where he became tight with Tiny, a roughneck member of the Casanovas street gang who made it known that the boy and his crew could rock the park whenever. Redubbed Grandmaster Flash after a local stick-up kid said he played records "like some kinda grand chess master," Flash became the first DJ to lay hands on a record while it spun, cutting it backward to extend the break, inventing that *zuka-zuka* sound that became scratching. Along with a former gang leader calling himself Afrika Bambaataa, they became the Holy Trinity of the South Bronx—Herc, Flash, and Bam, turning the DJ from a guy who played records into a one-man band with as many sounds as he could conjure from his equipment. Suddenly the South Bronx was known for something other than death, drugs, and fire: it was the birthplace of hip-hop.

It was more than turntables, of course. If you were historically inclined, you'd have to say the writers had come first, graffiti artists like "TAKI 183" and "LEE" Quinones, who scaled crumbling buildings to write their tags, and broke into the unguarded subway holding yards in the North Bronx where they had all night to paint epic, train-car-long murals that would be seen by thousands of people every day as they wound their course through the city. Then there were the break-dancers who kept the DJ parties going, and of course the rappers, more Bronx boys like the Cold Crush Brothers, Melle Mel, and the Furious Five. They talked trash and spat rhymes, and along with the rest turned hip-hop into not just a few records and a couple dollars, but arguably the most influential artistic and cultural phenomenon of the second half of the twentieth century.

While the kids were giving birth to new art forms, another group of Bronxites was laying the foundations for recovery of a very different kind. On Kelly Street in 1977, residents pitched in and renovated their dilapidated apartment buildings to keep the city from demolishing them. They went on to form Banana Kelly (named after the street's crescent shape), and over the last thirty years they have rehabbed and weatherized ten thousand units of housing, built a dormitory for homeless high school students, and helped bring a health clinic and small businesses back to the neighborhood. A few blocks away, Father Louis Gigante of St. Athanasius Catholic Church formed the South East Bronx Community

Organization, which has built and rehabbed more than eight thousand units of affordable housing in Hunts Point.

In the 1980s, Mayor Ed Koch introduced a housing program unlike anything ever proposed by city government. Instead of clearing vast swaths of land or unleashing the pent-up dreams of isolated planners, the program put development money in the hands of local community groups and nonprofits that used it to renovate, rebuild, and issue loans specifically tailored to individual communities. "I knew that a lot of the people who came from the South, like me, were used to having a small backyard," says Genevieve Brooks-Brown, who founded a development group that rebuilt devastated Charlotte Street with small ranch-style houses that sold like hotcakes and became the symbol of Bronx recovery. "People didn't think we could do it, but there was a group of folks from the city and HUD that were very cooperative, and we did."

Like "the rose that grew from concrete," as rapper and poet Tupac Shakur once wrote, or the Phoenix born out of its own ashes, over the last thirty years the South Bronx has taken the very things that the destruction of the War Years left behind, retooled and reshaped and repurposed them, and fashioned a recovery no one could have foreseen. Given up for dead, ignored by City Hall, slated for "planned shrinkage," the borough has showcased the curious ability of ordinary people to defy the best- and worst-laid plans of the elites who would analyze and model and decide for them. (As will likely happen again when artists, entrepreneurs, and deal-seeking home buyers fill up the city's stock of empty condos and offices in the coming years.) But their resilience is no excuse for not trying to understand how our governments and institutions can best encourage that native creativity and entrepreneurial energy. Or, at the very least, get out of the way.

ACKNOWLEDGMENTS

First and foremost, I'd like to thank the men and women of the South Bronx and the Fire Department of New York, who so generously shared their time, insights, and experiences with me. In particular, the people of 139th Street in Mott Haven, Jimmy Boyle, Tom Henderson, Vincent Dunn, Tom Von Essen, Sandy Sansevero, Jack Lerch, Daniel Maye, and Eddie Fahey. On the following page is information on two fine charities that support firefighting families in need and arts projects in the Bronx.

The photographs are courtesy of Ralph Bernard and Randy Barron at the FDNY Photo Unit, Harvey Eisner, Lisa Kahane, Henry Chalfant, Dan Comstock at Los Alamos National Laboratory, and Win Ruml and the Trombetta Agency.

For help with research, I'd like to thank Sam Hornblower for the time he donated and the angles he discovered; Jo Evans, Eileen Markey, and Emma Rebhorn for all their help; and Tom Robbins, who kindly opened up his arson files. I owe a great debt of gratitude to Charles Jennings of John Jay College, the rare person who can see things from both academic and operational sides, and to Emily Bell and Anna Jardine for handling far too many unruly details. I'd also like to thank all the members of the Lindsay administration, NYC-RAND Institute, and RAND archivists in Santa Monica, California, who shared their files and time even when they knew they wouldn't agree with my conclusions. Thanks also to Rebecca O'Brien, Dan Rosenheck, F. Reynolds, Dan Brook, Katharine Marino, and Jeremy Reff, who all read drafts of various lengths; and for showing a little faith, a special thanks to Larry and Sascha Weissman, Sean McDonald, Clayton Patterson, and Musa Gurnis.

Most important, I'd like to thank my sister, Caitlin, my mother, Mary—a longtime IT professional who used to bring me to work back in the Stone Age days of room-sized mainframes surrounded by rows of tape drives—and my father, Mark, recently retired from the Newton, Massachusetts, police department. They were teaching me about systems analysis and the civil service long before I knew.

The Arce-Boyle Memorial Fund is a nonprofit 501(c)3 corporation created for the dual purpose of preserving the memory of David "Buddha" Arce and Michael Boyle of FDNY Engine Co. 33, who died in the line of duty on September 11, 2001, and helping firefighting families who are in need. The fund makes contributions without personal recognition or publicity but with enduring love. Donations can be made to:

Arce-Boyle Memorial Fund
c/o Colleran, O'Hara & Mills LLP
1225 Franklin Avenue, Suite 450
Garden City NY 11530
Tel.: 516-248-5757

The Bronx Council on the Arts, a private nonprofit membership organization, is the officially designated cultural agency of the Bronx. For forty-eight years, the BCA has provided quality cultural services and arts programs to the multicultural constituency of the borough. The mission of the Bronx Council on the Arts is to encourage and increase the public's awareness of and participation in the arts and nurture the development of artists and arts organizations. Donations can be made to:

Bronx Council on the Arts
1738 Hone Avenue
Bronx, NY 10461
Tel.: 718-931-9500
Fax: 718-409-6445
www.bronxarts.org

NOTES

v   **We must be aware:** Trilling, p. 221.

ONE. THE WAR YEARS

1   **The War Years:** In this chapter, in addition to interviews with Louise O'Connor, fire investigators, and firemen who were at the scene of the Waldbaum's collapse, accounts of the fire are drawn from newspaper accounts compiled in DiMaria.

1   **"We cannot understand firemen":** Murray Kempton, "A Trip to the Hearts of the Fire," *New York Post*, 8/3/1978.

1   **"I saw flames":** Vincent Lee, Thomas Raftery, Albert Davila, and Donald Singleton, "B'klyn Blaze Kills 6 Firemen," New York *Daily News*, 8/3/1978.

1   **At 8:39, the call:** "What the Tapes Say About the Fire," New York *Daily News*, 8/4/1978.

2   **Before the terrorist attacks:** Dunn.

4   **about the rain roof:** Bart Mitchell, "Roof Collapse: A Legal Perspective," in DiMaria, p. 164 (originally published in *Firehouse* magazine).

6   **"All of a sudden":** John Kifner, "Six Firemen Killed as Roof Collapses at Brooklyn Blaze," *The New York Times*, 8/3/1978.

6   **From his shoe store:** Ibid.

6   **"When the roof collapsed":** Jimmy Breslin, "Intense Heat Then a Chill in Heart," New York *Daily News*, 8/3/1978.

7   **"We responded":** Jimmy Breslin, "Irish Wake: An Exercise in Grief," New York *Daily News*, 8/6/1978.

7   **In the parking lot:** Kifner, "Six Firemen Killed as Roof Collapses at Brooklyn Blaze."

8   **three hundred per year:** FDNY Annual Fire Reports, 1962–1977. Unless otherwise noted, all fire statistics are taken from the FDNY's Annual Reports, and from annual runs and workers statistics compiled by Ira Hoffman for the Fire Bell Club of New York, both of which are available at the Mand Fire Library at the FDNY Fire Academy at Randall's Island, New York City.

8   **$12 billion in debt:** Because of the complicated nature of the city's debt (hidden through a variety of short- and long-term bonds and lending schemes), exact figures tend to vary, but according to the city's own budget figures, as published in a memorandum submitted by Mayor Ed Koch to the Senate Banking Committee in 1979, and reprinted in Koch, p. 50, the city owed $12.3 billion in short- and long-term debt.

9   **The urban planner Robet Moses:** Chang, p. 18.

9   **Roger Starr:** Detailed in Roger Starr, "Making New York Smaller," *The New York Times Magazine*, 11/14/1976, and in Sternlieb and Hughes, p. 17

10 **Despite getting a call:** "What the Tapes Say About the Fire," New York *Daily News*, 8/4/1978.

10 **The department took so long:** John F. Burns, "City Is Accused As Fire Kills 10," *The New York Times*, 2/5/1976.

10 **Some people in Queens:** John Darnton, "City's Fire Alarm Boxes Are Called Undependable," *The New York Times*, 12/20/1974.

11 **"We charge that the city":** John Kifner, "Top Officials and Union Debate Handling of Blaze Fatal to 6 Firefighters," *The New York Times*, 8/4/1978.

11 **On the morning of October 5, 1977:** Descriptions of Charlotte Street and Carter's visit are drawn from author interviews with local residents, newspaper articles, and Jill Jonnes' excellent history of the neighborhood, *South Bronx Rising*.

11 **"Give us money!":** Lee Embart, "Carter Takes 'Sobering' Trip to South Bronx," *The New York Times*, 10/6/1977.

12 **"There had been so much life":** Jonnes, p. 248.

12 **"this entire area":** Ibid., p. 203.

13 **"You know that nice park":** Grace Paley, "Somewhere Else," *The New Yorker*, 10/23/1978.

13 **"That's the very area":** Major League Baseball, *The New York Yankees: 1977 World Series* (DVD, Collector's Edition).

13   "a spectacular set of ruins": Chang, p. 17.

14   "Everybody was gone": Jonnes, p. 339.

14   Youth unemployment rates: Chang, p. 13.

14   "Necropolis—a city of death": Martin Tolchin, "South Bronx: A Jungle Stalked by Fear, Seized by Rage," *The New York Times*, 1/15/1973.

14   "as crucial to an understanding": "The Trip to the Bronx," *The New York Times*, 10/6/1977.

14   "a condition of poverty": Chang, p. 17.

15   "who remember the Bronx": Berman, p. 219.

15   the city hemorrhaged: 1970 and 1980 census figures, and Morris, pp. 68, 71.

15   the murder rate: In 1963, the first year for which accurate citywide murder statistics are available, 548 murders were committed; the city's population was nearly 8 million. In 1979, there were 1,733 murders, and the population had dropped to just over 7 million. See Thomas J. Lueck, "Low Murder Rate Brings New York Back to '63," *The New York Times*, 12/31/2007, and Randy Young, "Death by Stranger," *New York*, 4/17/1980.

15   A new breed of rat: Newfield and Du Brul, p. 3.

15   measles and tuberculosis: Wallace, 2001, and Wallace and Wallace, 1998.

16   "It's the fucking blacks": Fitch, p. vii.

17   600,000 people's homes: Wallace and Wallace, p. 18.

17   The city's economic output: Budget Bureau, p. 39.

17   And while those blights: Wallace and Wallace, p. 81.

18   arson was taking its toll: Statistics compiled from FDNY Annual Fire Reports. Because of steep cuts in the number of fire marshals in the early 1970s, they were unable to investigate as many fires as in previous years, and the official arson rates are almost certainly too low from about 1972 to 1976. But by the late 1970s, when fire marshal ranks were expanded and new investigators felt the need to justify their own existence with high arson rates, arson stayed below 7 percent of total fires. The combined rate of arson and suspicious fires (a catchall categorization for fires whose cause fire marshals couldn't determine) peaked at 14 percent. The numbers were higher in many individual neighborhoods, some firemen estimate the arson rate was as high as 30 percent in the South Bronx, but many of those were small trash and nuisance fires, or were set in already burned-out or abandoned buildings.

19   There was ample reason: All figures taken from Moynihan, *Maximum Feasible Misunderstanding*, pp. 26–28.

20   75 percent decrease in American: From a rate of 40 to 45 deaths per million in the late 1950s and early 1960s (Committee on Fire Toxicology, p. 17) to fewer than 11 per million in 2008 (Karter, Table 6, p. 17).

21 **"You go into those pieces of shit":** Interview with FDNY Captain Tom Henderson.

21 **national fire fatality rate:** National fatality rates are from Committee on Fire Toxicology, p. 17. New York rates are based on fire death rates, which hovered around 18 to 20 deaths per million when O'Hagan took over as chief of department in the early 1960s, and rose to more than 40 per million by the late 1970s.

22 **fifty companies in all:** Denis Hamill, "Where There's Smoke . . ," *New York*, 2/13/1978, p. 14.

22 **Fire inspections were cut:** The number of fire inspections fell from 1,529,334 in 1965, to 474,331 in 1976.

TWO. THE FIREMAN AND THE REFORMER

27 **"Thus the city presents":** Quoted in Campbell, pp. 39–40.

27 **John O'Hagan was raised:** Descriptions of John O'Hagan's early life are drawn largely from interviews with his eldest daughter, Catherine.

27 **"a fresh, green breast":** Fitzgerald, *The Great Gatsby*, p. 115.

28 **$24 worth of trinkets:** The trade was actually for goods worth 60 Dutch guilders—a figure converted by a New York historian in 1848 to $24. "If recalculated in current dollars," historians Edwin G. Burrows and Mike Wallace wrote in 1999, "the sum would come out—so Amsterdam's Nederlandsche Bank tells us—to $669.42. Yet a variable-rate myth being a contradiction in terms, the purchase price remains forever frozen at twenty-four dollars." That the trade items were trinkets is probably another nineteenth-century myth. The letter doesn't specify what the goods were, but Minuit later "purchased" Staten Island with iron kettles, ax heads, hoes, and drilling awls, making the transaction less highway robbery than "high-end technology transfer," in the words of Burrows and Wallace (p. xv).

28 **"The nuns":** Smith, p. 193.

29 **What is forbidden by the Ninth Commandment?:** *A Catechism of Christian Doctrine.*

30 **Tall, elegant, and educated:** Accounts of the early life of John Lindsay are drawn largely from Cannato.

30 **graduate a year early:** Cannato, p. 2.

31 **"The war played a part":** John V. Lindsay, *Journey into Politics: Some Informal Observations* (New York: Dodd, Mead, 1967), p. 3, as quoted in Cannato, p. 3.

31 **"one of the bright hopes":** "Lindsay Victory Puts Him in Fore," *The New York Times*, 11/5/1958.

31   **"a dominant, rather cheerless":** Cannato, p. 27.

32   **"completely individualistic":** Lindsay, *Religious Aspects in the Life and Times of Oliver Cromwell.*

32   **"GOP's Big Winner":** Cannato, p. 18.

35   **When the city's Democrat-controlled:** Golway, p. 65.

36   **Americus Engine Co. 6:** Ibid., p. 69.

36   **In 1883, progressive:** Ibid., p. 142.

39   **After a wave:** O'Hagan.

39   **"builders, developers":** Ibid.

39   **steel-and-glass high-rises:** The real estate industry even turned one of the great successes of the codes into a reason why they should be relaxed. In July 1945, a massive B-25 bomber got lost in fog and slammed into the north face of the Empire State Building, between the seventy-eighth and seventy-ninth floors. The four main components of the fire codes—compartmentalization, masonry insulation for structural beams, reinforced elevator shafts, and standpipes—all worked magnificently. The department was able to knock the fire down in thirty-five minutes, preventing any fatalities beyond the fourteen crewmen and office workers killed by the initial impact, and keeping property damage to under half a million dollars. If buildings could sustain such a large and unexpected shock, the real estate industry's argument went, couldn't the codes be lessened somewhat?

41   **"a fantastic farm":** Fitzgerald, *The Great Gatsby,* p. 16.

43   **On a chilly afternoon:** *The New York Times,* 12/17/1964.

44   **"The papers and some people":** Riordan and Plunkitt, p. 118.

44   **"Why is it":** Fitzgerald, *This Side of Paradise,* p. 175.

45   **"branch" approach:** Lindblom, p. 198.

45   **"starting from fundamentals":** Ibid.

46   **The brainchild:** Jill Lepore, "Not So Fast," review of Matthew Stewart, *The Management Myth: Why the Experts Keep Getting It Wrong* (New York: W. W. Norton, 2009), *The New Yorker,* 10/12/2009.

46   **"not so much to jail":** Caro, p. 41.

47   **"È finita":** Caro, p. 444.

47   **"The New Deal":** Paul Krugman, "Not the New Deal," *The New York Times,* 9/16/2005.

48   *Herald Tribune:* The sources in this paragraph are as quoted in Cannato, pp. xi, 22.

48   **"behavioral sink":** Tom Wolfe, "O Rotten Gotham—Sliding Down into the Behavioral Sink," in Wolfe.

49   **trouble sleeping at nights:** Cannato, p. 27.

50   *Here is New York:* White, p. 32.

50   **"perpetual muddling through":** The "muddling through" line actually predates
     Charles Lindblom's "science of muddling through" by more than a decade.

51   **"For more than half an hour":** Martin Gansberg, "38 Who Saw Murder Didn't
     Call the Police," *The New York Times*, 3/27/1964.

51   **"Nobody can say why":** As quoted in Gladwell, p. 27.

52   **"insensitive to its failings":** Cannato, p. 30.

53   **William F. Buckley:** Buckley ran a vigorous campaign of ideas that presaged the
     rightward shift in New York and American politics in the coming decades, but
     he was never a serious contender. Asked by a reporter what he would do if he
     won, Buckley said he would "demand a recount."

53   **Lindsay's thirty-two-year-old:** Descriptions of Price and election night are
     from Cannato, pp. 19–20, 25.

THREE. THE HANGMAN'S TRAP

55   **"... by three fingers":** Robert Alden, "12 Dead: The Department's Worst Fire,"
     The New York Times, 10/19/1966.

55   **An hour earlier:** Cull, p. 9.

55   **Wonder Drug store:** Maurice Carroll, "Fireman Saved from Fall Mourns His
     Friends," *The New York Times*, 10/19/1966.

57   **"The walking was real slithery":** Ibid.

57   **Fire Commissioner Lowery:** Cull, p. 25.

59   **Within a few hours:** Author interviews with Catherine O'Hagan and Tom
     Henderson.

59   **"athletic 183 pounds":** *Long Island Star Journal*, 12/17/1964.

60   **"figure in a black velvet suit":** Burnett, p. 97.

61   **The morning after:** Robert Alden, "12 Dead: The Department's Worst Fire," *The
     New York Times*, 10/19/1966, and Cull, pp. 31–32.

61   **"This is the saddest day":** Cull, p. 32.

62   **"magic economy":** Wolfe, p. 24.

63   **"are, in fact, a 'leading indicator' ":** Moynihan, "Text of the Moynihan Memo-
     randum on the Status of Negroes."

63   **fire mortality rate:** Committee on Fire Toxicology, p. 17.

64   **The *Daily News*:** New York *Daily News*, 10/19/1966, front page.

64   **The public reaction:** Robert Alden, "Firemen Bear Their Dead Down Fifth
     Avenue in Silent Grief," *The New York Times*, 10/22/1966.

67   **shit for brains:** With all due credit to Nick Hornby's novel *High Fidelity*.

67   **In 1948, FDNY Deputy Chief:** Hashagen, p. 72.

67 **Brooklyn fireman Lester Bourke:** "Fireman Designs Safety Shield for Eyes by Accident—His," *WNYF* magazine, July 1968.

FOUR. OF WHIZ KIDS AND THINK TANKS

73 **Of Whiz Kids and Think Tanks:** This chapter owes a great debt to John Byrne's book *The Whiz Kids* and Errol Morris' documentary *The Fog of War* for information on McNamara and the Whiz Kids.

73 **"They believed":** *Pandora's Box*, episode 2, "To the Brink of Eternity."

73 **"If people do not believe":** Quoted in Song Y. Yan, *An Introduction to Formal Language and Machine Computation* (River Edge, NJ: World Scientific, 1998).

74 **Lovett needed men:** Byrne, pp. 29, 32–33.

74 **asking four different agencies:** Ibid., p. 34.

74 **"It was pulled out of thin air":** Ibid., p. 33.

75 **"charting the birth and evolution":** Ibid., p. 41.

76 **George Dantzig:** Joe Holley, "Vanguard Mathematician George Dantzig Dies," *The Washington Post*, 5/19/2005.

77 **20 percent of all bombers:** *The Fog of War.*

77 **Analyzing the new B-29:** Ibid.

77 **Henry Ford's modern assembly line:** Gilbert Burck, "Henry Ford II," *Life*, 10/1/1945, p. 112.

78 **In Ford's accounts-payable:** Byrne, p. 105.

80 **"Just as the student":** Whyte, p. 7.

80 **"It is from their ranks":** Ibid., p. 3.

80 **While the military veteran:** The early history of RAND is drawn largely from Fred Kaplan's *Wizards of Armageddon*, Jennifer Light's *From Warfare to Welfare*, the Adam Curtis documentary *Pandora's Box*, and David Jardini's "Out of the Blue Yonder."

81 **The Stat Control Whiz Kids:** Kaplan, p. 355.

81 **"investigate all the possibilities":** Ibid., p. 56.

82 **A child prodigy:** Ibid., p. 64.

83 **John Williams:** Ibid.

84 **Edwin Paxson:** Ibid., pp. 86–89.

85 **a hard-drinking:** Ibid., p. 86.

85 **As a bookish teenager:** Ibid., pp. 94–95.

86 **Strategic Air Command:** Ibid., pp. 96–99.

87 **"but they each might find":** *Pandora's Box*, episode 2.

88   **"If I see that the Russians":** Kaplan, p. 134.

89   **To the young pocket-protector:** Accounts of Wohlstetter's lifestyle are taken from Kaplan, p. 122, and Neil Swidey, "The Analyst," *The Boston Globe*, 5/18/2003.

89   **good friend Le Corbusier:** *Pandora's Box*, episode 2.

90   **"missile gap":** Kaplan, pp. 161–164, and *The Fog of War*.

91   **"This slide":** Halberstam, p. 217.

91   **"that fellow from Ford":** Ibid., p. 41.

92   **On August 11:** Marc Crawford, "There's No Easy Place to Pin the Blame," *Life*, 8/27/1965.

92   **When rioting broke out:** Ward, Clark, and German journalist Hans Herbert Götz quotations are taken from Light, p. 62.

93   **Urban Institute:** Jardini, pp. 390–400.

FIVE. ENTER THE POET

97   **"the New York mind"; "the bookstores":** Moynihan, 1969, p. 147.

97   **"the contrast between ideas":** Ibid.

98   **"What they wrote":** David Grossman, "Memories of Frederick O'Reilly Hayes," presented at Fred Hayes Celebration, 12/13/2002.

98   **"toughest budget men":** "Tough Budget Man," *The New York Times*, 8/2/1966.

99   **"of total supervision":** Caro, p. 1118.

100 **" 'brains, balls, and ignorance' ":** the word "balls" is used here metaphorically, and, Isenberg is quick to point out, on gender matters Hayes was one of the most progressive members of city government, happy to hire and promote women in the traditionally male-dominated Budget Bureau.

SIX. THE FIRE NEXT DOOR

107 **Past may be prologue:** Henry T. C. Hu, "Misunderstood Derivatives: The Causes of Informational Failure and the Promise of Regulatory Incrementalism," *The Yale Law Journal* 102, no. 6 (April 1993), p. 1477. As quoted in Lowenstein, *When Genius Failed*.

107 **Standing behind a lectern:** Quotations and descriptions of NYC-RAND's opening press conference are taken from Richard Reeves, "City Hires Rand Corp to Study Four Agencies," *The New York Times*, 1/9/1968.

107 **200 million pounds:** Cannato, p. 199.

108 **"During La Guardia press conferences":** Caro, p. 1118.

108 **"We'll explain that later":** Richard Reeves, "City Hires Rand Corp to Study Four Agencies."

108 **Under intense pressure:** Jardini, pp. 252–270.

109 **"One of John Lindsay's handicaps":** Martin Arnold, "Wagner Assays Lindsay: Much Talk, Little Action," *The New York Times*, 11/21/1966.

109 **$255 million:** Cannato, p. 101.

110 **"everyone's feelings":** Aaron Wildavsky, "Recipe for Violence," *New York*, 5/20/1968, p. 90.

110 **"no issue in this campaign":** Cannato, p. 61.

111 **with welfare enrollment more than doubling:** Morris, pp. 68, 71.

111 **"an attempt to use systems analysis":** Martin Arnold, "The Lindsay Inner Circle," *The New York Times*, 10/15/1967.

111 **"knew the city and how it works":** Cannato, p. 190.

112 **43 percent of the vote:** Ibid., p. 77.

113 **C. West Churchman predicted:** Light, pp. 44–45.

113 **"techniques that are going to put":** As quoted ibid., p. 96.

114 **"Every facility":** White, p. 33.

114 **Princeton defeated:** Hastorf and Cantril, pp. 490–495. For a readable discussion of the underlying brain functions behind faulty perception and analysis, see Burton.

115 **Returning home:** Author interview with Joseph De May, Jr. A fuller account of the case, written by De May, including witness testimony, can be found at http://kewgardenshistory.com/ss-nytimes-3.html.

116 **"I don't know where that came from":** Jim Rasenberger, "Kitty, 40 Years Later," *The New York Times*, 2/28/2004.

116 **"Yeah, people heard":** Ibid.

116 **"We didn't have what":** De May, on National Public Radio's *On the Media*, 3/27/2009.

117 **twenty-nine-year-old Juan Diaz:** All quotations and descriptions are drawn from Paul Hofmann, "Fire Kills 9 Children, 4 Adults in Brooklyn," *The New York Times*, 1/10/1968.

118 **The following day:** "8 Injured in Fire, One of Many Here," *The New York Times*, 1/12/1968, and "Alarms, Assignments Given in Manhattan, Bronx Multiples," *The Chief*, 1/15–1/21/1968.

118 **Just across the Harlem River:** "Boy, 15, Rescues 9 from Fire in the Bronx," *The New York Times*, 1/10/1968.

118 **Regina and Charles Schiebel:** "Eight Children Killed in 2 Blazes Here," *The New York Times*, 12/4/1967.

119 **Earlier that same day:** Ibid.

119   **But if there was any aspect:** His lone experience as a ghetto firefighter was a short stint in a company in Brooklyn's Bedford-Stuyvesant neighborhood.

SEVEN. HOW THE OTHER HALF THINKS

123   **"You say what is a city?":** *New York: A Documentary Film.*
123   **"good fortune":** Pete Hamill, speech at Broad Street Ballroom, 1/18/2008. Excerpts can be found at http://cityroom.blogs.nytimes.com/2008/01/18/pete-hamill-downtown-on-downtown/.
124   **"free market days":** Burrows and Wallace, p. 46.
124   **"Every four years":** *New York: A Documentary Film.*
125   *How the Other Half Lives:* Riis.
125   **"Jewtown":** Ibid., p. xi.
125   **"37,316 tenements":** Ibid., p. 216.
125   **"throw off a scum":** Ibid., p. 2.
126   **close down hundreds:** Schwartz, p. 8.
126   **virtual refugee crisis:** The Bowery's flophouse population grew to 180,000 in the 1890s, and Riis, in *How the Other Half Lives*, "blamed saloons for demoralizing patrons with cheap beer."
127   **cost of ten thousand:** Ibid., p. 9.
127   **translated into public policy:** Teddy Roosevelt may have been hinting at such blind spots when he coined the term "muckraker." In a speech on the importance of investigative journalism, he referred to a character from John Bunyan's *Pilgrim's Progress*, above whose head floated the "celestial crown" of Christ, which he could grasp if he just looked up; but he was unable to, because he "could look no way but downward, with a muck-rake in his hand." In Bunyan's book, the muckraker is a cautionary character, too concerned with earthly matters to seize divinity. To Roosevelt, though, investigative journalists performed a vital function, the shit-stirrers whose eyes are always searching for corruption, scandal, and suffering to bring to the public's attention. Yet while Roosevelt's speech transformed Bunyan's muckraker into a positive figure, it also gave a subtle warning about the role muckrakers should play in society. (This was, after all, the same man who in a more famous speech said that "it is not the critic who counts, not the one who points out how the strong man stumbled or how the doer of deeds might have done better.") Looking always downward at what is evil, what aspects of society do not work, muckrakers devote little time or energy to seeing or understanding what aspects of society actually work well. Great for pointing out problems, they acquire little of the wisdom necessary for devising new structures for fixing them.

128   **"The New Deal":** *New York: A Documentary Film.*

129   **longer life-span:** A sewer system is one of the best examples of this weakness. By the 1840s, as Steven Johnson documents in his book *The Ghost Map*, London was a public health nightmare, literally "drowning in its own filth." Enter the bulldozing, root-thinking health reformer Edwin Chadwick, who whipped the bureaucracy through the staggering creation of an enormous public sewer system. There was just one problem. Like most of his learned contemporaries, Chadwick adhered to the "miasma theory" of disease: that all contagions were spread through noxious smells, or, as Chadwick put it, that "all smell is disease." In reality, the stench of backyard cesspools did nothing to spread disease. It was only when the source of the smell reached drinking water that problems arose—which is exactly what Chadwick's sewer system did, by emptying directly into the Thames River. There was plenty of evidence that dumping in the Thames was a bad idea, from the devastation of the once pristine and fish-filled waterway to a spike in the rate of the very diseases the sewer system was supposed to prevent. But even after Chadwick was pushed from office, the root-oriented bureaucracy he left behind was unable to rethink his assumption or change course; it took two decades and thousands of needless deaths to undo the damage of a single faulty theory. See Johnson, pp. 113–136.

130   **Mumford called Midtown:** Mumford, Bauer, and Stein, as quoted in Jacobs, p. 21.

130   **"Under the seeming disorder":** Jacobs, p. 50.

131   **"Some of the poorest":** From Regional Plan Association, vol. 1, "Major Economic Factors in Metropolitan Growth and Arrangement," p. 32.

131   **"In the very heart":** The report does say that the confusing diversity of New York's economy was also a strength, but given the document's broader context, this concession reads like little more than lip service.

132   **The leaders of the RPA:** Fitch, pp. 60–66.

133   **named Robert Moses:** Descriptions of Moses and his career are deeply indebted to Robert Caro's brilliant *The Power Broker*, Marshall Berman's *All That Is Solid Melts into Air*, and Hillary Ballon and Kenneth T. Jackson's *Robert Moses and the Modern City.*

133   **fifty-thousand-strong:** Caro, p. 171.

134   **"the greatest, the gaudiest":** Fitzgerald, "The Crack Up."

134   **extorting bribes:** The most notorious scam involved sweeping up female bystanders from the street, charging them with prostitution, and demanding a bribe to drop the charges. It worked for years in poor neighborhoods, but scandals broke when policemen got too greedy and began arresting middle-class white women, who had access to power and the media.

135   **"The Bridge to Nowhere":** *New York: A Documentary Film.*

135   **Even the great public works:** Caro, p. 334.

135   **a million dollars in "beneficences":** Walker's honesty was commendable: one of his deputies testified that he had made his personal fortune not from such kickbacks but from $360,000 he had found in his own home, inside "a tin box . . . a wonderful tin box." This earned Walker and the lengthy list of corrupt officials who followed him in the witness box the nickname "The Tin Box Parade."

136   **Maine to Mississippi:** *New York: A Documentary Film.*

136   **627 miles of roads:** Caro, p. 940. Including highways built in New Jersey under a Port Authority partnership with Moses, by the time the Master Builder was forced from power in the mid-1960s he was responsible for 899 miles of highway completed or under construction in and around New York City. By way of comparison, Los Angeles, that most highway-centric of "cities," had only 459 miles of highway at the time.

137   **the Interstate Highways Act:** Though in fairness to Moses, Bertrand D. Tallamy, a former Moses hand and the chief administrator for the Interstate Highway System during the 1950s and 1960s, told Caro that the system was based on principles that Moses had taught him when he was a young civil engineer.

137   **Robert F. Wagner, Sr.:** A member of FDR's "Brain Trust," Wagner also introduced the National Labor Relations and Social Security acts.

137   **half a million people:** Caro, p. 7. Caro cites an official figure of 555,000 residents, though with the doubling up that became so common during the slum clearance era and War Years, the actual number was far larger. The New York City Housing Authority currently puts the official population (which includes those living in smaller-scale projects built since the 1960s) at just under 420,000.

138   **"Suppose we are entering":** Le Corbusier, p. 117.

139   **the city spent billions of dollars:** Moses himself controlled projects that spent an estimated $27 billion.

139   **a million of its own residents:** Exact figures are impossible to come by when determining the scale of Moses' clearance projects. The figure of a million is based on a combination of estimates. Moses and the City Planning Commission claimed 250,000 people were relocated for his highway projects, a number almost certainly too low (Caro, p. 19). A conservative study puts the number of people cleared for Moses' Title I projects in Manhattan and downtown Brooklyn alone at more than 100,000, with more than twice that displaced by attached public housing projects (Schwartz, p. 295). One of the few comprehensive studies performed by an outside agency at the time estimated that Moses, who held power for decades, evicted 320,000 people during a single ten-year period. Conservatively, Moses himself cleared more than half a million people, and

when that number is combined with the population cleared for the city's public housing projects, the total approaches one million.

139 **his personality did nothing to diminish:** Robert Caro's Pulitzer Prize–winning biography of Moses still stands as the most evenhanded account of both Moses and the political world in which he operated. In recent years there have been attempts to revive Moses' reputation, a move that not so strangely coincided with a return of government-backed clearance and redevelopment projects in New York City.

139 **he built his Long Island parkways:** Caro, p. 1952.

139 **"doesn't know what's in his own interest":** *New York: A Documentary Film.*

140 **"I don't think they were too bad":** Caro, p. 876.

140 **Nietzsche's explanation:** Nietzsche, p. 132.

141 **Tammany's George Washington Plunkitt:** Riordan and Plunkitt, p. 40.

141 **"legal graft":** Al Smith once diagnosed the practice while touring a law school library. Pointing out a young student diligently poring over his books, the governor remarked, "There is a young man studying how to take a bribe and call it a fee." Caro, p. 713.

142 **Moses paid the Kennedy family:** Ibid., p. 1014, and Schwartz, p. 285.

143 **By 1957:** New York had spent $267 million, the rest of the country $133 million. Caro, p. 12.

144 **vast swaths of the city:** La Guardia is generally portrayed as a counterbalance to Moses on the development front. There is Moses, the devotee of traffic and the never-ending flow, the man who once said, "We wouldn't have any American economy without the automobile business—that's literally true. . . . There have to be places for them to run, there have to be modern roads, modern arteries. Somebody's got to build them and in order to get things done and done properly, people have to be inconvenienced who are in the way." Then there's La Guardia, the jolly polyglot who spoke to the city's immigrants in their native tongue, danced polkas with the Poles, kibitzed with Jews, ate sausage with the Italians, and reveled in the congested street: "that Dago son of a bitch," Moses used to call him, who waged epic battles with the Master Builder over his public works program. It's a lovely way to look back at the comically mismatched pair—the stocky little ethnic firebrand and the cool, tall patrician who disdained ethnicity to the point of denying his own Judaism—but from a planning standpoint it's not really true. La Guardia certainly loved the city, and he fought bitterly with Moses over which of them *really* controlled public works, but the mayor believed as fervently as anyone that to create the city of the future he needed to clear slums, restrict industry, and build highways and high-rises.

144 **The Planning Commission:** Schwartz, pp. 232–233.

144   **cleared thirty thousand jobs:** Fitch, p. 100.

145   **600,000 industrial jobs:** New York City figures from Weil, p. 262. Detroit figures from Sugrue, p. 144.

146   **"If the city was to prosper":** Caro, pp. 858–859.

146   **half a million white New Yorkers:** On the basis of Moses' own estimate that 37 percent of his evictions were of nonwhites (Caro, p. 968), 63 percent of those cleared were white. Combined with the roughly one million people cleared by Moses and the City Housing Authority, half a million evicted whites is a conservative estimate.

EIGHT. RED LINES AND WHITE FLIGHT

149   **"On the method I call":** Engels, quoted in Berman, p. 153.

149   **"Sometimes I think":** *New York: A Documentary Film.*

151   **old-law tenement slums:** The borough did have new tenements built after New York State passed laws requiring light and ventilation in apartment buildings. They were far from luxurious, but the borough's oldest neighborhoods, like Port Morris and Mott Haven, were home mostly to brick townhouses, modern apartment buildings, even distinctive brownstone blocks. Mott Haven's main drag, Alexander Avenue, was known alternatively as "Irish Fifth Avenue" and "Doctors' Row" and was home to the Cathedral of the Bronx, the ornately decorated St. Jerome's Church. "My grandparents bought the house eighty-nine years ago, because it looked like Holland, it reminded them of home," says Carol Zakaluk, who grew up in a Queen Anne rowhouse on East 136th Street and still lives next door; hers is the only white family whom she or anyone else in Mott Haven can think of who never left the neighborhood.

151   **"He'd say":** Jonnes, p. 119.

151   **Clara Rodriguez watched:** Ibid., p. 117.

152   **"a conspicuous rectangular lawn":** Jacobs, p. 15.

152   **225-foot-wide:** Caro, p. 860.

152   **"When the postwar program":** As quoted in Jonnes, p. 91.

153   **"There are people":** Caro, p. 259.

153   **"For ten years":** Berman, p. 292.

154   **"The Rake Who Wrote":** Asked about Jordan Mott's renaming the area around his ironworks Mott Haven, Gouverneur Jr.—who had sold Mott the land—said it didn't bother him one bit, and while Mott was at it, "he might as well change the Harlem River to the Jordan."

154   **George Fox:** Legend has it that Fox himself preached in Hunts Point during a brief trip to the Americas in the 1670s.

154   **Home Owners' Loan Corporation:** The section on redlining owes a great debt to Craig Steven Wilder's *A Covenant with Color.*

155   **"has among the lowest":** Jacobs, pp. 10–11.

155   **"the North End had to be a bad place":** Such inflexible thinking had, just a few years earlier, led to the leveling of the nearby West End of Boston. To residents, the West End was a stable, if sometimes surly, working-class Irish and Jewish neighborhood. To progressive housing reformers and planners working in an isolated world of maps and statistics, it was a slum. (A reduction in city garbage removal and a newspaper photographer who overturned a trash can for photos of the "slum" didn't help matters.) The neighborhood was torn down to construct the much-reviled Government Center, a windswept plaza frequented mostly by derelicts and municipal clerks hustling to the new City Hall, an imposing concrete box built in the Le Corbusier–inspired "Brutalist" architectural style of the period.

157   **most segregated by the end:** Wilder, pp. 177–178, and interview in *New York: A Documentary Film.*

157   **Advocated by influential:** Krossney and Bartelt, pp. 711, 730.

159   **"the pressure he puts":** Jonnes, p. 111.

159   **apartments under rent control:** That said, the role of rent control in the dysfunctional housing market has been greatly exaggerated for political reasons, and by the mid-1980s, rent-controlled buildings were actually *less* likely than their unregulated peers to be neglected and abandoned.

160   **Overcrowding was the worst:** Wallace and Wallace, p. 65.

161   **An increase in fire rates:** Ibid., p. 74. Research scientists Deborah and Rodrick Wallace were able to predict with remarkable accuracy the spread of fires by tracking the public school transfers of children leaving burned-out neighborhoods. "I remember them telling the unions and the department that kids were transferring from P.S. 27 [in the South Bronx] to Highbridge [in the West Bronx]," says Captain Tom Henderson. "The Wallaces knew the fires would follow. The department didn't listen to them, but they were right."

NINE. OF RIOTS AND AIRMAIL

163   **East New York:** Descriptions of the riots are drawn primarily from Cannato, pp. 119–141.

163   **Louis "Lepke" Buchalter:** Raab, pp. 66, 72.

163   **"an abandoned neighborhood":** Cannato, pp. 120–121.

163   **"just as much a wasteland":** Ibid.

164   **15 percent of the seven-to twenty-year-old males:** Ibid., p. 127.

164   **"Whitey has done it again":** Ibid., p. 124.

164   **"Go back to Africa, Lindsay":** On the advice of an influential local rabbi, Lindsay's Youth Board actually reached out to gangster Albert "Kid Blast" Gallo to help pacify local Italian-American teens.

164   **The next summer:** Ibid., p. 132.

165   **fifty-stitch stab wound:** Ibid., p. 134.

165   **"He looked straight at the people":** Ibid., p. 212.

165   **"And there was no riot":** Contrary to Breslin's conclusion, there was, in fact, a riot in Harlem that night in 1968, and in other neighborhoods across the city and across the years of Lindsay's mayoralty, but the press's downplaying of those riots was a testament to the mayor. When riots flared, Lindsay provided reporters with a secure bus, which kept members of the press—generally less courageous than the mayor himself—simultaneously out of harm's way and out of view of the worst of the rioting. When they did see any rioting, Lindsay appealed to their civic duty to not promote more of the same, convincing reporters and photographers and cameramen to downplay the unrest and show New York as more united than perhaps it really was.

166   **long, slow climb:** But where old New Dealers like President Johnson valued job creation above all else, the educated liberals running War on Poverty programs tended to focus more on symbolic community-action programs and opening the bastions of educated progressivism (like Ivy League colleges) to the rare child of the ghetto who was qualified (often with a small assist from affirmative action) to join the mandarin class. The federal War on Poverty did provide jobs for inner-city minorities in New York, and nationwide it helped create much of what has since become the black middle class, but the programs were relatively small and relied on the fickleness of federal politics, with most of the funding pulled after Richard Nixon took the White House in 1968. The cuts were devastating for inner cities; during his visit to Charlotte Street, President Carter asked his HUD chief, "Most of this occurred in the last five years after Nixon cut off the [War on Poverty] funds?" and she said yes. It had taken a lot more than federal budget cuts to burn down the South Bronx, but it was true enough. Not that there wasn't a logic to the Republican cuts. Just as had happened with Tammany and the Irish, Depression-era make-work programs had helped create an enormous plurality of loyal working- and middle-class Democrats who owed their livelihood to the party. Blacks stayed loyal to the Democratic Party regard-less, but there was at least some canny political triangulation behind the cuts.

168   **114 attacks:** David Bird, "City Firemen Assail Police Inaction," *The New York Times,* 7/23/1968.

168   **"It made them seem":** Kenneth Gross, "Hot Under the Collar," *New York Post,*
      5/28/1968.

169   **police work in poor neighborhoods:** For Lindsay, it was a classic case of being
      caught between a rock and a hard place. Afraid of inciting further riots, City
      Hall urged police restraint in poor neighborhoods, but had to deal with the
      resultant low morale and lazy policing. On the other hand, the administration
      stymied investigations into what turned out to be massive police corruption
      (exposed by Officer Frank Serpico and later the Knapp Commission) for
      fear of losing the police completely, and dealt with the consequences of
      lower public faith in an often corrupt, abusive, and unresponsive police
      department.

170   **Fires in partially abandoned:** FDNY Deputy Chief Francis J. Ronan, "Vacant
      Buildings . . . A Serious Fire Problem," *WNYF,* no. 3 (1969).

170   **30 percent of multiple-alarm fires:** Ibid., p. 139.

170   **2,900 vacant buildings:** Ibid.

TEN. O'HAGAN'S CHOICE

173   **urgent phone call:** Greenberger, Crenson, and Crissey, p. 265.

173   **"has tensions":** Ibid., 253.

175   **workload increased about 60 percent:** A more accurate measure is the Fire
      Damage Index, which put the increase at closer to 70 percent. Developed in later
      years by research scientists Deborah and Rodrick Wallace, the index combines
      the number of building fires, the number of fires where all of the dispatched
      units were needed to fight the blaze, and total hours that firemen spent fighting
      blazes.

176   **"To relieve its workload":** Walker, "Performing Policy Analysis for Municipal
      Agencies," pp. 7–9.

179   **the number of "workers":** For the FDNY, "worker" numbers were complicated
      somewhat by the fact that the first company on the scene of a false alarm, which
      was responsible for resetting the alarm box, could technically report the false
      alarm as a worker. Theoretically the best measure of increased workload for first
      sections would be "work time," the amount of time companies spent actually
      fighting fires. The biggest problem with this statistic is availability, the statistics
      published infrequently in department literature. The accuracy of work-time
      statistics is also questionable. The numbers were based on fire officers' after-
      the-fact recall of how long a company spent fighting a fire, and were frequently
      underreported, particularly in busy companies, and occasionally overreported
      by zealous officers intent on proving how busy their companies were. That said,

where available, work-time statistics show that second sections had a positive impact on work time similar to that they had on workers.

180   **Alarmed . . . South Bronx Deputy Chief:** Charles Kirby, "Projection of Fire Occurrence—Borough of Bronx," memo to John T. O'Hagan, 3/17/1970. Copy of the report furnished by Deborah and Rodrick Wallace.

183   **"I remember when my mother":** Jonnes, p. 6.

183   **"the baron of a sweeping array":** Douglas Martin, "Ramon S. Velez, the South Bronx Padrino, Dies at 75," *The New York Times*, 12/2/2008.

183   **"physical destruction is inconsequential":** Jonnes, p. 266.

184   **"The South Bronx":** New York City Planning Commission, Comprehensive Plan, draft, n.d. [1968], pp. C-2, C-3, reproduced in Fitch, p. 120.

184   **The housing department:** A fact that the NYC-RAND Institute, to its credit, pointed out and tried to reverse in its work with the housing department.

ELEVEN. GOING ALONG TO GET ALONG

187   **Twenty-nine-year-old telephone repairman:** Unless otherwise noted, accounts of the New York Plaza fire are drawn from Lawrence Van Gelder, "Fire on 33d Floor of New Building Kills Two," *The New York Times*, 8/6/1970, and O'Hagan.

188   **"The thing that hinders us":** " 'Fireproof' Buildings Probed," New York *Daily News*, 8/6/70.

189   **Jack and Lew Rudin:** Decades later, Jack was an honorary pallbearer at O'Hagan's funeral.

189   **ways of New York power:** O'Hagan was no neophyte when it came to politics, of course, particularly within the FDNY and the Catholic Church. Other than Episcopalian La Guardia, every New York mayor from 1918 to 1966 was a Catholic; the Archdiocese Chancery at St. Patrick's Cathedral was known as "The Powerhouse" in Cardinal Spellman's day. In 1950 a college basketball point-shaving scandal connected to Mafia gambling rings broke, involving players from Long Island University, Columbia, New York University, and City College (which had won the NCAA tournament the previous year). Observers wondered how the fifth basketball power in the city, Catholic St. John's University, which pulled players from the same mob-ridden neighborhoods as the other schools, hadn't been implicated. Those who knew Spellman never wondered.

Catholic royalty were even rumored to have a secret hangout, Dropkick Murphy's—a New England farmhouse retreat run by a former professional wrestler nicknamed for his signature drop-kick move—where businessmen, fire and police chiefs, politicians, and priests from New York and New England could go to relax and tie one on for a few days without worrying about political blowback. (Although it's notoriously hard to cull truth from rumor concerning Dropkick Murphy's, members of a Boston band by the same name grew up hearing cautionary tales about Dropkick Murphy's being a brutal rehab facility where Boston's skid row winos were sent to dry out.)

The most powerful men in the FDNY all belonged to the department's Catholic fraternal organizations, such as the Knights of Columbus–affiliated Anchor Club. Some of the best firehouses in the city—Engine 69 in Harlem, Engine 35 in Midtown—and the fast-track officer posts in Manhattan's Third Division went almost exclusively to Anchor men. As with mob-movie funerals and weddings, the most important backroom deals, last-minute compromises, unofficial contract talks, and hush-hush cover-ups all seemed to take place at Anchor functions. There's even some debate among firemen over how the parties that follow such events became known as "rackets" (not to be confused with "collations," which usually follow more somber affairs, like funerals and memorial services)—whether it was the noise they kicked up or the deal-making that surrounded them.

A devout Catholic who went to daily Mass, O'Hagan joined Catholic organizations like the Anchor Club early in his career, and was helped along with good company assignments. As he climbed the ranks, O'Hagan returned the favor—helping members with transfers and good assignments, making sure the Church never had any trouble with fire inspections, helping out department chaplains, even donating an old fire engine to a Catholic monastery in western Massachusetts.

190 **Brooklyn and Queens Democratic:** Through the Brooklyn machine he made friends with political heavies like city council chairman Tom Cuite and the Brooklyn Democratic leader, judge-maker, insurance broker, printing-plant owner, alleged made man in the Gambino crime family, and self-proclaimed "boss of the fucking state" Meade Esposito.

190 **fight for his political life:** His primary loss to Staten Island Republican John Marchi and the Democratic nomination of comptroller Mario Procaccino were actually the best primary results Lindsay could have hoped for. Two-thirds of the votes cast in the Democratic primary were for liberals, like Bronx borough president Herman Badillo, former mayor Wagner, and novelist Norman Mailer, but because they were split among three candidates, the clubhouse conservative Procaccino won, leaving many liberal Democrats to begrudgingly turn to Lindsay as their best option. And many Republicans who would have voted for Procaccino in a head-to-head matchup with Lindsay stuck with Marchi, who was never a serious contender to win the popular vote. (He once told reporters, "I can't say that the burning ambition of my life has been to become mayor. . . .

You know sometimes I feel that the quality of life in this city is so disastrous that I just can't wait to get away from it—back out to Staten Island.") Lindsay's supporters did little to help him with middle-class voters—at a campaign rally for the mayor (who'd reinforced his "limousine liberal" image by leaving eastern Queens unplowed for weeks after a snowstorm), a young Woody Allen warmed up the crowd with jokes about Average Joe Procaccino: "Sure I want a mayor who cleans up the snow, but not by himself with a shovel." Procaccino, though, was able to "snatch defeat from the jaws of victory" (in the words of reporter Richard Reeves), once telling a Harlem audience, "On the outside my skin is white. But inside, my heart is as black as yours."

190 **$70 million consultant habit:** City Council of New York, Committee on Charter and Governmental Operations, "Report on Consultant Contracts," 12/21/1970, cited in Greenberger, Crenson, and Crissey, p. 244.

190 **$900,000 grant:** Greenberger, Crenson, and Crissey, p. 244.

191 **"Lindsay really believed":** Newfield and Du Brul, p. 154.

191 **"I remember that I once wrote":** Ibid.

192 **Harlem chief Joseph Galvin:** "A Fire Chief Near Tears at Story of Woe," New York *Daily News*, 2/18/1972.

TWELVE. QUANTIFYING THE UNQUANTIFIABLE

197 **Before RAND's studies:** This chapter owes a great deal to the work of Deborah and Rodrick Wallace, who first discovered the problems with RAND's studies and models.

198 **Earned run average:** ERA still depends on factors outside a pitcher's control, for instance how good his team's defense is, the size of the park he's pitching in, and plain old luck (statisticians have found that other than home runs, pitchers have very little control over whether a batted ball is turned into an out or goes for a hit). Looking only at the things a pitcher can control—like the number of strikeouts, walks, and home runs he gives up—is a better measure than ERA.

199 **Ed Ignall later wrote:** "What Is a Minute of Response Time Worth?" Undated NYC-RAND Institute memo, likely written in 1972 or 1973, based on data used.

202 **fifteen of the FDNY's nearly four hundred units:** Kolesar and Walker, pp. v, 3.

202 **didn't take into account the fire engines:** The reason no engines were chosen, according to RAND reports, is that none of them had odometers that were accurate to a tenth of a mile.

202 **"took one look at this dimpled kid":** Greenberger, Crenson, and Crissey, p. 274.

202 **"The RAND Model":** Ibid., p. 270.

203 **"Hell, I didn't think anyone":** Ibid., p. 130.

203 **"some stopwatches were thrown":** Green and Kolesar, p. 1005.

205 **"The residents of the low-demand region":** RAND Report 1566 (1975), Section 2.2.2, "The Location of Fire Companies."

205 **"hazard categories":** Wallace and Wallace, p. 33.

206 **"small variations":** Kolesar and Walker, p. v.

207 **"stepped through the looking glass":** *Pandora's Box.*

208 **"The glaring omission":** Corrigan p. 28.

208 **leftist ideologues:** The Wallaces' claims—specifically, that RAND was part of a conspiracy to *intentionally* burn down poor black and Puerto Rican neighborhoods—were certainly open to such criticisms. But while the Wallaces' conspiratorial contentions about *why* the RAND models were so flawed were unfounded, their technical criticism of the actual flaws were quite valid.

209 **"This is a female!"** Hartley C. Fitts, "HUD Review of R-1853-HUD, 'Deployment Methodology for Fire Departments' Under H-2164," sent to Dr. Jan M. Chaiken of RAND, 2/20/1976.

THIRTEEN. A DISPROPORTIONATE SHARE OF THE ECONOMIES

215 **In a column:** Michael Maye, "The 'Expert' in Firemanics," *Civil Service Leader,* 12/19/1972.

215 **"To the blacks and Hispanics":** "UFA Sues to Block Fire Company Cuts," *Civil Service Leader,* 11/21/1972.

216 **Columnist Pete Hamill:** Pete Hamill, "The Fire This Time," New York *Daily News,* part 1, 12/1/1972; part 2, 12/4/1972; Part 3, 12/6/1972.

216 **$15,000 renovating a firehouse:** Vincent Lee and Henry Lee, "Firehouse Goes Out in Stile," New York *Daily News,* 11/15/1972.

216 **Queens Borough President:** Jeff Forgoston, "Loss of Fire Companies Called Gamble," *Long Island Press,* 11/10/1972.

217 **after 233-2 was closed:** When available, work-time statistics show similar increases. After the 1972 closing of Engine 88-2, 88-1's work time increased by 85 percent over the next two years. After Ladder 41-2 was closed in 1973, 41-1's work time rose by 77 percent the following year.

218 **He missed all but one:** Paul Thayer, "Fire Flies," *Civil Service Leader,* 11/12/1974.

219   **Despite some serious miscalculations:** O'Hagan found out that new firefight-
      ers' union president Dick Vizzini had lost a secret-ballot vote by union mem-
      bership and couldn't legally call a strike. When city negotiators called Vizzini's
      bluff and backed out of a one-year contract they had agreed to, an enraged
      Vizzini called the strike anyway, nearly landing himself in jail when the results
      of the vote leaked to the newspapers.

220   **The day after O'Hagan announced:** "Mother and Two Children Die in
      Brooklyn Blaze," *The New York Times*, 1/9/1974.

177   **More than five hundred were rendered:** John Darnton, "City's Fire Alarm
      Boxes Are Called Undependable," *The New York Times*, 12/20/1974.

220   **"Believe it or not":** Ibid.

221   **"It's possible that with fourteen thousand boxes":** Ibid.

221   **"It's a toy":** Ibid.

221   **"diverted alarms":** Wallace and Wallace, p. 31.

222   **False alarms rose sevenfold:** Denis Hamill, "Where There's Smoke . . . ," *New
      York*, 2/13/1978, p. 14.

224   **(20 percent of uniformed personnel):** Vincent Lee and Mark Lieberman, New
      York *Daily News*, 11/21/1974.

225   **"The specific decision":** Warren Walker, "Result of Recent Court Case," NYC-
      RAND memo no. 0011, 1/6/1975.

225   *New York Times* **editorial page:** "False Alarm," *The New York Times*,
      11/29/1974.

225   **"being asked to carry a disproportionate":** John Darnton, "$8.3 Million
      Savings Due; 8 Fire Companies Will Shut in the City; Summary of Mayor's
      Budget Changes Personnel Reductions," *The New York Times*, 11/28/1974.

FOURTEEN. NEW MATH

227   **"Because the city's structures":** Starr.

228   **"a bad loan is better than a good tax":** Quoted in Cannato, p. 101.

228   **"The tradition in New York":** Steven R. Weisman, "How New York Became a
      Fiscal Junkie," *The New York Times*, 8/17/1975.

230   **erase nearly 50 percent:** Paul Krugman, "How Did Economists Get It So
      Wrong?" *The New York Times Magazine*, 9/6/2009.

230   **Wall Street lost $600 million:** Sobel, p. 61.

230   **66.7 million square feet:** Moody, p. 13.

230   **500,000 jobs disappeared:** Michael Sterne, "City Fiscal Crisis Feeds on Itself,"
      The New York Times, 10/27/1975.

231   **sold off billions of dollars 'worth:** Newfield and Du Brul, pp. 41–44.

231   **went belly-up with $2 billion:** Ibid., p. 12.

231   **"had the three shells":** Weisman, "How New York Became a Fiscal Junkie."

232   **"an exile in his own city":** Harry Stein, "An Exile in His Own City," *The New York Times Magazine*, 1/8/1978.

232   **16 percent of the vote:** Cannato, p. 568.

232   **"In a way, he's a rather sad figure":** Ibid., p. 565.

232   **liberal social welfare policies:** And whereas in every other American city the cost of programs such as welfare, Medicare, and Medicaid were borne entirely by the state and federal government, New York State passed about half of its share on to the city. Though in fairness to the state, New York City paid a much higher percentage of Medicare and welfare costs than did poorer southern and western states.

232   **Pete Hamill put it:** Pete Hamill, speech at Broad Street Ballroom, 1/18/2008. Excerpts of his speech can be found at: http://cityroom.blogs.nytimes.com/ 2008/01/18/pete-hamill-downtown-on-downtown/.

233   **Nine percent:** Newfield and Du Brul, p. 34.

233   **second-lowest welfare rate:** Morris, p. 186.

233   **$3 billion:** Fitch, p. ix.

233   **$700 million:** Moody, p. 59.

233   **28 percent in the mid-1950s:** Ibid.

234   **dropped assessments on the value:** Ibid., p. 58.

234   **"oversold and underfinanced":** Quoted in Isserman and Kazin, p. 192.

235   **"It's the fucking":** Fitch, pp. vii, 189.

235   **"local socialism":** Newfield and Du Brul, p. 30.

235   **firemen Thomas Newbert:** Ronald Smothers, "A Fire Hero Learns He's Dismissed," *The New York Times*, 7/2/1975, p. 190.

236   **five thousand laid-off policemen:** Selwyn Raab, "Laid-Off Policemen Block Brooklyn Bridge Traffic," *The New York Times*, 7/2/1975.

236   **"Beame Is a Deserter":** Mahler, p. 8.

236   **"We could be on the other side":** Raab, "Laid-Off Policemen Block Brooklyn Bridge Traffic."

236   **"the most well-organized wildcat strike":** Weisman, "How New York Became a Fiscal Junkie."

236   **"We called it Big MAC":** John Darnton, "M.A.C. in Trouble, Too," *The New York Times*, 7/19/1975.

237   **"The people of this country":** Transcript of President's Talk on City Crisis, *The New York Times*, 10/30/1975.

237   **$2 billion in debt:** Budget Bureau, p. 43.

238   **"On Fox Street":** Newfield and Du Brul, p. 3.

239 **"It's very difficult"**: Charlayne Hunter-Gault, "Rising Violence Creates Controversy Among Teachers at Bronx High School," *The New York Times*, 6/13/1977.

239 **Russian roulette**: Chang, p. 44.

240 **"suggest that, in the area described"**: Starr, p. 42.

240 **"provided only that a certain homogeneity"**: Ibid.

240 **"Stretches of empty blocks"**: Roger Starr, "Making New York Smaller," *The New York Times Magazine*, 11/14/1976.

241 **A "new means"**: Downs, p. 135.

241 **"The Future of Cities"**: The philosophy rose as high as the White House, with Nixon's Housing and Community Development Act of 1974 promoting "the spatial de-concentration of housing opportunities for persons of lower income" in U.S. cities in order to encourage "the revitalization of deteriorating or deteriorated neighborhoods to attract persons of higher income."

241 **"'blacktop' most of the South Bronx"**: Francis X. Clines, "Blighted Areas' Use Is Urged by Rohatyn," *The New York Times*, 3/16/1976.

FIFTEEN. THE FISCAL CRISIS KOOL-AID TEST

243 **"In a marvelous, sad way"**: Quoted in Chang, p. 17.

244 **he could for his department**: One of the most striking features of conversations with those who worked in the upper levels of city and state politics during the fiscal crisis is how removed their lives were from the impact that the budget cuts had on city departments and the neighborhoods they served.

   "Everyone talks about austerity cuts and all the terrible things that happened," says then state budget director Peter Goldmark. "But where are the dead bodies? Where are the houses that burned down? Where is all the damage?" When he is given a brief rundown of the effects of the cuts, the normally unflappable and fastidiously well-informed Goldmark's lower lip drops noticeably, a look of genuine surprise frozen for a moment on his face.

   Many in the fire service chalk up such surprise to government officials' tendency to play "country dumb" when it suits their purposes. "Open your eyes!" says O'Hagan's assistant, Captain Sandy Sansevero. "Ask him, during the cuts what did they call the shops out in Long Island City? They called them Red Square. You know why they called them Red Square? Because there was so much fire apparatus parked out there that they didn't have parts to fix, because they didn't have the money. He couldn't see where not having the money had the impact? Well, you see, that's the kind of answer you are going to get from a politician."

In Goldmark's case and many other cases, though, the ignorance seems genuine, the gap between City Hall and the rest of the service-starved city too far to see across. And Goldmark for one would have listened to O'Hagan seriously. When he was a young budget analyst working for Fred Hayes, Goldmark had worked with O'Hagan and regarded him as one of the most honest and competent administrators in the city. Most of the city councilors, deputy mayors, state assemblymen, and other powerful politicians O'Hagan knew from his years as chief and commissioner felt the same way about him.

245   **reopened a few years later:** Most famously "The People's Firehouse," Engine Co. 212, in the Polish neighborhood of Greenpoint, Brooklyn, where residents staged a sixteen-month sit-in; the city reopened the house.

246   **40 percent from 1974 to 1977:** Joseph P. Fried, "Serious Fires in New York City Have Jumped 40% in Last Three Years," *The New York Times*, 6/16/1977.

246   **Subsequent investigations:** The faulty fire fatality statistics (along with evidence of faked engine-response times) were brought to public attention by then State Assemblyman (and current U.S. Senator) Chuck Schumer. One fire union official, Schumer revealed, had told him that O'Hagan had admitted to knowing the numbers were far too low. One battalion chief told him that the department had an unofficial policy of counting many fire deaths as heart attacks and homicides. "Schumer Reveals: Fire Department Death Statistics May Be Falsified; Statistical Analysis Demonstrates Engine Response Time Figures Also Doubtful," press release from the office of State Assemblyman Schumer, 9/26/1977.

247   **"What we found ... Arson was only a problem":** Insurance fires had been a problem in the city's redlined neighborhoods for years, as policeman Howard Farkas had discovered in 1968, when he collared a superintendent who'd set fire to his own building on Charlotte Street. The trend remained relatively small, though, until a new set of economic incentives, most of them well-intentioned government programs sprung from the fire department's inability to stop fires in the first place, turned arson into the most profitable ghetto business this side of the drug trade.

One government-run program offered fire insurance in redlined neighborhoods where it had been unavailable for years. With insurance brokers making commissions on each policy they sold, and their companies no longer on the hook for the cost of fire insurance payouts (the money was drawn from a general fund that all insurance companies paid into), abuse was rampant. Landlords would buy exorbitant policies on usually abandoned buildings, give a kickback to the insurance broker to overvalue the building, strip valuables like copper wiring and lead pipes, and set the building ablaze. Politically connected developers even applied for city, state, and federal grants to redevelop burned-out properties, took out insurance on the partially reconstructed buildings, and torched them again.

Just as arson was becoming more profitable and pervasive in the early 1970s, O'Hagan slashed the fire marshal program as part of his early budget cuts, leaving marshals with barely enough time to investigate a fraction of the suspicious fires in the city, never mind untangle the web of insurance brokers, landlords, and real estate developers profiting from the destruction. Conspiracy theories sprang up in firehouse kitchens around the city, most of them overlapping variants on there being a "Do Not Investigate" order from City Hall to protect prominent politicians and campaign donors who were making millions on fires. Another story had it that the firehouse closings and arson were part of a plan to clear blacks and Puerto Ricans out of the city, and then redevelop the vacant land for middle- and upper-class whites. There was some merit to the idea. Urban planning theorists such as Roger Starr were advocating a non-arson version of the latter plan, and convicted arsonists included a number of wealthy, politically connected real estate developers, lawyers, former police officers, at least one Community Board official, and a handful of Democratic club regulars. Two judges presiding over arson cases were accused of taking bribes. A Bronx city councilman and later state assemblyman shared his offices with a real estate holding company whose heavily insured properties had a suspicious habit of going up in smoke.

"Holding companies, title companies, insurance brokerages—that was where half the guys in the [Bronx] organization made their money," says one former Bronx clubhouse member. "All those buildings burning and it was like this taboo thing, no one talked about it."

But there was no grand design from on high, just the uncoordinated activities of creative capitalists with few moral compunctions. Arson was ignored for the same reason fires in general were ignored: it required effort to stop it, and no one with the power had much incentive to bother. "I remember telling [Bronx Boss] Pat Cunningham, 'Stick your head out the window, you can smell the city burning,'" says Bronx fire captain Tom Henderson. "He told me, 'What the fuck do I care about firemen for? You all moved out of the city, and you don't work on campaigns—you got no votes behind you, so what do I care?' And he was right, we just didn't have the power to get things done."

Even the Bronx's Puerto Rican power brokers had little interest. Democratic Party boss Ramon Velez said arson was a law enforcement matter that was out of his control. "When we went into the community we ran into tough resistance," said the borough's District Attorney Mario Merola. "They refused to cooperate, to give me the torches. . . . The community leaders all wanted money to be invested the day *after* the fire." Merola's words are a tad self-serving: community leaders and activists including Genevieve Brooks Brown of Charlotte Street for years had been pleading with officials (among them Merola) to look into the arson problem, and had found local politicians unwilling. "From our experience," wrote research scientists Deborah and Rodrick Wallace, who studied the fire epidemic and fought firehouse closings in the late 1970s and the 1980s, "many [politicians] banked on certain results of the burning down of whole neighborhoods. . . . They all thought they would end up on top of the ashpile."

And it wasn't just landlords looking for insurance money. Junkies lit fires to get at the pipes and wiring more easily in abandoned, and sometimes even inhabited buildings. Tenants got in on the act as well after another government policy went awry. To lessen the burden on the tens of thousands of families being burned from their homes, the City Housing Authority put fire victims at the front of the years-long waiting lists to get into public housing. At city welfare centers, large signs in both Spanish and English informed: "The only way to get housing priority is if you are burned out by a fire." Families on welfare were also eligible for thousands of dollars in aid to offset the costs of moving and of replacing items after a fire. Like no-questions-asked insurance, it was an unintended incentive for arson, and firemen started showing up to fires to find the supposed victims outside on the street with their furniture and belongings packed up and ready to go.

Fire had been a fact of life for so long in so many communities that it became the default form of violence and mischief. Kids who might otherwise have tortured a cat or broken windows lit fires. In 1977 a *New York Times* reporter visiting Samuel Gompers Vocational-Technical High School found classrooms and furniture scorched by student-set fires. Firefighters on the Lower East Side called arson "Puerto Rican revenge" for all the fires started over petty disputes and lover's quarrels. "Instead of fighting a guy who was taking out your girl, or putting a baseball bat through his windshield, guys would light his car or apartment door on fire," says one fireman. "And he'd end up killing or burning up the homes of everyone else."

For all the horrors of intentionally set blazes, they remained a fraction of all fires: arsonists weren't burning down New York's poorest neighborhoods, just picking over the debris.

248   **"somebody had been drinking":** It didn't help that O'Hagan—despite a strict personal ban on coffee, tea, and tobacco—was himself a problem drinker. He didn't drink as frequently as many, but when he did, it was heavy. "Any celebration, anything, he'd get drunk, and he was awful," says one former assistant. "I remember walking back from a bar with John once and we were passing by [a firehouse], and he said, 'Let's go in there and shake them up,' and I asked him why. 'Fuck it, why not?' he said, and he meant it. He wanted to go in there and do an inspection, see if guys' shoes were shined or whatever. I just told him, 'John, I'm going home, if you want to do that, you can do it yourself.' He was just like that, a mean drunk."

Called in to command fires that went to three alarms or larger, he sometimes arrived after a night out on the town. "I remember one fire we had," says Captain Tom Henderson, "row houses with common cocklofts, and the fire just spread from building to building. On top of that, it was freezing cold outside, the hydrants freezing up, guys falling on their ass all over the place on the ice. And O'Hagan shows up with [a department chaplain], and they must have been out somewhere, because the two of them were legless. Here he was, screaming at guys in these miserable conditions and telling them to do this and that, and he's hammered! Now, O'Hagan almost never came up to the Bronx, and so, hell, that's the way a lot of those guys knew him."

After Regulation 202 was ordered, and particularly after the brass started surprise firehouse inspections looking for alcohol, conducting blood tests after accidents, and bringing firemen up on formal charges, the stories about O'Hagan's own drinking spread and were exaggerated throughout the department, to the degree that decades later, if the first word that comes out of firemen's mouths when they are asked about the chief isn't "innovative," "tough," or "smart," it's a variant on "drunk."

248   **broader culture wars:** In the case of women, O'Hagan said they were free to join the department so long as they took and passed the department's physical and written examinations. He also appointed a woman to head the department's Bureau of Personnel, the first high-ranking female in department history. For the long-hairs, he commissioned a report of questionable scientific veracity that said long hair was a fire hazard and facial hair interfered with the suction on air masks, and the bans stayed in place.

250   **nearly made O'Hagan a deputy mayor:** Interview with Chief Elmer Chapman.

250   **paid for his MBA classes:** Edward Ranzal, "Interest Conflict Is Linked to O'Hagan," *The New York Times*, 11/23/1977.

251   **O'Hagan returned in 1989:** Cull, p. 47.

251   **"If one listened carefully":** Ibid., p. 48.

SIXTEEN. WALDBAUM'S REVISITED

255 **"Is that Dad?"** Sharon Churcher, "'He Was on the Roof, He Waved to Us and We Waved Back—Then the Roof Collapsed,'" *New York Post*, 8/3/1978.

256 **"You mean, they couldn't recognize him":** Ibid.

256 **"The lockers are on the third floor":** Pete Hamill, "Flame Is Always There . . . Waiting," New York *Daily News*, 8/4/1978.

257 **Eric Jackson was convicted:** Joseph P. Fried, "On Retrial, Suspect Is Acquitted in Fire That Killed 6 in '78," *The New York Times*, 8/18/1994.

257 **"Death was the grim paymaster":** John Kifner, "Top Officials and Union Debate Handling of Blaze Fatal to 6 Firefighters," *The New York Times*, 8/4/1978.

257 **"It was almost classical":** Ibid., p. 207

257 **"When I heard on the morning of August 2":** Vincent Dunn, "Truss Collapse: Final Report," in DiMaria, pp. 162–163 (originally published in *Firehouse* magazine); Bart Mitchell, "Roof Collapse: A Legal Perspective," in DiMaria, p. 164 (originally published in *Firehouse* magazine).

CONCLUSION

263 **"The history books":** Johnson, pp. 231–232.

264 **But the last two hundred years or so:** Ibid., p. 231.

265 **"packed at the rate of 290,000 to the square mile":** Riis, p. 10.

265 **"that turned out in the last eight years":** Ibid., p. 6.

265 **"tenants died":** Ibid., p. 2.

266 **Jane Jacobs points out:** Jacobs, p. 218.

268 **"I don't care whether the man":** Schlesinger, p. 129.

269 **"Moloch whose buildings":** Ginsberg, p. 21.

270 **Tony Blair and Gordon Brown's Labour Party:** *The Trap*.

271 **"the first war that's been fought":** Neil Swidey, "The Analyst," *The Boston Globe*, 5/18/2003.

271 **"big-picture governance":** Ben McGrath, "The Untouchable," *The New Yorker*, 8/24/2009.

271 **1987's "Black Monday":** Lowenstein, p. 72.

272 **Long-Term Capital Management:** For excellent accounts of LTCM and its collapse, see Lowenstein, and Michael Lewis, "How the Eggheads Cracked," in Lewis, *Panic!* (New York: W. W. Norton, 2009), originally published in *The New York Times Magazine*, 1/24/1999.

274 **Stand on a South Bronx street corner:** Accounts of Grandmaster Flash's life are taken from Saddler.

276 **"like some kinda grand chess master":** Saddler, p. 98.

BIBLIOGRAPHY

BOOKS, ARTICLES, ESSAYS, AND DOCUMENTS

Abella, Alex. *Soldiers of Reason*. Orlando, FL: Harcourt, 2008.

Auletta, Ken. *The Streets Were Paved with Gold*. New York: Random House, 1979.

Ballon, Hillary, and Kenneth T. Jackson, eds. *Robert Moses and the Modern City*. New York: Norton, 2007.

Berman, Marshall. *All That Is Solid Melts into Air*. New York: Simon & Schuster, 1982.

Budget Bureau, City of New York. "Fiscal Crisis: Origins and Solutions." New York, 1979.

Burnett, Frances Hodgson. *Little Lord Fauntleroy*. New York: Scribner, 1886.

Burrows, Edwin G., and Mike Wallace. *Gotham*. New York: Oxford University Press, 1999.

Burton, Robert. *On Being Certain*. New York: St. Martin's Press, 2008.

Byrne, John. *The Whiz Kids*. New York: Doubleday, 1993.

Campbell, Helen. *Darkness and Daylight*. Hartford: Hartford Publishing Co., 1899.

Cannato, Vincent J. *The Ungovernable City: John Lindsay and His Struggle to Save New York*. New York: Basic Books, 2001.

Caro, Robert. *The Power Broker*. New York: Vintage Books, 1975.

A Catechism of Christian Doctrine. New York: Paulist Press, 1929.

Chang, Jeff. *Can't Stop Won't Stop: A History of the Hip-Hop Generation*. New York: St. Martin's Press, 2005.

Committee on Fire Toxicology. National Research Council "Fire and Smoke: Understanding the Hazards." Washington, DC: National Academy Press, 1986.

Le Corbusier. *The City of To-morrow and Its Planning.* New York: Dover, 1987.

Corrigan, William. "Travel Time Estimation for Emergency Medical Vehicles with Applications to Location Models." Ph.D. dissertation, University of California, Santa Barbara, 2005.

Cull, Frank. *The 23rd St. Fire As It Happened.* New York: Uniformed Firefighters Association of Greater New York, 1993.

DiMaria, Ernie (Lieutenant, FDNY, retired). *Fire: A War That Never Ends.* Las Vegas: Sunset Bookstore, 1993.

Downs, Anthony. *Opening Up the Suburbs: An Urban Strategy for America.* New Haven: Yale University Press, 1973.

Dunn, Vincent (Deputy Chief, FDNY, retired). *Collapse of Burning Buildings: A Guide to Fireground Safety.* New York: Fire Engineering, 1988.

Fire Department of New York. Annual Fire Report (various reports from 1960–1980 cited). Available at the Mand Fire Library at the FDNY's Randall's Island Training Academy.

Fitch, Robert. *The Assassination of New York.* London and New York: Verso, 1993.

Fitzgerald, F. Scott. "The Crack Up." *Esquire,* February 1936.

———. *The Great Gatsby.* Ware, England: Wordsworth, 1993.

———. *This Side of Paradise.* New York: Scribner, 1921.

Ginsberg, Allen. *Howl, and Other Poems.* San Francisco: City Lights Books, 2006.

Gladwell, Malcolm. *The Tipping Point.* New York: Back Bay Books, 2002.

Glanz, James, and Eric Lipton. *City in the Sky: The Rise and Fall of the World Trade Center.* New York: Times Books, 2003.

Golway, Terry. *So Others Might Live.* New York: Basic Books, 2002.

Green, Linda V., and Peter J. Kolesar. "Improving Emergency Responsiveness with Management Science." *Management Science* 50, no. 8, August 2004.

Greenberger, Martin, Matthew A. Crenson, and Brian L. Crissey. *Models in the Policy Process.* New York: Russell Sage Foundation, 1976.

Halberstam, David. *The Best and the Brightest.* New York: Random House, 1969.

Hashagen, Paul. *The Bravest: An Illustrated History, 1865 to 2002.* Paducah, KY: Turner, 2002.

Hastorf, Albert H., and Hadley Cantril. "They Saw a Game: A Case Study." In David L. Hamilton, ed., *Social Cognition: Key Readings.* New York: Psychology Press, 2005.

Isserman, Maurice, and Michael Kazin. *America Divided: The Civil War of the 1960s.* New York: Oxford University Press, 2000.

Jacobs, Jane. *The Death and Life of Great American Cities.* New York: Vintage Books, 1992.

Jardini, David. "Out of the Blue Yonder: The RAND Corporation's Diversification into Social Welfare Research, 1946–1968." Ph.D. dissertation, Carnegie Mellon University, 1996.

Johnson, Steven. *The Ghost Map*. New York: Riverhead Books, 2006.

Jonnes, Jill. *South Bronx Rising*. New York: Fordham University Press, 2002.

Kaplan, Fred. *The Wizards of Armageddon*. New York: Simon & Schuster, 1983.

Karter, Michael J., Jr. "Fire Loss in the United States 2008." Quincy, MA: National Fire Protection Association, 2008.

Kimmerly, Janet, ed. *The Bravest: An Illustrated History, 1865 to 2002*. Paducah, KY: Turner, 2002.

Koch, Edward. *Selected Documents from the Collection of Mayor Edward Koch*. New York: La Guardia and Wagner Archives, 2008.

Kolesar, Peter, and Warren Walker. *Measuring the Travel Characteristics of New York's Fire Companies*. RAND Report R-1449. New York: RAND, 1974.

Krossney, Kristen B., and David W. Bartelt. "Residential Security, Risk, and Race." In *Urban Geography* 26, no. 8 (December 31, 2005), p. 707–736.

Lewis, Michael. *Liar's Poker: Rising Through the Wreckage on Wall Street*. New York: W.W. Norton, 1989.

Lewis, Michael. *Panic!* New York: W. W. Norton, 2009.

Light, Jennifer. *From Warfare to Welfare*. Baltimore: Johns Hopkins University Press, 2003.

Lindblom, Charles E. "The Science of 'Muddling Through.'" Reprinted in Scott Campbell and Susan S. Fainstein, eds., *Readings in Planning Theory*, 2nd ed. Malden, MA: Blackwell, 2003.

Lindsay, John V. *Religious Aspects in the Life and Times of Oliver Cromwell*. New Haven: Yale University Archives, John Vliet Lindsay Papers, 1943.

Lowenstein, Roger. *When Genius Failed*. New York: Random House, 2000.

Mahler, Jonathan. *Ladies and Gentlemen, The Bronx Is Burning*. New York: Farrar, Straus & Giroux, 2005.

Moody, Kim. *From Welfare State to Real Estate*. New York: New Press, 2007.

Morris, Charles R. *The Cost of Good Intentions: New York City and the Liberal Experiment*. New York: W. W. Norton, 1980.

Moynihan, Daniel Patrick. *Maximum Feasible Misunderstanding*. New York: Free Press, 1969.

———. "Text of the Moynihan Memorandum on the Status of Negroes." *New York Times*, March 1, 1970.

O'Hagan, John. *High Rise—Fire and Life Safety*. New York: Dun-Donnelley, 1977.

Newfield, Jack, and Paul Du Brul. *Abuse of Power*. New York: Viking, 1977.

Nietzsche, Friederich Wilhelm. *Human, All Too Human*. Translated by R. J. Hollingdale. Cambridge, England: Cambridge University Press, 1986.

Pidd, Michael. "Just Modeling Through: A Rough Guide to Modeling." *Interfaces*, 29:2, 1995.

Raab, Selwyn. *Five Families*. New York: Thomas Dunne Books, 2005.

Regional Plan Association. *Plan for the City of New York and Its Environs*. New York: Regional Plan Association, 1927.

Riis, Jacob A. *How the Other Half Lives*. New York: Dover, 1971.

Riordan, William, and George W. Plunkitt. *Plunkitt of Tammany Hall*. New York: McClure, Phillips, 1905.

Roszak, Theodore. *The Making of a Counter Culture: Reflections on the Technocratic Society and Its Youthful Opposition*. New York: Doubleday, 1969.

Saddler, Joseph. *The Adventures of Grandmaster Flash: My Life, My Beats*. New York: Broadway Books, 2008.

Schlesinger, Arthur Meier. *A Thousand Days: John F. Kennedy in the White House*. New York: Mariner, 2002.

Schwartz, Joel. *The New York Approach*. Columbus: Ohio State University Press, 1993.

Smith, Dennis. *Report from Engine Co. 82*. New York: McCall Books, 1972.

Sobel, Robert. *Dangerous Dreamers*. New York: Bear Books, 2000.

Starr, Roger. *Urban Choices: The City and Its Critics*. New York: Penguin Books, 1967.

Sternlieb, George, and James W, Hughes. *How Cities Can Grow Old Gracefully*. Washington, DC: U.S. Government Printing Office, 1977.

Sugrue, Thomas J. *The Origins of the Urban Crisis*. Princeton, NJ: Princeton University Press, 1996, 2005.

Trilling, Lionel. "Manners, Morals, and the Novel." From Lionel Trilling's *The Liberal Imagination*. New York: The New York Review of Books, 1950.

Walker, Warren E. *Fire Department Deployment Analysis*. Santa Monica, CA: RAND, 1979.

———. "Performing Policy Analysis for Municipal Agencies: Lessons From the New York City-RAND Institute's Fire Project." New York: RAND, 1975.

Wallace, Deborah N., "Discriminatory Public Policies and the New York City Tuberculosis Epidemic, 1975–1993," *Microbes and Infection* 3, no. 1–10 (2001).

Wallace, Deborah, and Rodrick Wallace. *A Plague on Your Houses*. London: Verso, 1998.

Wallace, Rodrick, Deborah Wallace, with H. Andrews. "AIDS, Tuberculosis, Violent Crime, and Low Birthweight in Eight US Metropolitan Areas: Public Policy, Stochastic Resonance, and the Regional Diffusion of Inner-City Markers," *Environment and Planning* 29, pp. 525–555.

Weil, François. *A History of New York*. Translated by Jody Gladding. New York: Columbia University Press, 2004.

Whalen, Richard J. *A City Destroying Itself: An Angry View of New York*. New York: William Morrow, 1965.

White, E. B. *Here is New York*. New York: The Little Bookroom, 1949.

Whyte, William H. *The Organization Man*. New York: Simon & Schuster, 1956.

Wilder, Craig Steven. *A Covenant with Color*. New York: Columbia University Press, 2000.

Wolfe, Tom. *The Pump House Gang*. New York: Farrar, Straus & Giroux, 1968.

Yochelson, Bonnie, Daniel August Riis, and Daniel J. Czitrom. *Rediscovering Riis*. New York: New Press, 2008.

FILM

The Fog of War, directed by Errol Morris. Sony Pictures Classics, 2003.

New York: A Documentary Film, directed by Ric Burns. Steeplechase Films and Public Broadcast Service, 1999.

Pandora's Box, directed by Adam Curtis. BBC, 1992.

The Trap, directed by Adam Curtis. BBC, 2007.

INDEX